WHAT OT

"Jay Roberts is fearless and unflinching as he chronicles his personal transformation from a tortured child to a strong man who reluctantly finds himself on the path to forgiveness. Along the way, he grapples with life's most serious issues: family, faith, and even his own imminent death. *Break the Chains* is a deeply compelling story of endurance, courage, and ultimate transcendence. It will convince you that miracles not only happen, they are necessary."

—Julie Mars, author of *Rust*
and other novels and the memoir *A Month of Sundays: Searching for the Spirit and My Sister*

❧

"Dr. Roberts' story illustrates how human beings can endure unimaginable suffering and still bring themselves through it to prevail if they can draw strength from their own transcendent faith. His book inspires each of us to cultivate our spirituality and have confidence that it will ultimately guide us to a higher truth than ourselves and fill our lives with purposeful joy. As a physician myself, I was reminded by Dr. Roberts' life story that a doctor often discovers he heals his own wounds when he addresses the suffering of others."

—Allan J. Hamilton,
author of *The Scalpel and the Soul: Encounters with Surgery, the Supernatural, and the Healing Power of Hope*

❧

"Ironically, *Break the Chains* is written by a medical doctor whose whole life has been devoted to healing wounds and yet for many years was unable to heal his own. Like many victims of severe child abuse, Dr. Jay Roberts lived for years on the painful edge between faith and doubt. This vastly inspirational, beautifully written memoir not only demonstrates how traumatic issues from childhood can impact us as adults, but also proves that miraculous solutions abound for those who bravely seek to understand their faith. Follow Dr. Roberts' amazing journey from his turbulent childhood to his medical studies in the Philippines, to his practice among the rich and famous in southern California, to his near death experience, and his spontaneous healing when he finally 'Let go and let God.'"

—LeAnn Thieman,
coauthor of *Chicken Soup for the Soul: Answered Prayers* and *Chicken Soup for the Soul: A Book of Miracles*

❧

"A compelling, heart-wrenching story of one doctor's struggles to heal not only his patients' wounds but his own, literally carved on his back by an abusive parent. Whether battling his own childhood demons or overcoming a debilitating, life-threatening illness, Jay Roberts is proof positive that one man, committed to his faith, can transform his own broken spirit into a driving force for good in the world. *Break the Chains* is a powerful, inspirational memoir, a journey into the mystery of healing."

—Minrose Gwin, author of
the novel *The Queen of Palmyra*,
the memoir *Wishing for Snow*, and other titles

❧

"Dr. Roberts did not plan to do prison ministry work. In fact, in his darkest moments he had so little compassion for prisoners that when he first learned he was dying from a neurological disease, he actually wished his disease would be transferred to inmates. *Break the Chains* is the wonderful, honest, and spirited story, not only about how Jay Roberts came to defy death, but how he found the truths he needed to embrace inside a detention center."

—Joan Schweighardt,
author of *Virtual Silence* and other novels

❧

BREAK THE
CHAINS

Jay D Roberts, MD

BREAK THE
CHAINS

Transforming Shame into Forgiveness

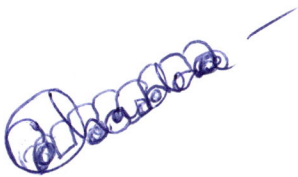

Forgive + be set free —

2/16/16

TATE PUBLISHING
AND ENTERPRISES, LLC

Published by Tate Publishing & Enterprises, LLC
127 E. Trade Center Terrace | Mustang, Oklahoma 73064 USA
1.888.361.9473 | www.tatepublishing.com

Tate Publishing is committed to excellence in the publishing industry. The company reflects the philosophy established by the founders, based on Psalm 68:11,
"The Lord gave the word and great was the company of those who published it."

Book design copyright © 2014 by Tate Publishing, LLC. All rights reserved.
Cover design by Allen Jomoc
Interior design by Caypeeline Casas

Published in the United States of America
ISBN: 978-1-62746-758-2
1. Biography & Autobiography / General
2. Biography & Autobiography / Personal Memoirs
14.07.22

PHILIPPINES

South China Sea

Pacific Ocean

Luzon

Baguio ● ●Banaue

Zambales●
(Province)

Manila●

Philippine
Sea

Visayas

Sulu Sea

Mindanao

Iligan ●

Zamboanga● ●Davao

Jolo●

N

DEDICATION

For Beverly, the love of my life,
and to you:
May you break your chains.

ACKNOWLEDGMENTS

I wish to thank:

My beloved family—Beverly, Ryan & Emily, Derek & Anna, Maxwell, Kate, Grant, and soon-to-be Sofia—for giving me reason to live. Mom, Rob, and especially Dona for prayers and support.

Cherished friends—Ed and Gwen Carpenter, Madeline, Ray & Lisa Nolta, Rene & Imelda Deza, and respected relatives—Cuyugans, Borjas, Barrettos, Novales, and clans of Roberts & Burns.

Harold Robbins for urging me to write my story, years ago, and Jann.

Julie Mars for her inspiration and guidance, and most importantly her friendship.

Joan Schweighardt for her advice and belief in my work and finding it a home.

Minrose Gwin and "The Gang" (Colleen Friesen, June Jackson, Sherri Burr, Judith Gelt, Alan Day) at the Taos Summer Writing Conference, for their early encouragement; and Cristina Garcia for her heartfelt advice at my subsequent Taos course.

Dr. Richard Tate for his faith in my book and all the staff at Tate Publishing who helped to make my book a reality.

My Kairos brothers, inside and out of prison, for their agape love.

Anyone else I might have forgotten. It's sounding like an Academy Awards acceptance speech. But my trophy will be to inspire and help someone through my story. Oh, Milo, my dog, for sitting by me as I wrote, and wagging his tail at just the right times.

As always, God, my Heavenly Father, for loving me!

AUTHOR'S NOTE

These are my memories. Some were buried for years and never meant to be unearthed.

I hope my mother will forgive me for revealing our family's secret. My greatest fear in writing my story is my mother will die reading it.

My intent is not to hurt or malign but to tell my story by breaking down the protective wall around my heart. I have dug deep to separate the spirit of my reality from the tales I had convinced myself to be true—some were easily mended; others held me hostage in my prison.

My prayer is that my book will help all who are bound by chains. *May you forgive and be set free.*

PROLOGUE

PALM SPRINGS, CALIFORNIA

1999

My eyes water as I stare at the whirling ceiling fan. The blades blur and transform into *bolos* (machetes) that slice through the air and my thoughts. The physician in me dissects my infirmity, orders treatment for cure, and demands to be in charge. The Christian in me calls for faith without understanding, to die to self, to surrender to Christ and his will. My medical and religious beliefs battle and clash like opposing bolo blades.

I lay wasting in my bed with muscles, once toned and defined, now atrophied and weak. I am wounded. I struggle to push the opened Bible away from my bedside. Beverly has placed the Bible next to me for weeks. She and I have been married since 1975, after a three-year courtship. I wonder if she wants to reconsider the "for better or for worse" part of our vows. How easy those words flowed from our naive mouths.

The Bible falls to the floor. The fight is over.

I smile.

My inner voice and friend, Buddy, warns me I am wrong to disrespect the Bible.

I tell him to go away.

He does.

My eyes close. My brain waves surge and scenes are projected on the back of my eyelids, reflections of my past. I am in fifth grade. It is late at night. I walk like a robot to the kitchen. My pajamas stick to my bottom. The dried blood from the bullwhip

17

lashings holds the fabric to my skin. My father is passed out, drunk. His right hand, with its thick, stubby digits and brownish-yellow stain between the long and middle fingers, hangs over the edge of the couch. He snores with the intensity of a train. I select the sharpest knife and walk over to the bullwhip that hangs on a wall near the living room. I remove it from the wall, walk back to the kitchen, and stand at the table. I methodically cut the whip into small pieces. It takes several hours. I return the knife to its proper place and put all the pieces of the bullwhip into a paper bag. I open the back door and hide the bag in the bottom of the trashcan.

I look up and see a million stars, turn, and then walk back into the house. I stop to pee and go back to bed. When I awake later that morning, I try to sit up but cannot. I stand and cautiously walk to the living room. My father is not there. A squished pillow partially hides his body imprint on the sofa cushion. Stale beer odor hangs in the air. I turn and walk over to the wall. The whip is not there.

I thought it was a dream.

My eyes scan more images from my life.

Wounds dominate the picture.

I have always tried to heal wounds, others' and mine.

Some wounds are not easily sutured, some impossible.

1

SAN FRANCISCO, CALIFORNIA

1971

I thought I would attend medical school in the United States. I was wrong.

I needed to get away from my father. He was a military man, strict in discipline; he taught me to be strong, honest, and loyal, and never to quit. He was also a mean drunk, my tormentor who forced me to keep secrets.

At San Francisco International Airport, I had trouble checking in for my flight. I did not have an important entry document and was denied boarding.

"I'm sorry, but I overheard you talking. I'm Senator Almendras, and I know Governor Barretto. Will you let me help?" asked a Filipino standing beside me.

"Yes," replied my mother before I could say anything.

The tall Filipino-Mestizo man, with light brown skin and dark, wavy hair, was dressed in an American sack suit, white shirt, and tie. He quickly conferred with the airline agent, turned to my parents, and then said, "Everything is fine. He can enter with the tourist visa he has and will have twenty-one days to change it to a student visa. And don't worry, we're on the same flight, and I'll see to it that your son arrives safely at the Governor Barretto's home. I heard you say that was where he was going to live in our country."

"Thank you, thank you, thank you," uttered my mother with tears.

"Thank you, sir," stated my father with a firm handshake and a stiff back.

I stood there with a smile pasted on my face. *Oh my God, I almost didn't escape.*

I was the last passenger to enter the plane. I looked out the window and saw my parents standing behind a large window at the terminal. My mom cried and leaned on my father. He stood straight. I wanted to look away. I didn't. I stared at my mother, who was still crying. He turned to face her, and there it was. My eyes focused like a zoomed camera lens on the nose. His nose.

My mind swirled, and I was now a child focusing on my father's straight, hard nose. I could not look into his eyes. He might read my thoughts. I was ordered to stand erect with eyes forward. I awaited the first blow. The waiting was the hardest. My shirt hung over a chair; my pants and underwear wrapped my ankles. I was cold. I dared not move or twitch. I could smell his stale beer breath and taste the ale from his spit as he shouted, his nose barely an inch from mine. Will the strike be from his fist, a metal coat hanger, his military belt buckle, or his favorite tool, the bullwhip? His nose was blurring, the stench of his breath was overwhelming. I must not vomit. I must not move.

His physical assaults stopped when I started high school, when he went to Vietnam for two years. But his mental cruelty persisted. The smell of his breath and the sight of his nose were enough to tie my insides in knots, twisting me into a little child. In college, I began to think of him as dead. It felt good until I returned home on holidays or summer vacations. Then he was like Lazarus returning from the dead.

Sometimes, his evil look and wicked words were more harmful than the physical beatings had been.

Wounds from beatings were visible; from words, invisible.

Both could scar and disfigure.

❧

"Sir? Sir, you must put on your seat belt." My memory was terminated by the kind voice of the flight attendant.

"Sure." I smiled. She was concerned about my safety.

I turned back, looked out the window, took a deep breath, and peered back at my parents. My mom still cried. My father was rock-solid and stood stiff.

The plane backed from the gate. I was not sad, not happy. Just relieved. Tears flowed down my cheeks, like cascading water out of a backed-up dam. I needed to be released, to escape. I closed my eyes and began to pray.

Lord, keep me strong. Help me.

I knew I could never quit. I had to get my medical education and make my family, mainly him, proud of me.

I always knew my father was ashamed of me. He did not like me or want me. He adored my year-older sister Dona and cherished my brother Robbie. "Now Robbie is a real son, a real man," he said on many occasions. "You should be like your brother. He's younger than you by four years, but he's a lot tougher. You need to toughen up. Come over here and stand up straight. Eyes forward. Do not move. I will teach you. You bet your ass I will turn you into a man." His stale beer breath nauseated me. His nose frightened me.

My mother was the enabler of our family. She looked younger than her years. She married early, I think at fifteen. "Jay, you know your dad loves you," she would say. "He's doing this for your own good. You must listen and learn. You be a good boy now. I love you, Jay. Do you love me?" Her eyes pleaded with me to believe in her way of thinking. She had suffered the stings of his slaps.

"Yes, Mom."

"Buddy, I hate the word Love. It is too painful to be loved. Maybe he can stop loving me so frequently," I reasoned with my inner friend.

"Be quiet. Your father is near," warned Buddy.

Buddy is my friend. He keeps me grounded and softens my heart. He tells me what is right and wrong and good and bad, and he encourages me to be strong and not to quit. He plays with me when I am in pain. He comforts me when I am sad.

I protect Buddy. I keep him deep within me where no one can see or harm him. He is safe. He is never harmed. He is loved.

"Jay, are you listening?" Each word was always emphasized, with hands on her hips, head protruding forward.

"Yes, Mom. I know. Be good. Be strong. Don't cry."

My mom was about five-foot-nine and lanky. She had flawless skin and beady eyes. She frequently puckered her lips and rarely smiled.

❧

The plane soared. My mind jarred.

I had left California.

I had escaped.

It seemed like yesterday, not a year ago, when my decision to attend medical school in the Philippines was made. Governor Manuel D. Barretto came to our home in Pleasant Hill, California. He was on a political trip to Spain, representing President Marcos, with Prince Juan Carlos and Princess Sophia, who in 1975, became King and Queen of Spain. On his way home to the Philippines, he stopped over to see my father. The governor was a handsome man, a mixture of Filipino and Spanish—a Mestizo. He was small in stature but large in spirit, with compassion and love that did not hurt. He sported a neatly trimmed, thin black mustache. I remembered, from my childhood in the Philippines, his infectious smile, gentle eyes, and comforting pats on my head. There was usually a group of men around him talking politics. As an adult, I admired his attention and love for his family and his devotion to his country. He gave me positive encouragement and a feeling of worth. He told me he was proud of me.

My father and the governor had a long friendship that had roots on the island I had lived on as a child. I would see them sitting around the square poker table. I was in third grade. Cigarette smoke filled the *lanai* (veranda). Overhead fans twirled and scattered the hot air. Screens kept the mosquitoes outside and allowed the ocean breeze to blow through the room. Attentive servants replaced empty San Miguel Beer bottles with fresh, cold ones, with a paper napkin wrapped around the bottle to absorb the moisture and keep the cards dry. A buffet of chicken *adobo*, *pancit*, shrimp, vegetables, and rice was on a large rectangular wooden table. A houseboy waved a stick with shredded paper attached to the end to keep flies from landing on the food.

My father, the governor, and two visiting politicians played into the early morning hours. One houseboy was replaced by another after several hours of patrolling for flies.

"Roy, I'm going on another hunting trip for two weeks. I really want you to come. I assure you of an adventure on our 'Filipino safari.' Can you get away?" asked Manoling, the governor.

"Sure. You bet," answered my father as he raised a beer bottle for a toast to good hunting. "I'll see if you still shoot as good as when we fought the Japs here."

My father fought in the Philippines during WWII. The governor was a prominent guerilla. They had a blood bond.

"I'll use that fine rifle you procured for me." Manoling laughed and raised his bottle.

The governor had won a handsome hunting rifle at the military base a month earlier. It was the grand prize at a formal dinner. He had the winning ticket but no Filipino, even the governor, was allowed to take an American weapon off the base. My father discreetly took his ticket, claimed the prize, and handed him the rifle at the governor's house the next morning.

"Manoling, I think a bet is in order. Let's see who is still the better marksman, you or Roy," said one of the politicians.

"Agreed." Manoling laughed.

"To the best," asserted my father, his back stiff.

Years later, in California, the two were in our living room talking about the good old days. I could hear their laughter. I sat at the kitchen table. I had to finish the paperwork in front of me.

I felt a firm but gentle hand on my shoulder. I turned and saw the governor smile at me. "Jay, what are you doing?" he asked with genuine curiosity.

"Applying to medical schools," I replied, pulling on my hair and rolling my eyes.

His response was immediate. "Why don't you go to school in the Philippines?"

"What?"

"Why don't you go to medical school in the Philippines?"

"I never thought of that."

"You can stay in my home, receive a first class medical education taught in English, and have no debt when you graduate."

My father stood off to the side. I felt the glare of his eyes on me. The smell of his beer breath twisted my insides. He spoke no words and left the kitchen, but as the governor was convincing me, the smell of his breath remained.

I smiled. I actually beamed. I could escape. I could go to medical school and be far away from my tormentor.

The laughter continued in the living room when the governor rejoined my father. My insides remained knotted.

That night, I threw the applications for medical school in the States in the garbage can. I applied to the University of the Philippines Medical School and was accepted.

In short succession, I had my passport, shots, and documents for travel.

2

PALM SPRINGS, CALIFORNIA

1999

I have miserable thoughts as I lie in my bed, my arms and legs scrawny and weak.

At least my casket will not be heavy to carry.

It seems like a month ago, not a year ago, when I dried my legs after showering and noticed worms crawling under my skin. At first a few in my left calf muscle, then came my right leg. Medically, I know they were fasciculations (muscle twitching) caused by involuntary muscle contraction and relaxation.

I dismiss my fasciculations as benign. I figure overexertion is the culprit. I know they will go away if I modify my exercise and get more rest.

I do. They do not.

Within a few months, the worms crawl up my legs to my arms and begin to consume my muscles.

I no longer dismiss the fasciculations as benign but refuse to admit they are pathological for a serious disease.

I perform a neurological examination on myself and note: fasciculations, weakness and atrophy in the major muscles of my arms and legs, diminished deep tendon reflexes, and sensory loss in my legs more than arms.

I also do an Electromyography (EMG) and Nerve Conduction Test (NCV). I have performed thousands and thousands of these tests on my patients. It is surreal to perform the test on myself. I have waited until all my patients and staff have left the office.

Before the last muscle and nerves are tested, I know it is serious. The worms have attacked my nervous system.

I submit to a full neurological evaluation by a neurologist. Male physicians are the worst patients, and I am no different. I reschedule my appointment twice, convincing myself that I am too busy. Dr. Stein does a complete and impressive physical evaluation followed by a multitude of tests, including blood studies, an EMG/NCV evaluation of my arms and legs, MRIs of my brain and cervical spine, and a biopsy of my sural sensory nerve in my leg. Diagnosis is confirmed.

I have Chronic Inflammatory Demyelinating Polyneuropathy (CIDP).

CIDP is an immune-mediated disorder of the peripheral nervous system. Immune cells, which normally protect the body from foreign infection, attack the nerves in the body instead and cause a loss of the myelin sheath (the fatty covering that protects nerve fibers). It is a chronic progressive or relapsing disorder. Although occasional complete remissions occur, quadriplegia and death may be the dreaded outcome.

Treatment is instituted: corticosteroids (Prednisone), plasmapheresis (plasma exchange), intravenous immune globulin (IVIG) infusions (antibodies added to the plasma), and immunosuppressive drugs.

Aggressive medical care is given but to no avail.

Worms continue to consume my flesh.

Our master bedroom looks like a hospital suite despite Beverly's decorating skills. Her original design, with peach and green decor, is distorted with infusion devices; trays of wound care supplies with gauzes, tapes, gloves, aseptic solutions, and antibiotic ointments; containers for medications; and syringes and needles. A small refrigerator placed in a corner, a chair taken away, a couch moved off center to the fireplace, and aluminum trashcans with lids and plastic liners add to the disarray. Less intrusive are the handsome glass water pitcher and etched water glass with lid cover on my nightstand, adjacent to fresh flowers in a crystal vase. Beverly knows the name of the crystal. I do not. Our king-size bed, with a tall headboard on an oriental-style ivory platform, stands between two long ivory bedside tables with large oriental lamps. Two plush sofas face each other in front of the massive fireplace. Built-in bookshelves occupy the walls on each side of the fireplace. An oversized lounge chair with an ottoman and a floor lamp is next to the wall-to-wall, twelve-foot glass sliding doors that lead to the expansive backyard. A large ceiling fan hangs from the center of the sixteen-foot-high domed ceiling with wood plank finish. Oil paintings and oriental vases add accent.

Beverly and I share the same bed. We always have. I am sick. But we are married. It is part of that "in sickness and in health" vow.

"I should tell Beverly and my sons I love them tomorrow or maybe the next day," I say to Buddy.

"No. You should tell them today. Don't wait," corrects Buddy.

I watch the ceiling fan for a few blank moments and then bring up something I've been thinking about.

"Buddy, maybe I should ask God to give my illness to prisoners. They're bad, right? I'm not. I'll just ask it to be given to the really bad ones, the multiple-life-sentence ones. They might even thank me for shortening their imprisonment time. Then I could get back to my practice and help heal wounds. Yeah, that sounds good. I'll ask God for this."

"Jay, you know better than that. Don't wish such a thing on anybody!" shouts Buddy.

"Mind your own business. God, please give my illness to prisoners. They are bad. I am not," I pray.

"Shame on you," says Buddy.

"Go away."

He does.

That Bible is next to me again.

Why can't Beverly understand that I do not want to read the Scriptures?

The fight to knock the Bible off the bed begins. It is a short bout. The Bible falls to the floor. I smile and wish I could raise my hands over my head in victory.

When will God answer my last prayer? I know he won't. I don't think he has time or cares. And I don't really care.

"Yes, you do," Buddy's voice echoes from deep inside.

"Self-pity is pathetic, but I don't care about that either," I blurt.

"Yes, you do," he repeats.

"Never mind. It's time for a nap. Go to sleep, Buddy."

We sleep.

3

MANILA, PHILIPPINES

1971

After five hours, there was a stop in Honolulu then a twelve-hour stretch to Manila. I tried to read, but it was impossible to concentrate. I tried to sleep but could not find a comfortable position. The packed seating lacked room for my six-foot-four-inch frame. I descended the stairs in Manila into the heavy heat. It was an outdoor sauna, and I sweated profusely. An endless line of people with luggage and boxes awaited the customs search in front of me. I heard Tagalog spoken, the national language of the Philippines and the language I spoke as a child living in the Philippines. I was edgy and exhausted. "Jay, come with me," Senator Almendras ordered. His right hand gestured with as much authority as his commanding voice. I found out later that he was a longtime friend and colleague of the governor and was returning home from a political meeting in the States.

I grabbed my suitcases and followed. We sped through the customs area. No questions from the inspectors, just nods to the senator. "Governor Barretto's car is not here. I'll take you to his home." The senator's convoy pulled up and doors opened. We entered his car. The air conditioner was on full blast and appreciated. Our luggage was loaded into one of the other vehicles. We exited the airport in a flash. As I rode in the backseat of the Mercedes with the senator, I was puzzled that I was not met at the airport, but I was grateful the senator kept his promise.

I stared out the window of the car. There was a sea of squatters living in shanties around the airport. I was overwhelmed by the number of kids living in trash sites, hungry, and struggling to survive. They were like ants, thousand and thousands of ants, descending upon a large dirt mound. Maybe the anthill was the same when I lived here as a child, but I didn't mind it, didn't know any difference or didn't care.

As a child in the Philippines, I didn't think about politics. I knew there were poor and rich people. That was just the way it was. At the governor's home there were usually lots of people eating. It was the tradition for a prominent politician to feed the poor and any visitor that came to his home. The cooks were always busy from early morning to late at night. Bodyguards kept us safe.

As an adult, I was glad I was not poor. I knew politics were corrupt and money could buy just about anything and anyone. The hand was not under the table but visible on top. I was aware of old stocks of rice in government warehouses that could be doled out to the poor but instead were rotting. Disputes and fights were often settled with guns. The strong ruled. Even I knew the president and first lady were corrupt, but I kept silent.

The car stopped. The senator lifted his head off the headrest and blinked, re-orienting his internal compass. "Good luck, Jay. Say hi to Governor Barretto for me. Call me if you need anything."

"Thank you so much." I extended my hand for a firm handshake.

The car door opened, and I entered the outside sauna that encased the island. I approached two large swinging metal gates that opened to allow cars inside. The gates, aged with years of weather damage, were attached to a six-foot rock wall that surrounded the Barretto compound. There were large pieces of jagged, broken glass cemented in the top edge of the wall to keep intruders out—the local version of barbwires.

I rang the bell to the right of the gate. Within minutes, a houseboy peeked through a small slot in a door that was built into one of the gates. The gate door opened and the servant bowed. Other servants rushed to get my luggage and escorted me into the large living room. I scanned the room as the servants vanished. There was a long, white leather, American-inspired sectional accompanied by seating areas of bamboo and *rattan* (climbing palm) chairs and tables and Filipino art on the walls. "Jay, what a wonderful surprise to see you," exclaimed the governor. His hair messed from sleeping. His long silk bathrobe tied in haste. "Didn't you get my letter?" I asked as we embraced. "What letter?" The puzzle solved. No wonder I was not met at the airport. I was welcomed with open arms and genuine warmth despite the hour of the day and the surprise of my arrival. From that moment on, I was part of the family.

After a tasty breakfast of fried eggs, *longganisa* (native sausage), steamed rice, ripe mangos, and instant Folger's coffee, I distributed my *pasalubongs* (souvenirs) to the family: Marlboro cigarettes and a bottle of scotch for the governor (*Tatay* or father), perfume and Sees chocolates for the governor's wife (*Nanay* or mother), blouses for their daughters, shirts for their sons, lipsticks for the female maids and cooks, and T-shirts for the houseboys and drivers. All the gifts were "made in the USA." It was very important that the labels revealed made in the States. It was part of the colonial mentality on the island. They think it is better if it is from abroad.

The next day, when I went to register at the University of the Philippines Medical School, I was informed that a new ruling had just been initiated. No foreigners were permitted to attend. I was flabbergasted by this news. My driver brought me at once to the governor's office. Tatay was outraged when I told him. But he called upon his lifelong friend, the minister of the Department of Education, and I was accepted into the medical school at the University of Santo Tomas (UST) in Manila before they got off the phone. I was rushed to the school and enrolled that same day.

UST was founded in 1611, ninety years after Ferdinand Magellan discovered the Philippines. It was seventy years older than Yale. Instruction was in English with the same curriculum as American medical schools. Most of the professors were educated and trained for their specialty in the States. The school was supervised by the Dominican order of Catholic priests. My acceptance to the school by order of the minister of the Department of Education caused the professors to wonder who I was.

Culture shock blasted me from the beginning. I went from living in a bachelor's apartment in California to the governor's home in Manila with the respect and duties as the eldest son living in the home. There were several inherent codes. Rules included never going barefoot, never sitting on the floor, always dressing up before meals including breakfast, letting maids serve me and stand behind me while I ate, never disagreeing verbally or nonverbally with an elder, and sitting in the back of the car, not in front with the driver.

Occasionally, my American blood would emerge, and I would break the code. Once, when the governor and his wife were with President Marcos and First Lady Imelda, I wore ragged jeans and a stained T-shirt I brought from the States. I had been sitting in the reception area of the home, barefoot, and had fallen asleep listening to music. I was startled when Tatay, Nanay, and their guests, all dressed in formal native attire, arrived at the house. I was introduced to the guests as their son. I bowed my head and promptly went to my room, ashamed of my behavior and appearance.

It was never mentioned. I was never punished. I was sheltered.

School was very strict. The teacher's desk was on a platform to ensure a height advantage over the students. You'd have to raise your hand for permission to speak and stand at the side of your desk to address the teacher. You should never disagree with a teacher. "Jay Roberts, come to the front of the class," ordered my professor in clinical pathology on my first day.

I stood in front of the class and looked around, astonished. It was my dream to be in medical school. I had entered the university campus early that morning. As I was driven past the Arch of the Centuries at the entrance of the campus, I was struck by the massiveness of the Spanish architecture, monuments, fountains, and gardens. "Why are you here?" asked the professor with the aid of a microphone. He was a short and thin elderly man dressed impeccably in white and perched on a tall stool. "To learn," I replied, surprised at the question. "You are an American. You should be going to school in the States. You Americans think you are better than everyone else. You should be ashamed of yourself for being here and taking up a seat that a Filipino student should have." My fellow students looked down.

I was dazed. "Get back to your seat." I sat and repeated the mantra of the Philippines in silence. *Show respect. Obey the rules. Show respect.*

At dinner that night, Tatay, Nanay, my sisters and brothers, and I sat around the large, wooden dining room table. The family had been called for this special weekday dinner. All were excited to hear about my first day at school. A massive chandelier shined overhead while large standing fans attempted to keep us comfortable. The cook made some of my childhood favorites: fried *bangus* (milk fish—the national fish), adobo (chicken and pork marinated in garlic, soy sauce, and vinegar—the most favorite dish in the Philippines), *pancit palabok* (noodle dish with seafood), *sinigang na baboy* (sour soup with pork and vegetables), *lumpia* (spring rolls), and lots of steamed rice. For dessert there was *leche flan* (custard) and *minatamis na saging* (sweetened banana plantain).

At the main house lived Tatay, Nanay, their two younger daughters, Nida and Elaine, their son, Nick (the youngest in the family), and me. The eldest daughter, Maribel, lived on an island in the south with her family. The second eldest daughter, Lina, lived a few miles away with her family. One mile away, Tatay built a compound for the rest of the family—eldest son Cesar and his family, and second eldest son Eduardo (Eddie) and his family.

Every Sunday, the entire family was at the main house. Some holidays and weekends, the family traveled to the second home in Zambales, north of Manila.

"What's wrong, Jay? I can tell something is bothering you." Tatay was either highly perceptive, or I was not a very good actor.

I did not want to reveal my shame. "What is it?" he persisted.

I told him of the incident in clinical pathology.

Nanay's eyes were sad. My brothers and sisters were quiet. Tatay turned to his second oldest son. He nodded. The nod was returned. I knew that meant to take care of the problem. Tatay and Nanay left the table and went to their master suite. I followed and begged him not to have the professor harmed. "When someone insults you, they insult the family," Tatay emphatically declared.

Nanay was quiet. She looked elegant and proud like a Filipina queen sitting in her oversized bedroom chair. Her eyes told me she agreed with Tatay.

A good wife by Filipino standards is one who looks after the best interests of her husband and manages the household and children efficiently. The Filipino macho husband is, usually, controlled by his strong-willed wife, who keeps him humble. The husband is teased as living under the *saya* (wife's skirt).

I never knew what happened. The word at school was that the professor suddenly decided to retire. My classmates accepted me with curiosity.

My dream survived.

I knew, even as a child, that Tatay was powerful. When I was in third grade, my father drove off the military base with my mother. A young native boy jumped off the end of a jeepney, was struck by my parents' car, and was severely injured. Filipino men ran to the site, some with bolos, and tried to break the window of the car to get my father. Military guards at the front gate fired warning shots. My father put the car in reverse and sped back into the base. He was confined to the base for his safety. Tatay informed the boy's family that my father was his close friend. He also gave money to the family. He then went to our home. My father sat next to Tatay in the backseat of the governor's car and drove off the base. Relatives and neighbors of the injured boy waited at the gate. The car windows lowered. The people saw my father with the governor. He spoke to the relatives in Tagalog. The boy's father came to the car and shook my father's hand.

My father was never harmed.

When the governor visited our home on the base, guards stood at attention and saluted. He never stopped at the commander's residence. By protocol, he should have. The governor didn't care. The commander kept quiet.

I studied hard. I did not want to disappoint family or myself. Because I was the American, I was relentlessly compared to my Filipino classmates. It felt like a competition between two countries. The vying became my fuel for knowledge; coffee and cigarettes, the stimulus that kept me awake late at night. I studied with the air conditioner and a fan on full blast. Occasionally, mosquitoes would enter through a defect in a screen. I swatted with precision as they attacked, barely breaking from my studies. We had a full staff of servants. There were cooks, maids to clean, maids to launder by hand, houseboys, nannies, gardeners, and drivers. The "dirty kitchen" was used for actual day-to-day cooking with woks. As in most Filipino homes, the "clean kitchen," complete with modern appliances, was rarely used and always ready to be viewed by visitors.

I favored the local food but developed a nutritional imbalance. A handful of hair fell out as I showered one day. I lost weight, causing great concern for Nanay. She ordered the cooks to fatten me up. The dirty kitchen was in a state of "emergency use." I was given double portions of more of my favorite foods. If I had a craving, I asked the cook to prepare the dish.

Filipino food consists mostly of vegetables, seafood, dairy, meat, and rice. Like Philippine fiestas, Filipino recipes are rich in flavor and color. Filipino culinary art is influenced by Chinese, European, American, Arabian, and Asian cuisines. Tropical fruits are abundant: mangoes (sweet and pulp-free), papaya (large, up to eleven pounds), coconuts, *macapuno* (mutant of coconut), star fruit (five angled, shaped like a star), *atis* (sugar apple), *dalandan* (orange), *mangosteen* (war of sweet and sour taste), *langka* (jackfruit), pineapple, *bayabas* (guava), *santol* (white pulp with brown seeds), and *durian* (large, up to ten pounds, tasty but stinky, known as the king of all tropical fruit).

I savored and devoured my meals. My body adjusted, my hair stopped falling, and I gained weight.

Nanay was pleased.

4

PALM SPRINGS, CALIFORNIA

1999

My once-toned body is emaciated, as if starved. I hide my withered muscles with long-sleeved shirts and pants. I am hot in my garments. It is summer. Most people are wearing short-sleeved shirts or T-shirts and short pants.

Burning pain and numbness in my feet add to the weakness in my legs. I stumble, stagger, and fall, as if drunk. Walking at night without any light is the hardest since I cannot feel my feet or see where they are. I am not able to reach for objects above my shoulders, as if my muscles are exhausted from hours of exercise.

I continue to practice medicine but with increasing physical difficulty. My mind remains sharp. I will not take any medication that could cause decreased mental alertness.

"Dr. Roberts, are you okay?" asks a patient as I stumble into the exam room. "Yes. I guess I'm just getting clumsy." I smile and lean next to the counter in the room.

"I'll get it. You dropped your pen," declares my patient with a concerned look on his face.

"Never mind. My nurse will get it later. I have another," I blurt. *It is better for my patient to think I'm lazy and quick to ask my nurse to do menial things for me than to fall down in front of him.*

I do not allow myself to be hugged. I have a central line, a port used to deliver medications straight into my heart, and I am afraid that it will be detected or disrupted from the force of an embrace. I wear extra large shirts to hide the bandaged line. I do not care if my friends and patients think I am not friendly. I have to protect the line, the access for my infusions. I also avoid handshakes. My grip strength has diminished. I do not want to offer a weak hand.

When I get home each day from the office, I collapse into my bed. The worms have begun to attack my facial muscles. I cannot hide my face. I continue the medical treatment and add alternative care to my regimen. When I try Nikken magnetic insoles in my shoes, my balance improves, temporarily. I take mounds of vitamins and antioxidants, and my fatigue improves, temporarily.

I become desperate.

Infusion treatments continue in my bed. I am often alone, but still, I am disturbed when Beverly returns to our master bedroom. The fan is still turning. The Bible is still on the floor.

I wonder if she will step over it to get to me.

"Can I get you anything, honey?" Beverly asks in a loving tone as she picks up the Bible and places it on the bedside table.

Beverly is a good person, sent to me by God. Her outward beauty with light golden-brown skin, black hair, dark eyes, perfect-shaped nose (a stranger wanted her nose to be like Beverly's and asked for the name of her plastic surgeon, but Beverly never had plastic surgery), sparkling teeth, and tall stature, is not as divine as her inner loveliness. She is a divine Mestiza.

Still I am annoyed with her.

"No."

"Are you sure?"

"Yes," I bark. I have tried for weeks to ignore her. I am mad at everything and everybody, including myself but mostly God. "I love you, Jay." No answer. "I love you, Jay," Beverly repeats and adds, "God loves you, too." No answer. "I'm going to fix us something to eat. What would you like?" No answer. She softly kisses my forehead and leaves the room.

I have shut out my family and God. I glance at my atrophied arms and legs. I am no longer in control of my life. "Be strong. Don't quit," Buddy says, always encouraging me.

I watch the ceiling fan again. I feel like one of the spinning blades.

Maybe an hour later, Beverly and our two sons enter our bedroom. Their eyes are red. No smiles.

"Jay, I have been praying for you. I know all the infusion treatments and medications have not helped. But God can heal. I want to take you to Fatima and Lourdes." Beverly's voice is soft and tender. Her right hand pats her chest over her heart.

"No," I shout.

"Please, Jay."

"I said no."

I do not mind the tears that flow down Beverly's cheeks. I also dismiss the gloomy looks of our two sons, their arms over each other's shoulders, as they stand beside their mom.

Ryan is in his third year at the University of Southern California, Derek in his first year. They are home for the weekend. They are best friends. They have exotic eyes, dark hair, and light milk chocolate skin that becomes a rich, darker chocolate from sun rays, large dimples that deepen with their infectious grins, smiles, and laughter. Ryan, the eldest by three years, is six foot two inches. Derek is six foot five inches. To me, they stand taller. They are good boys, good sons. We have raised them with love, love that does not hurt.

"Please Dad. Please go." Ryan's deep voice trembles.

"No."

"Please Dad." Derek's deep voice vibrates.

"No."

I close my eyes, my only means of control.

Discussion over.

I have never wanted to go to Lourdes. I know of the reported miracles, like most Catholics do, of people healed at Lourdes, but it is not for me. I am not special enough to be worthy of a miracle. As a child, I prayed for God to help me. He did not. As an adult, I prayed for God to give my illness to prisoners. He did not.

I believe "Blessed are those who fear the Lord." I fear the Lord. He is cruel. I believe "God looks down from heaven onto the earth." He looks down on me with hatred. I hear, "Happy are the sorrowing; they shall be consoled. Happy those who hunger and thirst for what is right; they shall be satisfied." I hunger and thirst. I am not consoled or satisfied. He does not care. I do not know why God is punishing me.

But he is.

Instead of "no," I should have said to Beverly, "I am not worthy. God hates me, and I hate him."

"Shame on you," Buddy cries.

"Shut up. I didn't ask for your opinion."

"God loves you."

"Go away."

I turn my head to the side and see the recording machine. I need to finish my fatherly advice tapes for my sons. Counsel for their use later. I'd best not put it off too much longer. The topics include:

- Importance of education, college and post-graduate school

- How to be a loving husband (I think I should erase this one)

- How to be a loving father

- Dedication to family

- Dedication to work

- How to ask a girl for her hand in marriage

- How to interact with in-laws

- How to know when God is talking to you (definitely have to erase)

- How to be happy (already erased)

Maybe I should get a new puppy that my sons can love later. A puppy might be better than tapes.

I am too tired to record anything right now.

I hope I can complete the tapes.

"You can. You will. Keep strong," encourages Buddy.

"Thanks, Buddy. Thanks for being my friend."

"I am not going anywhere."

I smile and close my eyes.

5

MANILA, PHILIPPINES

1972

"Jay, I know the perfect girl for you to meet. Her name is Beverly." Edwin's smile was enormous. His eyebrows elevated several times in fast tempo, conveying to me, "I really mean it."

Edwin was my classmate. He was tall for a Filipino and fit. His skin was milk chocolate and free of blemishes, skin I always wanted and never had, despite applying gallons of baby oil with iodine when I sunbathed. He had an infectious, somewhat devilish, smile. His pride and joy was his long, perfectly styled, black hair. He had mastered looking through strategically placed strands of hair in front of his eyes.

"I agree," chimed Erlinda "Peachy" Austria.

Peachy was a friend of Beverly and my classmate. She was a tall and pretty Mestiza with dark black hair, usually pulled back and away from her cheerful face. Edwin and Peachy thought Beverly and I would make a perfect couple, stating that we both had good hearts, bright minds, good looks, and would make "beautiful babies" with the combination of our races. The fact that Beverly was five foot nine inches added strength to their opinion. Also, they felt we came from good Catholic families (they only knew my Barretto family) and had the same morals. Peachy knew Beverly had had a premonition as a teenager that she would marry a white foreigner and leave the island.

"I'm busy with my studies. I don't know about this," I answered.

"Come on, Jay. You deserve a break, some fun," Edwin chuckled.

"Yeah, Jay. Anyway, we have already spoken highly of you to Beverly and her parents," added Peachy.

"You did what?" I raised my voice.

"We did. And you have permission to meet Beverly," boasted Edwin with a wide grin.

"Who is this Beverly anyway?" I asked. I tried to focus on my internal medicine journal.

"She is a first year medical student here at UST," cited Edwin.

"Yeah. And she is the stepdaughter of Dra. Carmelita Belmonte-Cuyugan," added Peachy.

"You know, Jay. Dra. Cuyugan, the terror professor in Pediatrics we will have to face soon." Edwin laughed as he slapped my back. "You might have it easier if you're seeing her daughter."

"Edwin, shame on you. Dra. Cuyugan is tough but a good person. Besides, it's Beverly that I want Jay to meet," scolded Peachy.

"Okay. Okay." I caved in, sensing their relentless determination. Besides, we were in the library disturbing others. Better to end the discussion. I did not want us to be accused having *walang hiya* (no shame) or being *bastos* (rude).

Seated in the backseat of Tatay's car, I knew why I was allowed to call upon Beverly. I was living in the governor's home and considered to be his son. If I was an American tourist or in the military stationed in the Philippines, permission would have been denied.

I was escorted by a servant into Beverly's house and was overwhelmed at the number of people present. It was her stepmother's birthday party celebration. Dra. Cuyugan sat with perfect posture, a picture of an Emily Post graduate, at the dining table with her husband and Beverly's father Dr. Angel Cuyugan, relatives, and friends. Servants hustled to begin dinner service but were stopped by a hand gesture from Dra. Cuyugan as I entered the room.

Dra. Cuyugan looked much younger than her years, a testament to her genetics and perfect makeup. She did not sweat despite the heat. Her hair and nails were well-groomed, as if she had just left a beauty parlor. Her silk dress, fashioned by the finest couture on the island, slightly flowed from the breeze of the overhead fan. Her shoes (I learned later they were size four) reeked expensive, Italian-made. The stones on her fingers and ears could blind you.

She spoke with perfect English and diction. No emotion. Her eyes surveyed me from head to foot as I stood and sweated, despite the coldness from her eyes.

Maybe I should have worn a better pair of pants and shirt or shined my shoes. A haircut would have been good.

Her stare shrunk me.

The flowers I brought seemed inadequate. I tried to conceal my dismay over not knowing about the celebration. After formal introduction to Beverly's father, stepmother, brothers, sisters, sisters-in-law, cousins, nieces, nephews, aunts, uncles, godparents, and close family friends, I was instructed to wait in a large *sala* (living room). I was grateful Edwin was at my side. The expansive room was inviting with native rattan furniture and oversized cushions, Filipino paintings, and a magnificent collection of antique jars that stood in sharp contrast to a large collection of Hummel figurines.

"I don't know about this, Edwin. Why didn't you tell me about the party?" I asked as I shifted in my chair.

"I did not know. Be patient. They are watching us," Edwin whispered, his head fixed forward.

The plan was for Edwin, his girlfriend Susan, who was also a classmate of ours, Beverly, and me to go to dinner. What I did not know was other female friends and cousins of Beverly were upstairs and would be joining us too. Chaperones galore!

After thirty more minutes and several more seating adjustments, a maid was sent upstairs to get Beverly and the other girls. Edwin and I stood. As the parade came down the stairs, I focused on the one girl I wished was Beverly.

My wish came true.

She was the one, the last to descend the stairs.

Beverly was the tallest and the prettiest, a Mestiza beauty with light, milk chocolate skin, full lips, straight nose, and oriental eyes. Her long, black, straight hair was pulled back to expose her face and ears. There was a hint of a smile.

Her steps were fluid and balanced, eyes forward, and shoulders level with the steps. Her right hand gently glided along the banister.

I took one step forward as she approached. There was a slight increase in her smile. I stared at her eyes. They appeared kind. Her eyelids lowered as she passed.

My heart pounded.

Beads of sweat dotted my forehead and back. I wiped my forehead with a white cotton handkerchief and was glad that I wore an undershirt.

I wanted to shake her hand.

No hand was offered.

The eyes of her relatives darted in rapid succession from Beverly to me.

My eyes remained focused on her.

I watched as she greeted her adult relatives with a gentle kiss on their cheeks. Young nieces and nephews ran to her to give *mano* (respect by placing Beverly's hand to their forehead).

With the last sign of respect given, Beverly sat between her female friends and cousins across from Edwin and me. Edwin sat, then I. My legs felt a bit weak but did not buckle.

I remained focused on her eyes.

Her relatives stared.

Her gaze remained slightly downward, the proper position for a shy, humble Filipina, particularly with all of the eyes focused on her.

My American blood stirred.

A smile consumed my face.

Edwin whispered, "Don't drool."

I mouthed, "Real funny."

More of my blood roused.

"It is nice to finally meet you." My voice tried to crack but a quick throat clearing aborted the potential embarrassment.

"I am sorry that you had to wait so long." Beverly's voice was soft but articulate.

"No, I didn't mean that I waited too long. It was worth the wait." A red flush covered my face.

The girls, our dreaded chaperones, giggled.

Beverly politely lowered her head a touch. No smile was evident. But no frown either.

Finally, we were permitted to leave. To my disappointment, Beverly did not sit next to me in the car. The traditional "no touch" was observed.

"Touch" referred to any physical conduct that could lead to sexual intercourse. I suspected the policy was supported and demanded by her stepmother. We were to keep a respectful distance from each other and be watched with multiple sets of eagle eyes.

I thought the no-touch rule sucked!

I did not know, until years later, how scared Beverly was that night. She had never met an American before, and I was her first non-Filipino suitor. I am sure she knew I was nervous. Although my voice had not cracked, my hands had quavered.

The evening went well. My conversational skills improved, and my trembles subsided. Beverly's shyness was revealed, her smile ideal. At the end of dinner, another custom was observed. I paid for everyone, including the chaperones. I was a proper gentleman that night, but I felt I would not be allowed to call upon Beverly again. After all, I was not a Filipino.

Back at the gate to Beverly's home and surrounded with our escorts, we exchanged smiles.

"Thank you for a lovely evening," Beverly said, breaking the silence.

"You are welcome. It was my pleasure." I felt the simplicity of my reply as I spoke.

"Good-bye then." Beverly turned as a door in the gate opened.

"Good-bye." I turned and entered the backseat of my car.

The eagles smiled, fluttered through the gate, and scurried off to give their report.

I was definitely not in Kansas.

The *dalaga* (young woman) is required by society to conduct herself with decorum and appear modest and shy, especially among men. Courtship in the Philippines is a game which both parties play. The young lady is supposed to play hard to get. Young men try to outdo each other in sweet talk or *bola* (bull). They send flowers, give presents, and call every night. Some suitors serenade at night, outside the dalaga's house. She listens but does not show herself in order to avoid hiya. A young man's devotion is measured by his overtures.

To my delight, I was allowed to visit Beverly once a week. I would arrive at her home and wait a "respectful" period of time before a maid was sent to get Beverly. We could not sit close, touch each other, or hold hands, in accordance with that ridiculous "no touch" policy. I could not call her my girlfriend. I was just a suitor. She had other suitors from rich Filipino families, suitors who gave her expensive gifts.

How could I compete?

A brilliant idea sliced into my mind. I would have a pizza made and delivered to Beverly. In our talks, I had learned that she'd never tasted a pizza.

My brilliant idea was difficult to execute. There were no pizza parlors in the country. My cooks were of no help. No one, it seemed, knew how to make a pizza.

A clerk at the US Embassy in Manila became my hero of the day. She had made pizza in the States and gave me the treasured recipe. Some of the ingredients for the pizza were not available. Substitution was in order. After several attempts, an acceptable pie was born. My driver delivered this "American treasure" to Beverly's home. I waited for a reply but there was none.

"Did you like the pizza?" I inquired after a week.

"You know about the pizza?" Beverly asked with bewilderment.

"I made it. Or I should say, I had it made."

"Oh. I was informed that someone else sent me the pizza. But yes, I really liked it. Thank you so much. You should not have gone to all that trouble." Beverly smiled.

"No trouble at all. It was my pleasure, and I am glad you liked it."

I wanted to get hold of Beverly's maid who misinformed her of the giver of my prized gift. One of her other suitors had received her grateful reply.

To this day, I claim it was that pizza that won me Beverly's heart. Her endearment to me is "pie."

I knew one day I would get involved with a Filipina. There were no Western women around. I was, after all, single and twenty-one and from a country that did not have that horrid "no touch" policy.

But I knew it would have to be a Filipina from a good and respectful family. I was now a son of the governor. The Philippines were very class-oriented.

There were many Filipinas from the lower-class that would want to be involved with an American for a green card. It was acceptable for me to "seek pleasure" with "that type of Filipina," but nothing more.

I had to obey the rules.

I did.

I hated the no-touch rule but obeyed it for Beverly.

I tried to break the rule many times. I offered bribes to her maids and drivers to look the other way and leave us alone for a while. I tried the line I used before in the States on Beverly. "If you love me…"

No success.

I thought the dating rules were old fashioned, but out of respect for Beverly and her family, I had to obey them. It did give me comfort to know that other suitors had to obey the same rules.

I was mad at, more than jealous of, one of the other suitors, Ed. He was tall for a Filipino and said to be cute. I didn't think so. He was from a rich family who pressed him to court Beverly. They wanted to strengthen their family's worth with Beverly's. He gave expensive gifts, walked and talked like he had already won Beverly's hand, and informed her many times, "You should stay with your own kind. Filipinos should be with Filipinos."

He was arrogant, *yabang*.

It did cross my mind to have my brother, Eddie, "take care of the situation."

I did not ask him.

I knew Beverly favored me.

So I stuck it out.

A lot of cold showers.

6

PALM SPRINGS, CALIFORNIA

1999

I turn off the recording machine.

I have several more tapes to complete but need to rest my eyes.

Our bedroom's sliding glass doors are open. It is early morning. I can hear the birds chirping. One is off-key and sounds like a crowing rooster.

My mind flashes to the island and the cockpits.

I am in third grade. My father has brought me, on the back of his motorcycle, to my first cockfight.

The fights on the island are in a circular structure with a central pit or arena and coliseum-style wooden bleachers. A roof keeps out sun and rain while the absence of walls permits light and ventilation. The fighting roosters, with a razor sharp spur attached to a leg, are placed in the arena and the betting begins. A bookmaker (*casador*) takes the bets as the crowd roars. A nod here and a quick hand gesture there verify the amount waged. The casador has a remarkable memory for faces. Reneging on a bet is inadvisable. The cockfight is over in minutes. The loser takes his dead rooster home and cooks it in a special dish called *talunan* (loser's repast).

My head spins, my ears ring, my eyes widen as I enter the arena. Men shout and push for a better view. Bets for the winning cock are yelled from around the ring. A sharp razor is strapped to their feet. I watch as two cocks fight to the death.

I try to turn away.

My father stops me.

"Watch it. This is great. You're lucky to be here," shouts my father as he gulps his beer.

I glance around. I am the only white boy, my father the only white man, in the pit.

The screams intensify.

I watch the fight and freeze at the kill. I want to leave but can't. My father has a firm grip on my shoulder with one of his hands, the other hand holds his fuel for rage. My eyes water. I smell death.

I do not speak. I stare forward. I do not move. I never look into the eyes of my father. He might see my weakness.

I become numb.

During the subsequent fights, I shout. I pick cocks for my father. I thank him for bringing me. I crave his respect. I receive none.

I do not pick a winning cock. He consumes countless bottles of San Miguel Beer and is mad that he lost.

We speed down a dirt road, a shortcut to home. The motorcycle staggers from side to side. The ride suddenly stops. I lie on the dirt road next to my father. His mangled motorcycle rests on one side a few feet away. I can smell his beer breath as I choke for air. Blood is on his face.

I feel no pain. I remain motionless and wait for him to stop breathing. He begins to stir.

"Buddy. I need you. We have to go play later tonight. He is going to be really mad," I whisper.

"I'm here. Don't be afraid. Be strong. We will go to our favorite place."

We do go away later that night.

In a few months, I become an expert cock picker. I do not know how I do it, but I choose winners. Tatay puts my gift to his benefit. I select cocks for him and the foreign diplomats he entertains. The foreigners' reaction to the spectacle of a cockfight amuses me. Some are alarmed, some disgusted, most excited. I profit. Tatay gives me *balato* (tip) with each win.

I remain numb at the fights.

"Jay, come here," calls the governor as he waves his right hand at me.

"I'm coming," I answer and run, tucking in the back of my shirt.

It is a weekend during my fourth grade, and I am spending time with the Barrettos. The sky is changing colors from blue to red to orange to violet as the sun disappears into the ocean. Trade winds stir the swaying coconut trees and refresh the night air.

I jump into the backseat of the car next to Tatay.

"Good boy." He pats my head and smiles. "Are you excited?"

"Yes, sir. I like cockfights. I'll pick you the winner," I boast.

"I know you will. You're the best," he affirms.

I smile and move closer to Tatay.

I never have to play with Buddy when I am with Tatay.

7

MANILA, PHILIPPINES

1972

The six-story charity hospital on the campus of UST admitted an endless supply of patients for our medical and surgical training. The hospital was sparsely furnished but clean. The surveying eyes of the nuns kept order, and the medical students were busy at all times. If not treating a patient, we made cotton balls from a large mound of cotton and four-by-four bandages out of large sections of gauze, repaired elastic surgical gloves with worn-out gloves and glue, and re-sharpened used injection needles and scalpels. Supplies discarded after one use in the States were precious and reused after sterilization. Modern medical equipment was not available to assist in our diagnosis. Proper history and physical examination were critical and our basis for medical care. Our clinical eye was perfected. Our proficiency was enhanced by rotations at San Lazaro Hospital, a government facility. There were rows of pavilions for sufferers of dysenteries, diphtheria, typhoid, tetanus with lockjaw, malaria, tuberculosis, and cholera. I stepped over rice-water stools that flooded the floor when buckets, placed under cots with large holes cut out for patients' buttocks, overflowed. Some patients vomited live giant roundworms, Ascaris Lumbricoides. Others, afflicted with elephantiasis, with enormous legs and testicles carried in a wheelbarrow, challenged our abilities. The rare and unusual were the norm at San Lazaro.

After my first day at San Lazaro Hospital, I made sure our cooks washed lettuce with Clorox then rinsed it in lots of boiled water to prevent ingestion of Ascaris Lumbricodes eggs and that servants sprayed our bedrooms at dusk to kill mosquitoes to prevent dengue fever, an acute febrile disease that can cause hemorrhagic death. Mosquitoes seemed to seek me out, as if attracted to my white skin or foreign scent. One night, I was assigned with several of my classmates to a pavilion at San Lazaro Hospital with malnourished, dehydrated, and dying babies. Feeble fans tried to provide comfort. Mosquitoes attacked relentlessly. Our white uniforms were drenched in sweat and soiled from the little ones. Long wooden tables with overhead beams nailed in every foot provided the stage for the factory line. Intravenous bags hung from the nails. Beneath each bag was a motionless baby, lying on its back.

"I can't find the vein." My voice cracked and my eyes watered, irritated with sweat. I struggled to insert an intravenous needle into a little one's head. No veins were visible. The limp baby was motionless throughout multiple attempts.

"Jay, move on to the next one. We can't save them all," advised Edwin as he stopped to wipe his forehead with his soiled cotton handkerchief. He struggled with another infant.

When an insertion in a baby was successful, we proceeded down the line. If we could not insert the needle, the baby was removed and replaced by another one. At the end of the table, we started back again. Exhaustion, not the lack of babies, caused us to stop.

Edwin glanced at me with a hollow look. He was right. We could not save them all. As I cried out, my head bowed, I questioned God's love that day. How could he allow babies and children to suffer and die?

My faith had heightened since I returned to the island. I worshiped daily and felt my spirit connect with God's spirit. I prayed for guidance and help with the babies, but he turned his back on me. He let little ones die.

I doubted God's kindness and mercy.

The faces of the babies haunted me as if they were etched into my brain. I tried to focus on my studies. Months passed but the images remained fresh. I knew anatomy was the key. I must know where veins and arteries are, even if collapsed or invisible. I must know. I had to know.

I settled down into my routine—attending lectures during the morning, doing clinical work in the afternoon, and studying late into the night—until the floods.

The Philippines have a tropical rainforest climate all over the country. The two main characteristics of this climate are high temperatures and high atmospheric humidity, both present the whole year. But June to October have torrential rains, like buckets pouring heavy streams of water. A third feature of the climate is the presence of strong typhoons that torture the land every year between June and November.

As a child, I played in the rain, which was like a massive warm shower. As a medical student, I saw its devastating effects. The typhoon rains were ruthless, causing major floods. I volunteered to give medical care to the flood victims in villages accessible only by *bangkas* (native canoes). The care was directed through my medical school and sanctioned by President Marcos. The floods left villages submerged and victims without food and fresh water. Huts on lower ground were only visible by their roofs. The water had consumed the village and distorted the landscape. Life was halted. It was like a scene out of a movie, but I was in it, thrust into mission work before I felt prepared.

I was in a bangka one day with two classmates and a villager who paddled through the filthy water. "My God, how can we help all of these people?" I asked not really expecting a response.

My classmate, Edwin, answered, "We can't."

"We have to try!" My voice cracked. His head nodded in agreement. "Careful," I shouted as our bangka almost tipped over. We had limited precious supplies. Most of the seriously ill were babies and small children. We stepped out of the bangka. The water came up to my waist and to the chests of my classmates. The fear of water snakes caused my heart to pound like a drum.

Dog-faced water snakes, hidden below the murky water, could strike without notice.

We carried the supplies over our heads and entered the first *Nipa* (palm) hut. Pitiful eyes of children and terrified eyes of adults were fixed on us. They had been trapped for days. The bamboo-slatted floor dipped as if to break as we added our additional weight.

The Nipa hut, also known as the *bahay kubo* (house-hut), is an indigenous house used in the Philippines before the Spaniards arrived in 1521. They are still used today, especially in rural areas. The native house is constructed out of bamboo tied together, with a thatched roof using *nipa/anahaw* (palm) leaves and built on stilts. I struggled to insert IVs in babies without visible veins and with lack of a proper sterile environment. There was no running water, no indoor plumbing. I was resolute but overwhelmed.

I would like to say that we saved thousands of lives that day, but we did not. I must be content with the babies we did save and all the treatment we were able to give in the midst of horrific conditions. I wondered whether God was there. When I prayed, there was no answer. "What are we supposed to do?" I asked Edwin as we headed back to Manila aboard the bus.

We were too exhausted to be hungry, too overwhelmed to sleep. "We could pray." Edwin's hair was in disarray. Sweat drenched his shirt. His skin was darker brown, matching the murky color of the floodwater. "I have been." I looked at my skin, now a patchwork of white and brown. "Jay," Edwin whispered.

"Yes."

"We did our best."

"I know. Try to get some rest. We have class tomorrow." I turned my head away from Edwin and looked out the window of the bus into the dark night. It was still raining. Tears flowed down my cheeks.

Edwin was my *pare* (buddy) and a member of my *barkada* (peers). Filipinos enjoy close friendship with those of the same gender, usually stemming from childhood. A male arm on another man's shoulder and males holding hands, particularly among pares, is not considered gay. It is the accepted norm. Barkadas go everywhere together and develop their own slang and private jokes. They exercise control over the behavior of fellow members mainly by teasing, having a powerful force with group pressure and conformity. They operate with *pakikisama* (getting along with others), requiring a member to yield to group opinion, pressuring him to do what he can for the advancement of his group, sacrificing individual welfare for the general welfare. There is usually no formal leader, though one or two members may be more respected.

The next morning, it was difficult to concentrate on the lecture of the anatomy and physiology of nerves. I didn't care about neurons, dendrites, and synapses. My eyes watered as I remembered the babies in the huts.

The lecturer's slides went out of focus with superimposed images of the little dead faces.

I looked over at Edwin. His head was down. I did not know if he was sleeping in the cover of the darkened classroom or praying, but his hair was back to perfect form.

I closed my eyes.

But I could still see the faces of the little ones.

I prayed for understanding and peace of mind.

And then it began. The word spread like the plague.

Martial law. Martial law.

On September 21, 1972, President Ferdinand Marcos issued Proclamation 1081, declaring martial law over the entire country. Marcos blamed communist insurgents with their network of front organizations "among the peasants, laborers, professionals, intellectuals, students, and mass media personal" for the demise of the Philippine democracy and the need for martial law.

We ran out of our classroom into chaos. Drivers sent to retrieve their students narrowly dodged other students and professors.

"Jay, Sir Jay!"

I recognized the voice of my driver over the thunderous noise. I turned around and around, searching for its location. I had an advantage being taller than my classmates and professors. I spotted him after a few more turns and followed him to the car.

"There. Keep down and cover up with the blanket," he pleaded.

"No. It's too hot to be under a blanket."

"You must. Your Tatay gave me explicit instructions. Now hurry."

Shouting, gunfire, and blaring horns overwhelmed my sense of perception. I pulled back the blanket and looked out the window. We were on side streets, attempting to avoid checkpoints erected quickly, weaving between barricades and thousands of people running in every direction like a chaotic, choreographed dance. Tanks entered the scene at stage left and right. Military men marched alongside with weapons drawn. I concealed myself under the cover and prayed. When the racket lessened, I popped my head out and recoiled at the sight of armed soldiers approaching the car. I held my breath as I heard fist-like poundings on the car, then I began to pant as if I had run a marathon. Hours passed. I sat up, my body drenched, as the car sped through the opened gate at the house.

I was helped from the car, entered the house through a side door near the clean kitchen, sat at a rectangular glass table used for early morning breakfasts, grabbed a pitcher of ice water and guzzled two glasses. Servants scurried about, some packing food, others clothes, in preparation for a possible immediate departure to the governor's provincial home in Zambales, Northern Luzon. Nanay and Tatay emerged from their bedroom after being told that I had just arrived. Their children were in the upstairs bedrooms. Tatay asked me to tell him what I had seen or heard on the streets. I did while drinking more water. Nanay was upset it had taken so long for me to arrive. She had thought the worst. She wanted me to eat something but never told the cook. She stopped a servant girl to make sure that my things had been packed, brushed back a few strands of hair that had fallen in front of her face, turned and reassured me that everything would be fine, and tried to smile. Tatay nodded but did not smile. His breathing was deepened but controlled, as if getting ready for a fight.

Foreigners and those considered political threats to President Marcos were targets. Our family was politically in favor with Marcos, but I was a foreigner. Plans were instituted for my escape from the island if necessary.

Four days passed with no official news—news blackout.

"Jay, we do not want you to leave either, but you might have to," Tatay declared as he paced back and forth in the master bedroom with short, strong steps. It had been a few days since martial law was declared. "You are a foreigner. There is talk that all foreigners are to be seized. I may not be able to protect you. Things are changing so fast. I don't want you to be taken away to prison."

Nanay sat on the bed and sobbed.

"But Tatay," I pleaded.

"No, Jay. Plans are being made to get you off the island by boat or even in a bangka if needed. There is panic everywhere. People are disappearing from families we know. I first thought of bringing you to the ranch in Zambales. But there are too many NPAs in that region. You would not be safe there. I must keep you safe."

The NPA, the New People's Army, was the military arm of the Communist Party of the Philippines. For years the rebels had led guerilla attacks, vowing to overthrow the government by revolutionary insurrection. The strength of the NPA quickly spread through the Philippines during the dictatorship of Ferdinand Marcos.

Tatay sat next to Nanay, put his arm around her, turned, and stared at me with tears in his eyes.

"I do not want to lose you, Jay. But it may be necessary for you to return to your family in the States, to your father."

I sat on a comfortable chair. My insides twisted. I could not speak.

I never told Tatay or Nanay of my perils at home in the States.

I also did not want to leave Beverly. I was in love. Her love did not hurt.

I did not want to quit my medical school.

We stayed in the master bedroom for hours, as if to postpone the inevitable.

Eventually, I returned to medical school. "Jay, you must be extremely careful. Try to blend in with your classmates. Do not speak ill of Marcos. You and the family will be punished if you do." Tatay spoke in a strong, deliberate tone at the breakfast table. Darkness under his eyes showed his lack of sleep. It had been a few weeks of martial law.

"I will be careful," I assured Tatay as I fought to control my tears.

The strained look on Tatay's face pained me.

"Good. Do not trust anyone outside the family. You will be watched."

"Okay."

"Do not break the curfew. You will be arrested."

"I won't."

"If you were taken, I couldn't bear it." His eyes watered, his voice cracked.

"Please don't worry. I will be careful."

I stood, went over to Tatay, and hugged him with an embrace of love, son to father.

❧

The plans for my secret departure were made but never executed. Tatay had been reassured by a general of the Armed Forces of the Philippines that I was not a target.

The military arrested opposition figures, including politicians, journalists, student and labor activists, and criminal elements. Weapons were confiscated, and "private armies" connected with prominent politicians and other figures were broken up. Most powerful families complied by giving up some of their weapons but keeping enough for arming their private bodyguards. The rest were hidden to avoid discovery during random home searches by the army and Philippine Constabulary. Newspapers were shut down, and the mass media were brought under tight control. With the stroke of a pen, Marcos closed the Philippine Congress and assumed its legislative responsibilities. During the 1972-1981 martial law period, Marcos, invested with dictatorial powers, issued hundreds of presidential decrees.

Most Filipinos—or at least those well-positioned with economic and social clites—initially supported the imposition of martial law. Before the martial law, the rising tide of violence and lawlessness was apparent to everyone. Guns were carried and used to settle disputes and arguments.

To gain support of the masses, Marcos confiscated businesses owned by the Chinese and Mestizo oligarchs to redistribute to Filipino businessmen, and he seized privately owned lands and distributed them to farmers, including some rice fields belonging to Beverly's family. But it led to graft and corruption via bribery, racketeering, and embezzlement.

Marcos used his power to settle scores against old rivals. Leading opponents such as Senator Benigno "Ninoy" Aquino, Jr., Jose Diokno, Jovito Salonga, and many others were imprisoned for months or years. Other political opponents were given the opportunity for compliance or were forced to go into exile. Some were taken and never seen again. Marcos' regime was marred by rampant corruption and political mismanagement by his relatives and cronies, which culminated with the assassination of Benigno Aquino in 1983. My Tatay had met with Aquino in San Francisco the night before he went back to the Philippines. They had been childhood friends, barkada. Tatay pleaded with Aquino not to return to the island. He feared for Aquino's life. Aquino was assassinated at the Manila International Airport upon his return to the Philippines after a long period of exile. Opponents of Marcos blamed the president directly for the assassination while others blamed the military and his wife, Imelda.

Tatay remained unharmed and continued to serve as the chairman of the National Power Corporation. He walked a fine line between being loyal to President Marcos and true to his buddy, Aquino.

For the years under martial law, I obeyed all of Tatay's commands although it was difficult for me to "blend into the environment." Marcos' "spies" were everywhere, ready to turn you in as payment for disloyalty. Curfew was enforced. Being caught outside after midnight meant arrest and not being seen for a while, sometimes never. A few times, I was out late past curfew. My driver drove through side streets with headlights off, avoiding military checkpoints at all cost. One time, it did cost me a lot. I was stopped and explained who my Tatay was, but I still handed over a roll of Filipino pesos. After that incident, it took me years after I left the Philippines for me to stop looking over my shoulder in public before speaking.

I still do it at times today.

Private communication, without government control, was difficult. I was asked by my family to smuggle four CB (Citizens' Band) radios into the country. CB radios were *bawal* (prohibited, forbidden) during martial law in the Philippines. Having an American passport allowed me leave the country and return. Those with Filipino passports were barred from leaving. I obediently left and a few days later returned with the radios hidden inside one of my suitcases, marked to alert an inside customs official who was loyal to the family not to open that luggage. The antennas were pulled apart and disguised as parts to fishing poles, namely their rods. The sweat on my back and brow were an ordinary sight on a foreigner entering the island with the sultry air, not of a frightened smuggler.

"Be strong. Stand straight," Buddy commanded as I stood in front of the final inspector.

If caught, I would go to prison for life.

"Thank you, sir." The customs inspector handed me my passport, smiled, and nodded.

"Thank you," I replied with a slight smile.

My sweat was now more than could be explained by the heat. I strolled straight to my waiting car. A run would have enhanced my excessive sweat and prompted suspicion.

"Let's get out of here." My smile was now replaced with a grin.

The car scrambled.

I vowed never to do that again.

I kept that promise.

We settled into our life under martial law. I went back to school and my studies. At the charity hospital, there was an increasing number of patients with brutal bolo wounds. Since martial law and the restriction of guns, there had been an escalation in bolo assaults.

The Philippine bolo could be either a long knife or short sword. Normally, the bolo was a farm implement to cut wood, clear jungle bush, slay animals, cut down banana trees or harvest their fruit, and open coconut husks. The bolo could also be a deadly weapon used historically by farmers to settle disputes, by the revolutionaries against the Spaniards, and by the military and guerilla unit against the Japanese in World War II.

The "Kampilan" bolo was the weapon most favored by the Moros (Muslims) in Mindanao, a southern island of the Philippines. It had a fearsome look and was meant for battle, the equivalent of the Japanese samurai's "katana." The mystical "kris" was another favorite of the Moros. The wavy shape of its blade gave it distinction; according to lore, it was indicative of a lightning-bolt strike to earth from the heavens, or a snake. It allowed for easier body penetration, made a nastier wound than a straight blade as it slipped easily between bones and through joints and facilitated retraction for more attacks

I became an expert bolo-wound healer. I used my knife, the scalpel, to repair damage from the cruel cuts of the swords.

8

PALM SPRINGS, CALIFORNIA

1999

My eyes open.

The blades of the ceiling fan appear larger and sharper as they slice through the air and my thoughts.

I am spellbound.

The walls in the ward are bare except for a crucifix. It is hot, humid, and stifling, a typical day at the charity hospital in Manila. Old, flat, metal-framed beds with thin mattresses, small pillows, and mosquito nets line the perimeter. Fans struggle to circulate the sticky air. A lizard flees across the bed of a fortunate patient. The reptile consumes unwanted insects.

I inspect the hack wounds of a young man sliced by a bolo sword. Two nurses assist. There are mutilating blows to his upper limbs as he attempted to ward off the attack. There is a near amputation of his right upper extremity and some missing fingers. His back is sliced open with massive loss of tissue, including skin, subcutaneous tissue, connective tissue, muscle, veins, arteries, and nerves. Suturing is a challenge, grafting impossible.

I despise wounds. I need to heal them.

We try to keep our freshly pressed white uniforms free of blood and antiseptic solution. Our wet foreheads are wiped frequently.

Suddenly, voices explode.

I look up to see a group of men waving bolos and rushing into the ward shouting, "He must die! He must die!"

"Oh my God!" yells a nurse. Another stands frozen and mute.

I grab their arms and pull them down to the next bed. Around us, patients are wide-eyed and mute. The nurses recite the Lord's Prayer. We watch in horror as multiple bolo strikes dismember our patient. One of the attackers turns and stares into my eyes. His sword drips blood. I remain motionless and find myself repeating the Lord's Prayer in silence.

Finally, the killers turn and flee. Their bolos splatter blood on our uniforms as they wave them over their heads.

We return to our patient and stare at his mutilated body: legs hacked off, more massive back wounds (no defensive wounds in his prone position), and a split-open skull exposing the brain like an open coconut displaying fruit. An expanding pool of blood creeps across the floor.

The silence of the other patients is replaced with wailing prayers. I begin to ask myself, "My God, what am I doing here? Why didn't I fight to protect my patient? Is a doctor supposed to put his life on the line for his patient? Did I make the right choice to attend medical school in the Philippines?" It is not the first time I questioned my ability to be a doctor. Nor would it be the last.

9

MANILA, PHILIPPINES

1972

I was not allowed to openly participate in political elections, provincial or national, since I was an American citizen.

During a provincial election, our family was at the governor's home in Zambales, Northern Luzon. The house was bustling with activity. Election officials ran about. Frantic chatter became frustrated shouts.

I wanted tranquility and needed to work on my tan. The obvious solution to me was the beach. My tactful pleading worked, and Tatay allowed me to go to the beach but insisted on extra bodyguards for my protection. Reluctantly, I surrendered to his demand, gathered my belongings, and jumped into the car. We were like sardines in a can, but I was happy to get away.

"There. This is a nice place to swim," announced the driver as we pulled up to a pristine section of white sand. Coconut trees lined the edge and swayed in the hot breeze. A towel was laid in the sun for my use. The driver and guards sat under the shelter of some coconut trees. No sunbathing for them.

The ocean water refreshed me. Despite being warm, it was dramatically cooler than the intense heat of the day. The guards surveyed my every movement. Thumbs-up were exchanged as I left the water and walked to my towel. After a few adjustments to the sand under my towel, I relaxed.

I fell asleep listening to the sounds of the waves in my sand cradle.

"What are you doing here, G.I Joe?"

A native male straddled over me, his breath laden with alcohol. The nose of his rifle bored into my back.

"Hey, G.I. Joe, what are you doing here?"

Shots fired.

"Get off him," shouted one of my bodyguards.

More shots.

"Get the hell off of him," yelled another bodyguard.

The weight of the man shifted as the pressure of his rifle dug deeper. He struggled to dismount from me, using his rifle as a cane planted into my back. He staggered a few steps and fell into the sand. A guard pinned him into the sand. Another guard tossed his rifle toward the coconut trees.

Two guards grabbed my arms, helped me to stand up, and rushed me into the water, where they released their grip and rushed back to assist their comrades.

My guards and driver had fallen asleep and never saw the man coming. They awoke with his shouting.

Rifle butts struck the man's head.

The pristine white sand splattered red.

"Stop it! Stop it!" I screamed running out of the water. "You're going to kill him. Stop it."

They halted the beating.

The car had been turned around. The back door opened. I jumped in. My heart pounded, my legs and arms shook.

I stared out the window of the car. Coconut trees and rice fields were blurred by the speed of the vehicle. Shouts between the guards, blaming and cursing each other, deafened my hearing.

I closed my eyes and put my hands over my ears.

The stench of the man's alcohol-breath lingered in my nose.

I felt like vomiting.

The guards stopped their shouts and repeatedly said "Sir, sorry *po.*" (Sorry with utmost respect.)

Their apologies fell on my deaf ears.

I remained mute and focused on not vomiting.

"Sir, sorry po."

I opened the window to get rid of the stench.

It did not work.

I vomited.

I ran into the house through the main entrance, interrupting Tatay and some officials' meeting. I tried to run past Tatay but was stopped by his quick commanding eyes.

"Jay. Jay. What's wrong?"

"Nothing, Tatay. Sorry I disturbed you." I stood still.

Tatay turned to his company and nodded. His eyebrows raised and mouth protruded (a common Filipino way of pointing) toward the door. They were proper signals, for a man of his position, to command the officials to leave the room.

"Why are you back so soon? What happened?"

We were alone, his tone now more intense.

"Nothing, Tatay."

I wanted to leave, but I had too much respect for Tatay.

Elders were respected and revered by Filipinos as the living links of tradition and family roots. To embarrass your elder in public was inexcusable. A respectful greeting, particularly for family elders, was to hold your elder's hand and press their hand on your forehead while saying *mano po* (permission to do the gesture). It was the traditional Filipino acknowledgement of respect for elders.

There was also a respectful way of crossing a room where there are people conversing, or cutting in between them. Your hands should be clasped together in front and used to advance with lowered head. Or you could extend one hand in front, fingers together as in a karate chop, elbows bent, and head bowed.

I had broken these rules today.

I told Tatay what happened at the beach. My two older brothers were called into the room. The eldest son, Cesar (*Kuya*, or older brother*)*, was instructed to take care of the situation.

I knew what that meant.

Cesar looked like a young Spanish Casanova, and he was one. Eddie, the second eldest son, was taller and stockier than Cesar with a Mestizo look and distinct mischievous smile.

I learned later that the guards were beaten and fired. Tatay was outraged that I was not watched closely. I could have been killed if the man had fired by reflex when the guards fired their guns.

I never blamed myself for the incident. It was the guards' job to watch and protect me, whether at home or at the beach. They did not.

I did not want them beaten. I did not like wounds on anyone. I did not care that they were fired. I felt they should have been.

I did not return to the beach for the rest of that stay in Zambales.

The following morning, I rested on a bamboo and rattan lounge chair under a mango tree. Roosters crowed and Maya birds sang. No sunbathing, but I was content.

"Tito Jay, what are you doing?" Vicky, a petite, playful, young granddaughter of Tatay and Nanay, stirred some soil with her foot.

"Thinking."

"About what?"

"That I am hungry, and I am going to eat you."

I jumped out of the chair and grabbed her arm. It was then I noticed the small, flat, red spots and raised bumps on her arm. I had seen these spots on children at the charity hospital and knew of possible causes for the rash—scarlet fever, measles, heat rash, skin reaction to antibiotic drugs, meningitis, and dengue fever.

I felt her forehead, and she was warm.

"Vicky, do you have a headache?" I asked calmly.

"Yes, Tito Jay."

"Does it hurt here and here?" I inquired as I pressed on muscles in her arms and legs.

"Yes."

I walked her inside and applied my blood pressure cuff and inflated it to a point between her systolic and diastolic blood pressure. I suspected dengue fever. After five minutes, I inspected her skin. There were countless petechiae (small red spots). A test is positive for dengue fever when there are ten petechiae or more per square inch. The test was highly positive. My suspicion confirmed.

Cesar (Vicky's father and my Kuya), Charito (Vicky's mother), and I rushed her to Manila. The driver was ordered to go faster. And he did.

It was a frightening two-hour ride on streets with cars, buses, dogs, motorized tricycles, jeepneys (converted passenger jeeps), pedestrians, *kalesas* (horse-drawn carriages), and *carabao*s (water buffalo). And there were no rules of the road. The most vital part of your vehicle was the horn. The most vital part of your driver was his big testicles.

"You saved this little girl's life," a doctor at the hospital announced to me in front of Cesar and Charito.

My diagnosis was correct. She had severe dengue hemorrhagic fever.

After a platelet transfusion, intravenous fluids, and a lot of close observation and rest, Vicky was released from the hospital.

"Thank you, Tito Jay." Vicky, nudged by her mother, ran and jumped into my arms.

"You're welcome, squirt." I smiled and squeezed her gently. The exhaustion from my studies was alleviated by a little hug, the power of pure love.

It was not the only time I saved the life of a Barretto.

As a medical student, I also saved the life of my sister, Maribel, the eldest daughter of Tatay and Nanay. I had just watched the birth of Carlo, my godson. Buddy hollered at me to turn around. Maribel was whiter than her hospital bed. I threw back the sheet. She was in a pool of her blood. She had uterine atony, relaxation of an enlarged uterus with hemorrhage, and was bleeding to death. I began massaging the uterus and screamed at the nurses for IVs and a blood transfusion. Her doctor rushed over and continued where I started. He told the family I had saved Maribel. She was fine except for weakness on the right side of her face.

Tatay thanked God for having me as a son. He told me it was God's will that I came back to the island.

It felt great for a father to be proud of me. It felt great to be loved by a father. It gave me strength to study harder. And I did. "Buddy, Tatay loves me," I whispered.

"I know he does."

"Never let me tell him about the other one in the States," I pleaded.

"I won't. You're a good person. I am proud of you."

"Thanks," I cried. "I love you, Buddy."

"Me too."

10

PALM SPRINGS, CALIFORNIA

1999

My eyes are closed as I lie supine in bed, and the ceiling fan whirls its blades.

His eyes come into focus, as if seen through my Nikon camera's zoom lens. The power of my father's stare paralyzes my pathetic, wounded body. I can do nothing. I cannot move. I cannot cry. I am weak. I pray.

But he comes back, refocused.

My father stands erect at five foot seven inches. Chest out, chin tucked in—a military stance. He walks with short deliberate and strong steps. His muscular arms are trained weapons. Scars from World War II and the Korean War, some from bayonets, are badges of honor. More scars later, from two years in Vietnam, add to his collection. He shows no emotions. He is strong and to be feared.

To me, my father is the ruler, the enforcer. I feel safe outdoors. He does not strike me in public.

Outdoors, he scans the surroundings, surveys the terrain. He is always in a protective mode and ready to strike. He shows no fear. I see that neighbors admire my father. I am told, "You're so lucky to have such a wonderful father. You must feel so safe."

Inside our home, I try to be invisible, which is often difficult. He has the same posture as outdoors except when drinking. Then his shoulders begin to drop a bit, his back is a little less stiff, and his stride is a bit unsteady. But his hardened eyes remain the same, although red. If he enters our home at night drunk, my insides twist; I attempt to go to my bedroom, and pray that he will not enter. Often my prayers are not answered. I doubt the existence of God or at least that he is a loving God and cares about me.

Buddy tells me to be perfect, to make my father proud of me.

At the kitchen and dining table, he sits erect, both feet firmly on the floor. No talking. All plates of food are to be eaten before being dismissed from the table.

He sits erect in his easy chair or lies flat on his back on the sofa. The sofa is usually reserved for him when he is passed out.

I can be called to him from my bedroom any time. I do not know why. But I know it is not good. He often has me stand on my toes, draws a circle on the wall where my nose hits, and orders me to keep my nose in the circle. At my back, he shouts; his beer breath felt with occasional spit at the back of my neck. I cannot see him but know that he stands erect; weapon arms posed to strike and hardened eyes glaring as if to pierce my spine. He shouts my offenses. I might have answered a question earlier with the wrong tone of voice, or did not complete a chore to his satisfaction, or did not mind my mother enough, or simply had stood or walked wrong, usually not strong or manly enough.

My mind wanders as Buddy and I play in a peaceful place but not for long.

My heel drops.

My nose moves off target.

Strike.

"Buddy, I can't go with you right now. I can't move. But don't leave me."

"I understand. I'll stay with you. Be strong."

"I'm trying. But he hates me."

"Be strong. Stay focused. It will be over soon then we can go play."

"Okay."

My legs shake.

Strike.

11

MANILA, PHILIPPINES

1972

I joined the College of Medicine's swimming team. I swam well, winning gold medals and a few silvers. I had an advantage over my competitors with my longer stretch. Weekly swim meets were held at universities throughout the Greater Manila Area and in some provinces. In the provinces, we were housed in dormitory facilities and some local homes.

"Jay, Jay, wake up. Can I get into bed with you, please?" Rene begged.

He was my classmate, fellow swimmer, and barkada.

"What? What's wrong?" I asked still half-asleep.

"The coach grabbed me. Please. May I stay with you?"

"Sure. Come on."

It was not strange that Rene wanted to get into bed with me. There was no sexual connotation. It was a pure, male-to-male friendship bonding.

A lot of homes on the island, particularly of the poor, had very few beds and a lot of relatives and friends to accommodate. It was usual—rather than unusual or strange—for relatives and friends of the same sex to sleep together, even in twin beds.

I felt Rene's body tremble as he snuggled into my single bed. Rene was big for a Filipino, large in stature and kindness. His ebony skin contrasted sharply with my ivory tone, like piano keys. His chiseled chest and upper back muscles propelled him ahead of others in his swimming heats of the Australian crawl (butterfly stroke).

I fell back to sleep and awoke later that morning, initially surprised that Rene was next to me. Then I remembered. "Rene, wake up. We have to get ready."

"Thanks, *pare ko* (my mate). I could not stay in that room with coach."

"Why?'

"I was asleep and awoke with his hand inside my underwear."

"What?"

"Yeah, I wanted to hit him, but I couldn't." Rene shook his head. *Hiya* was in Rene's face and voice.

"Rene, you did nothing to be ashamed of," I comforted.

Hiya was a Filipino sanction, an uncomfortable feeling of being in or performing a socially unacceptable position.

"*Walang hiya ang* coach (the coach has no shame)," added Rene.

Walang hiya was the worst condemnation directed at someone who does not know proper behavior and therefore behaves without any regard for his self-esteem.

Our coach was also the dean of our medical school. Rene was smart for not retaliating that night. He might have been expelled. There was that strict rule about ultimate respect for your elder and a person of authority. Better to be quiet.

I was not surprised that Rene told me about our coach. We were barkada. We watched out for each other.

I never confronted our coach. He knew Rene and I were barkada. He knew Rene came to my bed that night. He knew I knew. He never showed anger toward me. He showed respect.

I held his secret.

I did not tell Tatay. Barkadas tried to solve their own problems.

If he tried it again, I would have told Tatay and Eddie would "take care of the situation," especially if it involved me. That would have insulted the family.

He never did it again.

The coach was married with children. His wife was a close friend of Beverly's mother and was a professor at our medical school. In retrospect, I remember the frequent talks our coach had in the locker room at the meets. My stomach turned recalling the times coach had discussed my performance or plans for the next competition while I showered. At the time, it did not bother me.

Most Filipinos were curious about my anatomy, wondering how "big" I was.

One day, I was walking in front of three Filipina nursing students at school when one loudly declared, "*Siguro malaki ang tete niyon.*"

She had bet that I had a big dick.

"*Talaga* (for sure)," replied one of the other students.

They did not know I spoke Tagalog.

"*Gusto kayo makita?*" I asked if they wanted to see it.

The nursing students froze for a moment then bowed their heads and walked away briskly.

I smiled and resumed my walk.

My studies continued, and the swimming season was coming to an end. The final meet was the talk at our medical school. We were in position to make history if we took first place.

"Come on, guys. We have this, our final race. Jay, finish strong. You know what this means." It was the short jubilant speech by our coach. His eyes focused on me and not on Rene.

The four of us bowed our heads briskly at each other and pumped our fists. Rene and I spoke with our eyes. We were doing this for our school, not for our coach.

I could hear the roar as my head turned to gasp air. I shot up out of the water after I touched the wall. My head turned from side to side, my eyes still blurred from the chlorinated water.

"Jay, we did it," shouted Rene as he jumped like a gazelle.

Students and faculty at our university surrounded us in jubilation. It was the first time in one hundred years that the College of Medicine at the University of Santo Tomas had won the intercollegiate swimming competition.

It was also the last time we had to endure the coach's stare while showering.

Back on dry land, I had another problem, Dra. Carmelita Belmonte Cuyugan, Beverly's stepmother. She was a professor and chairman of the Department of Pediatrics. I was determined to be victorious in this contest—or battle.

"Answer," commanded Dra. Cuyugan.

I stood at the side of my desk. Her snapping fingers distracted me.

"Mr. Roberts, you need to study more," declared Dra. Cuyugan. The intensity of her snapping increased.

I concentrated and gave the correct answer.

She stopped snapping her fingers and went on to the next student.

I stared at her and did not smile.

Nor did she.

The next week, we had clinical rounds.

"Mr. Roberts, give me your findings and diagnosis." Dra. Cuyugan snapped fingers louder than before.

"Yes, doctora." I stood at the bedside of an infant in the charity clinical hospital. Sweat poured down my face and back. "This child has a relentless cough, loss of weight, fever, night sweats, crackling sounds in the lungs, and a positive tuberculin skin test. He has tuberculosis."

My fellow student physicians stood still.

The mother of the patient appeared frozen in her chair.

"What? Are you ignorant or just not studying enough?" barked Dra. Cuyugan.

I looked down.

I thought I was right in my findings and diagnosis. I had studied hard, reviewed the patient's chart meticulously, and thoroughly examined the little one. I did not know what I missed.

I bit my lip.

I knew she would prefer for me to study all the time and have no time for Beverly.

"I suggest you reevaluate this patient," she remarked, as she took her stethoscope out of her ears and placed it into a pocket of her pristine white lab coat.

All of us student physicians sweated.

She did not.

"Beverly, your mother was impossible today. As soon as she asked me a question, she began snapping her fingers."

"I'm sorry, Jay."

"No, she's sorry."

"What?"

"I knew the answers. She tried not to show it, but I could see annoyance in her eyes."

"Maybe she was proud that you knew."

"No, Beverly, she hates me. You know she thinks I am not good enough for you and that you should only court Filipinos."

"Jay, remember I told you she has to be hard on you at school. She cannot show any sign of special treatment to you because of us."

"Don't worry. She's not giving me any special treatment. But Beverly, at your home, who does she have to show that I'm not getting special treatment? Your brothers, sister, or the maids?"

"Jay, you are a good person. She will come to realize that. Give her time."

"But sometimes, I just want to scream."

"But you won't. I know. Be patient with her and pray instead."

"Yeah. But I don't have the patience of Job."

Beverly smiled and I melted.

I studied harder. Coffee and cigarettes continued to keep me alert. I had wanted for years to stop smoking, had tried many times since college but always failed, usually in less than a day.

The time I searched the ashtrays and trashcan for a butt to smoke, I knew just how low I had sunk. But I still smoked it.

The more Dra. Cuyugan pressed me, the more I studied. My only defense was to know the answers. I could not go on the offense. I had to remain respectful. I bit my lips many times during my time in pediatrics.

I shined in pediatrics.

My lip sores healed.

Months later, I stood in the waiting room of Dra. Cuyugan. It was the first time I entered her medical office in the private hospital at UST. Beverly asked me to accompany her to her stepmother's office. I initially objected but gave in on the second request.

"Your mother is expecting you. Go on in," announced the receptionist as she smiled at me.

I remained motionless.

Beverly opened the door to the private office. Her stepmother was at her desk. She looked up and smiled at Beverly. Her smile stopped when she saw me.

I remained in my position.

She slightly bowed her head and Beverly closed the door.

After a short while, Beverly came out. She was not smiling. Her eyes were wet.

"She said I have to study harder. And that it is scandalous for me to be seen with you."

We left the office and sat outside on a cement bench under a large mahogany tree.

"Jay, I have shown her respect all these years out of honor to my father. I do not know how much longer I can hold my tongue." She trembled.

I wanted to hug her but couldn't.

Eyes were watching us.

I wanted to scream.

Buddy told me to behave.

I did.
I bit my lip.
More sores to heal.

12

PALM SPRINGS, CALIFORNIA

1999

"Dad, can't they do anything else for you?" Ryan asks, sitting on the bed next to me.

"No, I am afraid not," I answer and place my hand on his hand. He squeezes my hand.

Derek sits next to Ryan. His eyes are full of tears.

"Sons, don't worry. You'll be fine. Remember that I have always loved you, and I always will."

All of ours eyes water.

"We know you love us, Dad. And we love you," Derek sobs.

"Yeah, Dad," Ryan cries.

"I will always be with you in spirit. I am so proud of you boys." I weep.

We all weep.

"Dad?"

"Yes, Ryan."

"I still think you're going to make it."

"Me too, Dad. You're tough."

They both stay next to me for hours. No more words have to be said that day.

My sons are also best friends. They are roommates in an apartment in college. They love, like, and respect each other. Not that they don't argue at times. Of course they do.

Our home is the "center home" for my sons and their friends. We are fortunate to have a large house. Their bedrooms are larger than most master bedrooms. There's a pool table room. Our back-yard includes an Olympic-sized pool for swimming and water sports and volleyball and basketball courts.

It is not uncommon on a Saturday or Sunday morning to have two to six additional boys to feed breakfast after spending the night.

I hear laughter from the boys and their friends and music blaring from their bedrooms or the family room. I feel like my father when I shout, "Turn down that music. How can you understand those words anyway?"

As I am more ill, I hear Beverly at times say, "Shhhh. Your father is resting."

From my bed, I hear birds singing in the mornings, my dogs' toenails click on the hardwood floor down the hallway, water cascades from the spa into the pool. Today, I hear the dogs bark, my boys and their friends splashing water in the pool. I can see the spa, a portion of the pool, and lots of palm trees.

When I was in better shape, I talked to my sons' friends everywhere in the house.

When I got sick enough to have medical devices in our bedroom, I did not allow any of their friends to enter the master bedroom. On good days, I sat and talked with them in the family room, kitchen, living room, my sons' bedroom, or outside. Later on, I stopped visiting their friends.

To their friends, I always have a happy face.

To my family, I do not.

❧

I hear a knock at the bedroom door.

Derek enters with a concerned look.

"What is it, son?" I ask.

"Dad, I really need a tattoo." He is starting his second year in high school.

"What? No."

"But Dad, all the other guys have tattoos. I need to show intimidation on the basketball court. I must rule the court. I need a tattoo."

"No. Absolutely not."

"But Dad."

"But what? I said no, and I mean no. Your body is a temple of God. Do not desecrate it. You'll thank me later."

Besides, my father had tattoos. Not my sons.

"Dad, please."

"No. And don't ask again."

Derek leaves the room quicker than he entered.

I know he is disappointed. But I have to be his father, not his friend.

"Buddy, I hope he'll understand."

"He will. You did the right thing."

"Yeah. But it was hard."

I close my eyes and try to sleep but scarred memories stir in my mind. I shake my head to dislodge the visions. But they persist.

My sons need to be disciplined. Ryan is in third grade, Derek in first.

They have been warned three times not to throw apples and lemons, like baseballs, at our home or our neighbors' home. My warnings have come with a threat of a spanking if they do it again. Our neighbors are furious with the last blast of lemons to their home.

"Maybe I should make them keep their nose on the wall like I had to," I tell Buddy.

"You don't mean that. You promised that your sons will never know that kind of punishment," he reminds me.

"I know. I won't. Help me to be a good father."

"I will."

"But Buddy, I have to spank them. They have to learn to be good. I warned them several times not to do it or they would be spanked. They have to learn consequences."

"You can give a little spanking, but don't hurt them. You know that is wrong. You know what that feels like."

"I know. Make sure you stay and help me."

"I'm with you."

I enter Derek's bedroom.

He sits on his bed, tears in his eyes.

"Derek, you know I don't want to do this."

"Then don't, Dad."

"I warned you three times. I told you if you did it again, I would have to spank you."

"I know."

"Now turn over."

He does. I use my open hand and give his backside a whack. He cries out. Quickly, I leave and enter Ryan's room. He also is on his bed with wide eyes.

"Dad, don't."

"I have to. Turn over. I warned both of you."

A whack with my opened hand.

He cries.

I leave and go to my bedroom, fall to the floor, and bawl.

"I tried to hold back when I spanked them," I tell Buddy.

"You did," he reassures me.

"I never want my sons to experience pain from my hands. No wounds from me."

I weep for hours.

Buddy stays with me.

Years later, my sons tell me they knew they were about to be spanked. Ryan told Derek to put on a lot of underwear.

They both did.

Ryan also told Derek to scream with my first hit, that I would stop.

They both did.

It worked.

I stopped.

The vision fades.
I still cannot sleep.

❧

Another old wound in my heart opens into my thoughts. My sister and her family visit us in Chico, California. I hear Kelly, my niece, scream. She is maybe in sixth grade, and her older sister, Tracy, is in the eighth. I run to Kelly and discover that Ryan bit her on her arm. He is in kindergarten and has never bitten before.

I know Kelly teased Ryan, but he still should not have done it.

I try to give a quick slap to his mouth and shout, "You don't bite." But I strike harder than I meant to, and his nose bleeds. He runs to the bathroom. I run after him. I hold and hug him on my lap and cry.

"Buddy, I can't believe I hurt my son like this."

"You did not mean to," he reassures me.

"I know. But do you see his eyes. He cannot believe that I did it."

"I see. He knows you did not mean it. He was just startled and afraid when he saw the blood," Buddy continues to comfort me.

"I never wanted to hurt him like this. I drew blood."

"Stop it. You did not mean to. He knows you love him," he shouts.

I hug Ryan harder.

"I love you, Ryan. I'm so sorry. I didn't mean to give you a nosebleed. But you mustn't bite."

"I know, Dad."

We sob for a while.

My heart breaks that day.

I just want to be alone with my boy.

I do not want to let him go.

"I love you, Ryan."

"I love you too, Dad."

I hold tight.

Later that night, I tell Buddy, "You need to help me to be a good father."

"I will."

He did.

The father-to-son abuse would stop with me.

My paternal grandfather was an alcoholic. He also beat his sons to make them stronger. He taught them real men drink, fight, and rule the house. If his sons lost a fight, he would beat them.

My father and his two older brothers became just like their father.

My father fought in three wars. I am sure he saw and did things he tried to forget by drinking. He probably suffered from post-traumatic stress disorder but was never treated.

As a teenager, I once asked my father if he ever killed anyone in the wars. His eyes bulged and seared into mine, the veins in his neck expanded as he shouted, "You don't ever ask me that."

I never did again.

About a year later, he told me that one day he would tell me something about the war when he retired.

He retired.

He never told.

I never asked.

As he drank more beer, occasionally whiskey, his breath reeked. He barked orders and demanded immediate responses. With each can of beer he consumed, my insides twisted more, my throat dried, my back stiffened as I waited for the one thing that would send him into a rage. It might be the tone of my voice, how I handed him his beer, how I took away the empty beer, if I walked in front of him and did not say "excuse me," if I looked at him wrong, or nothing at all.

If he drank several beers, I prayed that he would drink more and pass out. Then I could go to bed and be safe for that night.

His command, "Go to your room," made my heart pound like a drum. The beatings occurred in my bedroom. A punch or shove could occur anywhere in the house or in the backyard. Stabbing stares with his eyes delivered their strikes anywhere.

As I marched to my bedroom—sometimes quickly—I would tell myself to be strong and not to cry. If I cried, the beating would be worse.

I would call upon Buddy, who told me, "Everything will be fine. Come play with me. You can come back when your father is finished with you." And I would leave with him to our imaginary playground with ankle-high, green grass that tickled my feet as we ran to the swing set, and I felt the gentle breeze against my face as I soared higher and higher, laughed as we rolled in the grass and into a cool pool pond that soothed my body, floated on our backs, and hummed as we gazed at the sky.

I always returned in time for the lecture.

The "lecture" after a beating was the worst. I had to remain on my stomach, my pants still down around my ankles.

After each sentence he would add, "Do you understand?"

Then whip me again.

"Yes, sir."

"Are you sure?"

Another strike.

"Yes, sir."

Sometimes, the lecture would be a few sentences.

Sometimes paragraphs and paragraphs.

At the end, he added, "This was for your own good."

He left the room.

My mother, who was usually in the room and stood in one corner, would come to my side and help me get into bed.

She always kissed my forehead and said, "Your father does this because he loves you. Be a good boy."

She left the room.

I learned not to cry when I was alone. He might be outside the door.

Instead, I played with Buddy.

My sister and brother were never in the bedroom for the beatings. They were somewhere in the house but not in that room, and they were never flogged. The sound of the TV in the living room increased before each bedroom incident. The walls seemed to vibrate from the escalated sound.

My father demanded loyalty to country and family from my early years. "To be disloyal and dishonor your country and family is treason." And, "You do not betray your country or family by telling secrets. What goes on in my house is family business. God forgive you if you betray our family."

My mother reinforced the command for loyalty to family. "Whatever goes on in our home is family business and must never be spoken." And, "Jay, you do not want to get your father really mad at you."

The fear of telling the "secret" was embedded deep within me at an early age.

I never told anyone, not a friend, grandmother (both grandfathers were dead before I was born), relative, or neighbor. No one.

I also would not let any friend be at my home by late afternoon. My father might come home early. He might be drunk. I did not want them to make my father mad at me if they did something wrong in his mind. I did not want them to witness an angry attack. I was afraid and ashamed. No friends at home on weekends or holidays.

Absolutely no sleepovers.

Our neighbors and relatives knew my father drank. But he was always kind in front of them. I never knew if they were aware of his anger and treatment of me. People at that time and in our area believed that what goes on in one's home is family business and should be left alone.

I was alone. Except for Buddy.

13

MANILA, PHILIPPINES

1973

My need to provide medical care to the poor intensified. Despite being a busy medical student, I joined Medical Missions Inc. (MMI), a charity organization of UST medical students and faculty physicians that provided medical and surgical care for the indigent. I studied harder to gain medical knowledge for the missionary work. Caring for the impoverished provided me with clinical experience beyond medical schooling. I gave to the point of exhaustion but was renewed by the unconditional appreciation from the poorest of the poor. On weekends, I attended missions in the Greater Manila Area. Nuns and, occasionally, priests accompanied our team. Clinics were held in run-down school classrooms, vacant buildings, and church annexes. We also went into homes of the poor. Most of the dwellings were one-room shacks made of discarded materials and without electricity and water. I drew a crowd, especially with the children. I was the first tall, white American the kids had touched. My white uniform was full of little dirty handprints by the end of each day. We treated all types of illnesses and performed minor surgeries. I learned to be gentle while pulling out live cockroaches from ears. Flies, mosquitoes, and filth were our enemies. There were always wounds, and more wounds begging to be cared for.

Wounds I needed to heal.

The smiling faces of the children gave me strength. It became routine to deliver babies in the most deplorable conditions. I witnessed the genuine love of a mother and father for their child despite their despair. During longer breaks from medical school, I went on missions to remote areas of the islands and perfected my surgical care and expertise with the use of a scalpel. Sliced with precision.

I found beauty in providing pure medical care for the needy without the burden of keeping hospital medical records, charging for services, or fearing malpractice litigation. Despite operating in less-than-sterile conditions, the outcomes were free from major complications.

The medical team, priests, nuns, and patients' relatives offered prayers to guide and protect us. Shouts of "Praise the Lord, Thanks Be to God" reverberated around the mission site.

My prayers had always been self-centered. They were prayers for God to bless my wants and needs. I did not pray for his will to be done but to grant my will.

I never really talked to God.

But God talked to me through his power of healing. I could not ignore what I witnessed. Wounds healed that should never have. Operations were successful that should have failed.

A priest told me the Bible said, "Commit your works to the Lord, and your thoughts will be established" (Proverbs 16:3, NKJV). So I began to pray to God for wisdom and guidance as I performed surgical procedures or administered medical treatments, most of which I had never done before, on gravely sick patients. I felt my mind cleared, judgment heightened, and hands guided.

"There, I got it. I do not know how I did it, but here it is," I remarked as I placed the cantaloupe-sized goiter onto a surgical tray. It was the first goiter I had removed. It was also the largest one I had ever seen.

"I know how you did it. You're a good doctor, and God is with you," announced a surgical nurse at my side.

"Thanks. He must have been. It was scary there for a while. Now, I have to secure the trachea," I replied as I focused on the exposed soft trachea.

I placed a suture around a cartilage in the trachea. The relatives of the patient were instructed to gently pull on the string if their loved one had sudden difficulty in breathing. The large, heavy thyroid gland had pressed and softened the trachea for years, and it was in danger of sudden collapse with resultant death to the patient.

I removed several goiters over the next few days, all without complications despite horrific conditions and my lack of experience. I felt I was a witness to God's work. I was learning to be a servant for him.

A little girl, maybe six or seven years old, beamed as she looked into the mirror. Tears rolled down her checks when she gently patted her upper lip. It was the first time she ever saw her face closed. I had repaired her severe cleft lip and palate a few days earlier and had just removed the surgical dressings. She turned and hugged me. Tears welled up in my eyes.

I had questioned my ability to be a doctor. I had questioned God's love because he allowed the little ones to suffer. I had questioned my decision to be in the Philippines. But my questions were answered that day in the beautiful face of that little precious one. God had shown me his power, his love.

I was meant to stay in the Philippines to do medical missions, to be his servant, to be his healing instrument. The harsh conditions, long hours, and danger did not matter. I was to heal wounds.

Buddy confirmed my feelings. "Don't quit, be strong, they need you."

I needed them.

I also found natural beauty on the islands. There was the dancing of the trees when the trade winds blew, causing them to rub against each other; their leaves turned up and over like puppies wanting a belly rub or scratch. The dancing tropical trees included mahogany, banana, giant acacia, coconut, teakwood, mango, papaya, ficus, *sampaloc* (tamarind), and bamboo. The rustling sound varied in pitch and tone, depending on the shape and size of the branches and leaves; but it was in rhythm, as if conducted. The tree recital was accented by distinct animal sounds from screaming monkeys, chirping Maya birds, rooting wild boars, and croaking *tukos* (large geckos). A break of a twig from slithering snakes and giant lizards added a snap to the tempo.

There was the light show. The sunlight shined through changing pathways of the stirred leaves. Thumb-sized raindrops on large leaves from an afternoon shower intensified and dispersed the light, producing a panoramic colorful and shifting pattern of light. It was a colossal kaleidoscope.

I was in paradise, a piece of heaven.

During one of my vacations from school and apart from my medical missionary work, I went to the Banaue Rice Terraces in the most northern part of Luzon. I was accompanied by Chuck Curtis, a "cousin" of mine.

He was the son of Jack Curtis, a longtime friend and poker pal of Tatay and my father. Tito Jack was the superintendent of Baguio Gold and Cooper Mines. Chuck was fluent in the local dialect.

To reach this remote area, we rode a bus that had one side open for people to jump in and out; hard, unpadded wood benches; no air-conditioning; and no suspension. The lack of suspension proved to be brutal as we journeyed on poorly constructed roads with large holes. The narrow road was twisted like a snake and edged next to a steep gorge. Chickens and pigs occupied some of the space inside the bus. We were sandwiched between bundles of dry goods. Young native men on the roof of the bus held onto a metal pipe railing.

The ride took the whole day. Chuck and I crawled out of the bus and hobbled into the Banaue Hotel, the only hotel in the entire region. Our beds felt like feather mattresses, despite being hard and lumpy, compared to our rigid, rock-hard bus seats.

After resting that night, we walked onto the rice terraces.

I felt so small, like an ant on the Great Wall of China.

The terraces were built in 1 B.C., a feat beyond comprehension. Large boulders carried up steep sides of mountains, stacked twenty feet high without known machinery. A local native man from the Ifugao tribe, dressed in G-string and barefoot, guided us. He was an expert with his bolo, which he used to clear the tropical bush for our path, cut stalks of a banana tree for our snack, slice coconuts for our drink, and kill a few intruding snakes—or were we the intruders?

We passed by several primitive villages. In the past, the Ifugao were feared headhunters. Their ancestors constructed the fascinating rice terraces with the perfect irrigation system. The Ifugao built their houses on piles. The pyramid-shape-roofed hut was used as a bedroom, kitchen, and storeroom. To please the gods, the skull of a sacrificed pig was fixed on the outside of the house.

Out of reverence and as instructed by our native guide to please their gods, we stopped at each village to visit and rest. Naked children stared at the tall, white man, the first they might have seen. Or maybe they thought I was from Siguijor, an island province of the Philippines in the Central Visayas region where there are tall, white natives.

Siquijor is called the "Island of Fire" because it gives off an eerie glow. Many Filipinos consider it to be a mystical island, full of witches and other supernatural phenomena. Actually, the glow from the island comes from the great swarm of fireflies that harbor in the numerous Molave trees on the island.

The primitive dwellers offered us what food they had. We ate out of respect more than hunger. At one village, I looked into a treasured, ancient, metal pot that hung from a bamboo pole over a wood fire. My eyes widened, my right hand was quick to cover my mouth as I gagged. A haunting baby monkey's face bobbled in the boiling water. The children looked bewildered at the tall, white native from Siquijor who did not eat. I could not eat despite the concern of disrespect to the villagers. The children shrugged their shoulders and ate.

We continued on our journey deeper into the mountains. We came into a clearing and stared at a massive waterfall and pool. The aqua-blue water, surrounded by the emerald-green hue of tropical plants and trees, produced a mystical picture. Flashes of blue and white darted in and out of view as Kingfisher birds with their blue bodies and white heads chased each other like little children in the air. I felt honored to be in such a place.

The Ifugao tribesman chanted a prayer to the gods. After a refreshing and dreamlike swim, the vigilant native informed Chuck that we had to head back. It would be getting dark soon. It was treacherous to be in the jungle at night with dangerous animals about. The most feared were headhunters with the savage skills of their ancestors.

Sounds of the jungle are louder at night, at least to this white boy.

On our way out, we saw glimpses of Ifugao male natives between trees and behind bushes. They were dressed in their G-strings, barefoot, and with bolos in hand. Spine-chilling cries emitted near our path. The sounds from the jungle intensified in volume and eeriness as darkness approached. Some of the creepy calls were now ahead of us.

After passing the last village and at the end of the trail, our Ifugao guide departed. His right arm raised in farewell. His broad smile exposed blackened gums devoid of teeth. As he turned to return to his village, I imagined his ancestor waving a bolo at me instead of his hand.

"Jay, run! I mean it. Run for your life!"

Chuck did not have to repeat his command. We both ran to the jeep that would take us back to the Banaue Hotel. The jeep sped off as we jumped into the back. I turned and saw a group of native men running after us, their large bolos swinging in the air.

"Chuck. Why? What just happened?" I shouted, panting.

Chuck explained that those natives saw us early in the morning when we started on our adventure into the terraces. They waited for our return and drank tuba (local coconut wine). They planned to rob us and dispose of our bodies in a rice field. Fortunately, the driver waiting for us was a friend of Tito Jack. He overheard their plans and was quick to tell Chuck of the situation. They intended to behead us.

I never knew if our guide was one of them.

I preferred to think not.

14

PALM SPRINGS, CALIFORNIA

1999

"Dad? Are you awake?" Derek whispers.

"What?" My eyes open.

The blades swirl.

My head is still attached.

"Yes, son. What is it?

"Nothing really. I just want to spend some time with you."

He jumps back on the couch and assumes his favorite position. He grabs a smaller throw pillow, places it on his chest, and hugs it.

"Okay." I smile.

"Does it hurt?" Derek's tender eyes stare at my infusion apparatus.

"No. But it's good you came in. You see the infusion bag?"

"Yes." His stare hardens.

"Well, it's almost empty. And if it's empty and continues to infuse, air bubbles will enter my central line and kill me." I stare back into his eyes.

"Oh my God. Shouldn't you call Mom?"

"No, we have time. Now what can we talk about?"

I take a deep gasp of air, keep my mouth open, fix my eyes on the blades above me, and remain still.

"Dad. What's wrong? Dad. Dad!"

Derek jumps to my side and shakes me.

Ryan hears Derek's cry and runs to the room.

I can no longer hold my breath. I smile then say, "Nothing."

"Dad, that was horrible. That was mean. Do not do that again," pleads Derek tearfully.

"Yeah, Dad. That was awful," shouts Ryan.

"I'm sorry. I'm sorry. You're right. Bad joke. My bad."

Ryan and Derek just look at each other and shake their heads, as if to say, "There are bad jokes and then there are really bad ones."

"I said I'm sorry."

"Okay," Ryan replies and flops on the couch.

"Okay. But don't do that again," Derek adds and sits back down.

"Well. What should we talk about today?" I ask, trying to recover from my bad act.

"Anything, but no more sex talks," answers Derek.

"Yeah. No more sex talks. We get it already. We know the dangers," adds Ryan.

"Okay. Your choice today."

I guess I should erase the tape on sex talks.

I cherish the talks with my sons.

Later on, I lay alone in bed. Beverly is fixing dinner, our boys are playing basketball. My heart is still warm from our earlier talk. I never had a father-to-son talk. Only his hand spoke to me.

Just one kind word would have been enough.

My mind drifts back in time. I am thirteen and have acne on my face.

My mother sits in the waiting room at Oak Knoll Naval Hospital in Oakland, California. It was created in 1942 to handle casualties from World War II. Oak Knoll later served as the primary stateside hospital for the Korean and Vietnam wars and then provided health care for Navy personnel in California and Nevada.

"Take your shirt off," orders the middle-aged dermatologist.

"Yes, sir." I reply.

I take off my shirt and lay it across the end of the metal examination table.

I shiver. The room is cold and smells of chloroform.

The doctor excuses his young female nurse. She leaves and closes the door behind her. He goes to the window and closes the blinds.

"Sit on the edge of the table."

"Yes, sir."

He begins to examine my face then turns to a metal surgical tray. When he turns back to me, his long, white lab jacket is opened. With one step forward, he stands between my legs, a scalpel pressed against my face.

"Do as I say, and I won't hurt you."

I remain mute. My insides twisted.

"Did you hear me?" The scalpel presses a bit onto my cheek.

"Yes, sir."

"Get down slowly."

As I do, I see his erect penis.

I knee him, grab my shirt, and bolt to the waiting room.

"Mom, I want to get out of here," I shout. My shirt is in my hand.

My mother's mouth is wide open.

Other people in the waiting room stir and mutter noises.

"I mean it, Mom."

I try to put on my shirt as we leave.

My mother repeats, "Jay, Jay, Jay, what the hell happened?"

I stare out the car window. No tears.

"Jay, you have to tell me what happened."

I do.

My mother tells my father when he gets home that night.

I sit on my bed and stare at the wall. I wait for the doorknob to turn and my father to enter.

Buddy tells me to be strong, not to worry. It was not my fault.

I stare for hours.

My father does not enter my bedroom that night.

Days pass.

My father does not speak of the incident, nor does my mother.

I am ordered to sit in the front seat next to my father as he drives us to the military base at Treasure Island, California. No words are spoken. I sit like a statue, bent at the knees, hands in lap, eyes forward. My intestines twist.

At Treasure Island, my father and I are questioned separately about the doctor at Oak Knoll. I recount the incident several times.

"You may go, young man," states one of the military men.

I leave the room almost as fast as the examination room at Oak Knoll.

No words are spoken during the ride back to our home.

I sit still again. A statue.

A few days later, my father attends the military proceedings at Treasure Island. There are prior incidents with teenage boys. My testimony seals the case. The dermatologist is dishonorably discharged and loses his license to practice.

My father never tells me what he said at Treasure Island. But my mother informs me that he told the military men that I was not "queer."

My next beating is bad.

15

MANILA, PHILIPPINES

1974

Tatay was the governor of Zambales from 1956 to 1967. Then he was appointed chairman of the National Power Corporation of the Philippines (NPC or Napocor), a state-owned company. NPC was created and approved by President Manuel L. Quezon on November 3, 1936. The law nationalized the hydroelectric industry and reserved all streams, lakes, and springs in the Philippines where power may be developed, subject to existing rights.

I occasionally accompanied Tatay on business trips during short breaks from school. One time, we traveled to northern Luzon by military helicopter with guards. Three other helicopters, full of marines, provided protection. Tatay was about to head a critical meeting in a remote area of the island. National Power Corporation wanted to build a dam as part of a hydroelectric power plant. The plans called for the flooding of an entire village, including a sacred native burial ground.

The atmosphere was tense. Local tribesmen stood tall dressed in native war attire. The meeting erupted with anger, bolos and spears drawn by the chiseled tribesmen. Our military bodyguards surrounded us. We were led to the waiting helicopters. The blades had never stopped turning since our arrival. I looked down at the victory war dance as we lifted away. My heart pounded. My throat parched. My mind made up.

No more dam meetings on sacred ground for me.

Anyway, I had more studies.

I also attended political parties with Tatay and helped entertain local and foreign politicians.

Then the French landed, the Loygues and Toutays of Paris.

These French officials were offering to build nuclear power reactors in the Philippines. President Marcos insisted that Tatay show them a good time.

A yacht trip was in order.

While Tatay and the French dignitaries had a power meeting, the wife of the French leader was busy seducing me on deck. She enjoyed fresh watermelon juice squeezed on her while sunbathing.

I kept thinking, "What would Marcos do?"

I kept squeezing watermelon.

The ship docked at one of Marcos's beach estates. I jumped into the tepid, turquoise water to rinse off the juice. I selected one of President Marcos's new water skis and was thrilled to be skidding across the calm water, but I wanted more excitement. I motioned to the driver of the ski boat to go out of the protective cove. I felt honored that General Romualdez, the brother of Imelda Marcos, had insisted on operating the ski boat, I think to show off in front of the blonde French lady with blue eyes and white skin. A boy servant stood in the back of the boat with a vigilant eye.

I flew through the air as I jumped waves, seemingly unable to fall, defying gravity. I felt free. Paradise was around me.

I gave the signal for the boat to go faster. The servant was jumping up and down waving his arms overhead.

I gave the sign again, but no response, just more animation.

I glanced to my side. And there it was, a large shark scoping his potential dinner, the hot dog on the ski. I momentarily thought of the many jumps that could have served me up to the shark. I crouched down on the ski. The shark focused on me and zoomed closer. My eyes were fixed on the cove. I crashed onto the beach and tumbled head over heels. The shark turned. My skin and ski slashed.

After my cuts were cleansed, I went to my guest room. My mouth dropped. A fourteen-carat-gold-handled toothbrush and stateside toothpaste were next to the sink for my use. I felt the toothbrush to be sinful. I thought of the poor I treated on medical missions and the medical supplies that could be purchased and used to heal wounds from the sale of the toothbrush.

But I was at President Marcos's (and First Lady Imelda's) home. It was martial law, and he was a cruel dictator. She was no better. In fact, many thought she was worse. It was dangerous and potentially fatal to insult or displease the Marcoses.

So, as a young man, an American and son of Tatay, I quickly thought, "What would Marcos do?"

He would brush his teeth.

I shrugged my shoulders and brushed my teeth. When in Rome, do as the Romans do. I was in "Marcosland."

At dinner that night, I could feel the eyes of the general on me as the French lady stared at me.

Lord, please have her turn away. I like my limited freedom despite martial law. Please have her pay attention to the general.

Salamat po. My prayer was answered.

The blonde giggled with the general. His eyes were no longer on me but focused on his dessert for the night.

Paradise almost lost.

A few days later, I visited Tatay at his National Power Corporation office. When I entered the expansive office, decorated with rich, reddish-brown mahogany furniture, I saw a Filipino man, a newly hired office assistant. He sat in Tatay's chair, his feet on the desk, worn soles of his shoes exposed, and talked on the telephone. He was short in stature. He looked at me but did not move. He did not know me. His slang Tagalog and repulsive laughter irritated my ears. He bragged over the handset that he was "a big shot now" as if the receiver was a microphone and the desk was a stage. I was sure he thought I was an American visitor and could not understand his language. He bolted out of the chair when the noise of my Tatay and his entourage heightened behind the closed door. He scrambled to reposition the phone and chair and then stood motionless at the side of the desk. His eyes pleaded for me to keep quiet. The door opened.

He froze.

I smiled inside.

"Jay, what a nice surprise. Do you need something?" Tatay asked.

I glanced over at the assistant. His eyes showed fear.

"Yes, Tatay. I need to talk to you," I answered in Tagalog.

"Have you all met my son?" Tatay inquired.

"Yes. Yes. Yes. Yes. Yes," each stated in turn except the assistant. He stood mute and appeared smaller.

"Please excuse us for a moment." Tatay dismissed his entourage with a polite head nod. They exited in unison except the assistant. He darted. Tatay's eyes widened at the sight of this scurried creature.

I never told on the assistant, on purpose. I planned to use hiya and bastos to my advantage. On subsequent visits to the office, he carried my books and bags, fetched me a drink, or typed me a needed paper. I was his *boss* (used to address a person in a higher position or to flatter). In time, I did release him of his bondage to me. However, he continued to call me boss. And that was proper.

❧

I was selected for the sixth annual search for the three most outstanding international students in the Philippines for 1974. Without hesitation, Tatay insisted that I accept. I wanted my family to be proud so I joined the contest.

Thirty-three international scholars representing fourteen countries and twenty universities were selected from the more than 25,000 foreign student population distributed in the provinces and large cities. It was the Philippine International

Friendship Organization's yearly search for outstanding international students, aimed at promoting friendship and better understanding among Filipinos and foreign students and among foreign students themselves. We toured cities and provinces for several weeks, gave speeches, and were eliminated one by one. I was drained. I studied during breaks from the competition, afraid of getting behind academically.

I struggled during my final speech entitled "My Idea of a Great Man." I was given my topic thirty seconds before I was to start.

So I talked about my father, a military man, strong, a veteran of three wars. But the father of my speech was also kind, showed me love, played with me, and was proud of me. He was beaten as a child but vowed not to abuse his sons. He was a "great man."

I heard my mother's voice as I delivered my dissertation.

Do not tell family secrets.

I did not.

Buddy also spoke to me.

"Keep strong."

I was.

At the final selection, I was glad I withheld the secret. It would not have added value to my presentation or standing in the competition. The student from the Arab Republic of Egypt gave a better performance at the end of his speech—a large sum of money to the officials—and bumped me from third to fourth place, a shining moment for the Philippine International Friendship Organization's mission to foster good relationships and understanding among foreign students.

Hindi (Not)!

It showed that money talked more than my speech.

❧

Another school break, another medical mission. This one was to Iligan City on the island of Mindanao in the southern part of the

Philippines. Twenty-two medical MMI missionaries boarded a Philippine Air Force plane with all of our supplies to perform major and minor surgical operations. The medico-surgical team included doctors, nurses, nuns, and priests.

I had a special interest in Iligan. It was Beverly's hometown. Her father, Dr. Angel Cuyugan, would be there at his medical clinic. I hoped for some quality time with him. I also yearned to be in the place where Beverly was as a youngster.

My love for Beverly had been tested and remained strong.

"Young man, get away from her," shouted an anatomy professor and chairman of the department on the first floor of the medical school as he pointed to me on the second floor.

"I mean it, young man. Get away from her."

I did.

Beverly and I were talking next to the cement banister around a quad area of the school. We were close enough to touch.

I was frustrated with "no touch." I thought I would explode.

I was a young man. I wanted it.

I knew she wanted it.

It was hard, but we waited.

I never said the words "Stop seeing Ed." I wanted to.

I did say, "I can't stand him. He is so yabang," which he was. "He is *pangit* (ugly)," which he wasn't.

Beverly would reply, "Oh Jay, be nice."

But she knew I wanted her to stop seeing Ed.

And she did.

I loved that Beverly was confident.

She was wicked at *pelota* (ball), a court sport played with a hard rubber ball and a wooden racket, like a cutoff tennis racket, against a two-walled court (front and left side). She left her modesty and reserve in the locker room. On the court, it was pure aggression.

Beverly was mischievous in her youth. I would have loved to witness that.

Once, Beverly and Sylvia, her close first cousin, were bored and wanted to go to the family-owned movie theater. They were at Sylvia's home. There were no cars or drivers, all taken by the other members of the family.

Sylvia's father owned a large trucking company. There was a large semi-truck across the street in a lot. Sylvia grabbed the keys and drove Beverly and herself to the movie theater.

Beverly and Sylvia were tomboys. Beverly's older sister, Alice, and Sylvia's older sister, Tina, were the "young ladies" and the "prettier ones." Despite always being told that her sister was prettier because Alice was slimmer and had fairer skin, Beverly loved Alice.

Beverly was bright, kind, and spiritual. I loved that.

She did medical mission work in the Greater Manila Area as part of her clinical training. She was caring and compassionate with all patients. Her medical and surgical skills were excellent.

She was a giver. She provided shelter, food, uniforms, books, and money to a female medical classmate. The classmate had been accepted to medical school but was from one of the poorest parts of Manila. Some classmates made unfavorable comments about the appearance of this student. Beverly befriended her, supported her for the next four years, and never expected anything back in return.

Beverly had a strong faith and prayed often.

She prayed a lot for me.

When I was exhausted from my studies and the medical mission work, Beverly encouraged me to continue. "Jay, you're so good. You're doing God's work. He has plans for you. Let's pray."

We did.

❧

In Iligan, I became the cheiloplasty (surgical repair of cleft lip) and palatoplasty (surgical repair of cleft palate) king of the island.

There are approximately 4,400 native-born Filipinos born with cleft lip and palate deformities annually in the Philippines due to genetics and maternal malnutrition and vitamin deficiencies (B6 and folic acid).

The kids were brought to me in bangkas. Their male relatives paddled for days from nearby smaller islands to reach our missionary site. We operated in an old schoolhouse with dirt floors. Old wooden tables and World War II metal tables acted as operating tables. They were placed end to end in two rows in the largest classroom. Ropes tied from wall to wall served as intravenous bag holders. Old desks and used crates held the surgical supplies. The days were long, the nights short. Our uniforms had traces of white that shined between sweat stains. Sterilization was attempted but not always perfect.

Prayers were offered before, during, and after all treatments and provided comfort in a tough setting. The local impoverished gave thanks to God in the face of horror and tragedy in their hard lives. They bowed their knees to Christ. Their eyes showed sorrow for their loved ones, but their hearts were full of his Spirit.

I felt his Spirit.

I repaired many cleft lips and palates. The children's disfigurements were horrible; my results always better than the defect. The kids cried when they looked into a mirror and saw their faces without gaps for the first time.

No major infections or complications.

Prayers answered.

Tears flowed.

We were unable to treat all the needy people. Triage helped to assure attention for the most desperate. Our team cared for severe sufferers of malaria and bacterial and parasitic dysentery with appropriate medications and intravenous fluid replacements. Preventive education was addressed once a life was no longer in danger. Countless infectious and traumatic wounds were tended. Surgery for deformity injuries, large hernias, massive cysts and tumors, and severe lower genital lacerations from birthing in Nipa huts was a full-time operation. Those not cared for on that mission would wait a year for the next team. Our scheduled time on the island was over. Our medical mission was a success.

My personal mission was not as successful. I had little time to spend with Beverly's father and experienced few of her childhood spots.

"Good-bye, Jay. I wish we had more time together." Dr. Cuyugan was gracious to come to our mission site.

"Me too, Dr. Cuyugan," I replied, off-balance.

Dr. Cuyugan was a fine physician and successful businessman. He owned and ran a hospital clinic in Iligan with his wife (Beverly's blood mother). They were both OB-GYN doctors but also did family medicine.

After the death of Beverly's mother, her father continued to practice in Iligan and to conduct business as an owner and board member of the family enterprises. The children were sent off to boarding schools. Beverly and her sister went to another island, Cebu. The boys went to school in the Greater Manila Area.

After her father remarried several years later, he wanted his new wife to join him in Iligan. But she had a prominent medical career in Manila. A home was built for her in Quezon City, near Manila. The children joined her in this home. Beverly's father began his commute every month between Iligan and Manila.

We were about to leave for the airport to go back to Manila. Children clung to my pants, not wanting me to leave. Dr. Cuyugan smiled at the sight of me as I tried to maintain my balance and composure while the smallest children climbed on me.

"Well, maybe we can spend more time together on your next mission here. You need to come back. These kids are going to miss you." The doctor patted the head of a little boy that was attached to me like glue.

"I am going to miss them too. I hope to see you soon, Dr. Cuyugan." I tried to give a handshake, but I was off-balance.

"I'm sure you will." He smiled then turned toward his car.

I wondered if he meant I was sure to miss the kids or to see him soon.

I liked to think he meant both.

16

PALM SPRINGS, CALIFORNIA

1999

The whip cracks and hits its target.

Another crack and perfect strike.

The hand holds the whip firm with controlled and deliberate slashes.

More cracks and strikes.

The hand begins to tremble as the cuts gape and expose deeper matter.

"Great job, Jay." My whip instructor pats me on my back. "You are a master of the whip."

I am in college majoring in zoology. In my extracurricular class, ancient weaponry, we are instructed in the art of bows and arrows, swords, axes, and whips.

I am best with the whip.

I take a lot of PE classes and lack a few credits to obtain a double major degree in Physical Education.

I stare at the target, a stuffed dummy, and smile.

My hand still shakes.

My instructor notices my hand.

"Are you okay?" he asks, still focused on my hand.

"Yes, just a little hand cramp. I'm fine."

I glance at my exposed skin. There are no open wounds. I grin, coil my whip, and retreat to the locker room. My whip hangs in my locker, safe, not to be cut. I stare at the whip. It looks like a rope.

My mind moves on to another memory.

I climb over the edge of the cliff.

It is a sunny day with a few scattered clouds, a mild ocean breeze, and a fine mist in the air. The fifty-foot cliff drops to large boulders that are sprayed by crashing waves. There is one large bush between two rocks. It is the only vegetation within a hundred yards.

I have done this many times.

I set my rappel anchor, tie my rope in a double figure eight knot, attach the rappel device to the rope and my harness, plant my feet on the cliff's edge, sit back into the harness, pump my legs on the face of the cliff, and rappel. Five feet into my descent, my rope gives way. I fall backward and see the sky with a thin white cloud formation.

I do not panic. I just free float for forty feet. It seems like minutes as I wait for my spine and head to smash on the rocks. After several seconds, I crash onto the bush. It feels like a large sofa cushion with springs poking through.

I do not break my spine, and my skull is intact. I lie there motionless as seagulls fly overhead.

A splash of a wave startles me, and my legs and arms move as if on their own. I crawl off the bush, slide down a smaller boulder to the sand and walk a hundred yards to a lower part of the cliff that I have climbed up before. My legs shake, but I make the ascent in good time.

Peter and Jerry, my college friends, run to me at the top of the cliff. They wrap me in a large beach towel and help me back to my car.

"Shit, Jay, that was unbelievable," shouts Peter as he slaps me on my back.

"Are you alright, Jay? I think we should go to the ER," Jerry says, scratching his head.

"I'm fine. Let's just go back to the dorm. And stop with the slaps to my back," I bark.

"Wait. What about your rope and anchor?" Peter asks.
"Never mind, I never want to see them again," I respond.
I never rappelled again.

17

MANILA, PHILIPPINES

1974

I was elected president of Medical Missions Inc. I was the first foreigner to hold that position. I was considered *parang* (as if I was) Filipino since I had lived in the Philippines as a child, spoke the national language, and honored the customs. I was *puti lang* (just white), but a *tunay* (genuine, real) Filipino at heart.

My involvement intensified in the mission work, adding to the demands of my medical school schedule. I tackled the challenge head on. I could not fumble. I flourished. I continued to learn the real meaning of medical care, the essence of being a healing servant, as I once more witnessed God's work physically and spiritually in our medical care to the poor.

Wounds healed and lives were saved that should not have been.

I felt a sense of peace despite the threat of danger.

The impoverished natives thanked us with smiles, tears, and bows. On their knees, they gave glory and honor to God.

Their steadfast faith sparked a light inside of me to glorify God through good works.

God was present everywhere.

I recognized we were all equally filled with the spirit of God. He died for all of ours sins, not just the rich and famous.

Good works could be performed everywhere.

God had brought me to that place to labor and learn.

I did.

Our teams operated in any available building or shelter. Medical care was given indoors in buildings and huts and outdoors amongst coconut trees. Military planes, trucks, jeeps, or boats transported us. At times, local bangkas were requisitioned.

We awoke in the early mornings, prayed, worked all day, and ate late at night. In gratitude, villagers presented us with food offerings, usually chicken and fish, freshly caught that day. We ate abundant tropical fruits and lots of rice. Sometimes, a prized goat or pig would be slaughtered. Depending on the island and local native customs, a dog would be offered, but I quickly refused it.

On one island, I contracted acute gastroenteritis from eating raw fish. Intravenous fluid ran simultaneously in both arms and legs. Two days later, I rose from my bamboo-slatted bed, left the hut, and vowed never to eat raw fish again. To this day, I cannot eat sushi.

During dinners, young native boys shimmied up coconut trees in a race to bring down the first coconut and present the milk for us to drink. Their bolos swung with precision at the coconuts in the tree as they balanced with one arm and both legs wrapped around the trunk. Their descents were effortless as the trunks slid past their hands and feet. Powerful blows to the coconuts held between their feet exposed the fresh meat and milk. They ran to the finish line, to our open hands. Laughter and applause ignited the victorious boy, who pounded his chest to the delight of the elders.

I pictured myself as a young boy, much like these boys although I was taller, competing in coconut races in Zambales. Our finish line was the first coconut to strike the ground. No missionaries rooted for us, just little brown half-naked children cheered. My coconut hit the ground first many times. But there was one native boy that climbed with the speed and agility of a monkey. I proclaimed an unfair race every time he won, claiming that a monkey could not compete. Laughter overruled me, my laughter the loudest. Then we all would make monkey sounds, sway our arms, scratch our chests and armpits, and head for the beach to swim.

We were kids, all brown-skinned except for one. We climbed coconut trees like monkeys, ate bananas like monkeys, and imitated the walk of monkeys. I wanted to belong, to be one of them. I did not feel superior or inferior to my native friends. I did not feel my friends were prejudiced toward me. We were just young boys. At first, they were curious about me, the white one. In a short time, we were the same.

But I always wanted to be the best. To make my father proud of me even at a coconut race.

He never was.

I went to school on a military base with American children. I did not have a close friend on the base. I did not want any friend to come over to my house. I made friends with native boys through the cyclone fence that surrounded the base. We would sit on opposite sides of the fence. We smiled, laughed, and traded toys through the fence. The patrol guards never stopped us.

I was the one who felt caged on my side of the fence. I wanted to climb over and play with my friends on their side. I wanted to be free. I wanted to be like them. They usually wore only shorts and were barefooted. I took off my shirt and shoes. They spoke Tagalog. I learned Tagalog.

We met and played at the beach. My mother did not mind me playing with the natives. I think she was just glad I had some friends and was happy.

I did not know if my father knew. He never came to the beach with me.

I also played with native boys at the Barrettos' home. Tatay and Nanay knew and were happy for me. My mother knew and was happy.

My father knew but never said a word about my friends.

But I was never beaten for having friends.

We made another mission to Jolo on Sulu, a southern island, considered to be the "Vietnam of the Philippines." Muslims and Christians had been at war for years. The whole island was military-controlled, including the governorship. President Marcos gave us clearance that included a special note allowing me, a foreigner, to be on the island. We were dispatched to treat civilian victims with transportation of a military operation. In Manila, we were loaded into a C-130 transport aircraft. On board and secured into place, we headed to Zamboanga, a large city in Mindanao and near the island of Sulu. The airport at Zamboanga, with the third Air Division of the Philippine Air Force and sixth Naval District, would serve as our entry point to Sulu. The secured cargo included military jeeps, weaponry, Filipino soldiers and marines, and our medical team and equipment. The seats were narrow and hard. My knees bent toward my chest for lack of room. No air-conditioning, no movies, no meals served.

In Zamboanga, we were transferred to a smaller plane, a DC-3 converted into a military C-47. Machine guns were mounted to each window and door space. Long cot-like seats flanked each wall with shoulder seat belts attached overhead. Every inch of space was crammed with equipment, medical and military.

Jolo was in sight. Our plane dived and veered left. Rebels were spotted in bangkas. We tried to get out of the way of the military men and avoid being burned by the hot casings of ammunition scattered around us in an endless stream of gunfire. But there was no place to go. The firing stopped. The plane made one more pass over the bangkas. All rebels were down. We landed.

The soldiers sprung out of the plane with their rifles slung over their shoulders. I exited the plane and stretched, glad to finally be in Jolo. I turned and smiled at the rest of the team as they crawled out in their cramped positions. A few of their eyes suddenly widened.

A rifle poised at my back encouraged me to comply with the local military command, "Move!"

My legs trembled as I was forced into a hanger. I glanced over and saw everyone else on my team being escorted to a small, dilapidated airport terminal.

I squinted into the bright light. A gun pressed harder into the back of my head.

My arms and legs were tied to a metal chair. Sweat poured off my face.

"Admit it! You are a CIA spy," shouted a military officer, his words accompanied by a spray of spit.

"No, I'm a doctor with the Medical Mission team."

"Admit it, or I will crush your head." More spit showered my face. "You're an American spy."

"No, I'm a doctor. I'm here to do medical work."

"You're CIA. Admit it." Veins protruded from my interrogator's neck and forehead. If the babies at San Lazaro hospital had his veins, I could have saved more lives.

The interrogation lasted hours. He threatened to disfigure my face and remove body parts. My clearance papers had been misplaced. I was guilty and condemned the moment I stepped foot on their soil because I was white. The only white one on the entire island. And to that brainless armed man, white meant spy.

Members of my team pleaded with the guards for my release. They were warned not to interfere or be shot.

"Let him go. He is telling the truth," the sadistic officer finally ordered.

My identity had been verified.

I drank water like a camel the moment after. My peers helped me to a jeep. My hand shook as I dragged on a cigarette. A military procession brought us to our residence on the island, the Notre Dame of Jolo College. This once magnificent building stood beaten and worn. Scattered bullets had pierced holes in window screens. Motor shells had perforated walls to the point of decay but provided cross ventilation. Mosquito nets hung above our cots in a large secured room, void of any additional furnishings. We treasured the one functional bathroom. In the back of the school, old metal roofing covered a tunnel entrance to a bomb shelter. Debris and palm branches scattered on the roof provided camouflage for the refuge.

We had military protection by the Armed Forces of the Philippines. Ruthless, rough Filipino prisoners released by presidential order and trained by the American Green Berets for "special services" were assigned to us. Their current mission was to keep us safe and prevent kidnapping by the militant Muslims. The Moro National Liberation Front (MNLF) was a militant Islamist separatist group in and around the southern Philippines (Jolo, Basilan, and Zamboanga). Later, Abu Sayyaff, which means "the bearer of sword," broke from the MNLF. These terrorists carried out bombings, kidnappings, assassinations, and extortions in what they described as their fight for an independent Islamic province in the Philippines. They were feared for beheading foreign captives if ransoms were delayed. One blow with a bolo and the ransom was nullified.

On our mission to Jolo, I was in the most danger of being kidnapped, being a doctor and a foreigner. I was told to blend into my surroundings, a difficult task when you tower above everyone and you're the only white person on the island. My price would be high, but more likely I would be kept and not sold. The rebels needed a doctor for their injuries. I was an easy target. I was not a chameleon. Their previous doctor did not save one of the Islamic leaders and was killed. Extra guards were assigned to me. They watched me round-the-clock in shifts. Twenty armed soldiers stood guard while I slept, showered, ate, and performed surgeries and medical care. These convicted criminals, who might have sliced me with a bolo prior to their deployment, were now my protectors, prepared to die for me.

I had my own little army of "bad asses."

Our mission was to provide care in Jolo and the surrounding area and to villages on smaller nearby islands. We were the first medical doctors to be on these islands. The local "doctors" watched us in anger and suspicion and waved idols at us. When the first idol was thrust in my face, I prayed. *God protect us. I know you sent this army but please help.*

The next morning, a transport barge brought us to a nearby island. The metal front wall of the boat unfolded onto the white beach. I felt like General Douglas MacArthur as we stormed the beach.

Bamboo huts and coconut trees lined the shore. Bangkas with outriggers were poised near the clear, teal-blue water. The native children jumped and turned circles. They approached but darted away laughing when my arms reached out to them.

The laughter of children is the same everywhere.

We were to dispense medical care that day, no surgery. Surgical care was scheduled for the next day back in Jolo. There were plenty of wounds to heal and tropical diseases to treat. Tropical infections were prevalent and included roundworm, hookworm, whipworm, elephantiasis, tuberculosis, trachoma, cholera, malaria, leprosy, and scabies. I became an expert in rural tropical medicine. My clinical eye and stethoscope were my instruments of detection. No laboratory. No X-rays.

Our pharmacy was quickly erected in a Nipa hut, a thatched window propped by a short bamboo pole. Examinations occurred in huts and under the shade of coconut and mango trees. Native drums pounded out the message of our arrival. Overwhelmed with the mass of natives that came from the forest and nearby beaches and weary of the bolos carried by every adult male native, our safety was threatened. Our pharmacy, no longer secured, was moved to the back of a military truck the soldiers had unloaded on the island.

The army commanded order. My army, the bad asses, with rifles drawn, surrounded me and surveyed the natives. Their sharp eyes ignored the beauty of the island and focused on possible bandits with hidden firearms. We were in militant Muslim territory. Rebel terrorists might be among the natives seeking treatment.

After a long but successful day, we headed back to Jolo. A goat had been sacrificed for us and placed in the barge next to our medical supplies. Blood from the bolo slice to its throat sizzled on the scorching metal floor. Its body seared. Our army debated which regional Filipino recipe for goat was tastier. Goat was the preferred meat entrée for the soldiers that night. Fortunately, the medical team was to have dinner at the estate of the mayor of Jolo, Colonel Madrino C. Muñoz.

My team and a group of soldiers left in military jeeps ahead of me for the mayor's home. I stayed behind on the pier with my own personal army. As president of MMI and responsible for the overall success of the mission, I wanted to be sure our supplies were moved off the barge, into the military trucks, and transported back to our residence.

Gunfire erupted.

A guard forced me down with a rapid extension of one arm as he held his rifle forward and fired. Two of my guards stood in back-to-back positions and straddled over me. The other soldiers dispersed in crouched positions, their rifles blazed in fire. I wanted to run and dive into the ocean, deep.

"Stay down." The intense command allowed no reply from me. I gasped for air. My head spun, vision blurred, thoughts fogged into a trance.

Ammunition shell casings covered me, burned my skin. A guard fell on top of my head. Another guard assumed his position. The weight of the dead soldier smothered my thoughts of running. My concentration on breathing displaced any need to escape. With a desperate thrust with my right arm, my head was freed.

The militant Muslims crept closer.

More shell casings.

More burns on my skin.

Another guard fell.

"Buddy, they're going to get me."

"Jay, stay strong and pray!" he shouted.

I did.

More soldiers were down. My face was pressed into the pier. A gap in the wood plank allowed for some air. I was weakened, parched, and petrified. My eyes closed against the madness.

Childhood flashbacks flooded my brain in rapid succession.

Men, their heads covered in black hoods, flog themselves with whips attached to thin razor-like pieces of bamboo and slice their bare backs to shreds for penance on Good Friday. Dozens of jellyfish cover me when I dive into the ocean after I win a coconut race. The stings of jellyfish stab me like a thousand knives. Natives roll me in the sand. The gelatinous bodies release their tentacles from my body. The torturous stings remain. My horse throws me against a coconut tree. My hold on his mane fails to keep me on his bare back. He rears and kicks at the python snake and bolts to the beach. The long tortuous snake slithers toward me like an uncoiled whip ready to snap. I stand atop a carabao while my bolo slices at the enemy. My barkada, brave child warriors, attack atop their beasts. Our enemy, the Maya birds, retreat and take flight. My carabao, the national animal of the Philippines, important draft-animal in the rice fields and puller for heavy chores in the forest, is my cherished chariot that day.

I glanced around. More guards were down. The militants advanced. Their white target was in sight.

Increased gunfire.

A rebel dropped, then another, and another.

Rebels retreated.

More fell.

The escort soldiers of my medical team had returned to the pier, concerned by our delay. Their barrage banished the remaining bandits. My heart pounded as some soldiers removed their dead comrade off of me. I was freed from my pinned position. They surrounded me, and we shuffled as a unit to a jeep. Their rifles positioned forward with quick side-to-side movements in unison, ready for any rebel that might return or rise from the ground.

Inside the jeep I turned to the soldier in charge of my private army.

"I'm so sorry about the death of your fellow soldiers. I should leave so no one else will be harmed or killed because of me. My Tatay warned me of the danger. I did not think of this kind of loss. I am sorry, po."

"Sir, it was not your fault. We are soldiers doing our mission. My comrades did their duty. They died honorably, not in a prison, where we were before this mission. Do not quit. I am from this area. My people need you," stated the hardened soldier. His back was straight, head forward, chin tucked, and eyes sharpened and pierced into my wet eyes. He was in his early twenties. His skin was dark chocolate. A rifle slung over his right shoulder.

"Don't quit. Be strong. You have work to do," Buddy insisted.

"I'll stay," I answered.

My dazed state dissolved.

"Here, you need this," exclaimed the mayor as I entered his home. A bottle of Chivas Regal was shoved in my face.

"Thanks. I do, sir. Thanks."

A shot of Chivas downed in a flash, another to follow.

"It tastes better than the water after my interrogation." I coughed and wiped my mouth.

"Sir, I also thank you for the official letter you were kind to give me," I acknowledged between gulps of Chivas.

The letter the mayor wrote and signed authorized me to go anywhere in Sulu with my team. It helped at checkpoints during the rest of our stay and averted further interrogations.

"You are most welcome. Now, let's eat. I hope you are hungry." The mayor smiled.

"Yes. But I feel a little light-headed."

Maybe water would have been better than the Chivas.

During a short break the next afternoon, I explored the central town plaza area of Jolo. My soldiers, more numerous since the assault at the pier, were my tour guides. Crowds dispersed as we passed. The air was tense, destruction everywhere. No coconut trees, no houses, no buildings, no children playing, and no laughter.

Paradise had been lost.

Jolo's apocalypse had a date: February 7, 1974. First the MNLF (Moro National Liberation Front), then the military burned Jolo to the ground.

A Mosque and a Catholic Church, with its large cross adorning the highest steeple, stood untouched amongst the rubble. What a miraculous sight.

God is powerful.

A refreshing surprise awaited my return to our residence. An outside shower built for me looked like it belonged on the *Swiss Family Robinson* movie set. Long bamboo poles guided water down a hillside and into an upside down metal bucket pierced by multiple nail holes. The flow of water was continuous, strong, cool, and refreshing. Supportive bamboo poles provided height for me to squat under the bucket. A bamboo floor added comfort, the lush vegetation serenity. Ah, paradise found. Several guards watched as I showered. A vision of toughness in tranquility.

Militant Muslims were sighted daily for the remainder of our stay, but no further attacks occurred.

When I was interrogated by the military and ambushed by the rebels, I questioned why I was there.

When I saw the happy faces of the little ones, I knew why. This was a divine mission, and we were helping to do God's work.

At the airport, my private army formed two rows and saluted me as I passed. My interrogator stood off to the side and saluted. I turned, saluted, paused, and then boarded the plane.

A far better farewell than reception.
I took one last look at my protectors as the plane veered.
I prayed that they would be safe. I honored their service to me.
Those bad asses had my gratitude and respect.

18

PALM SPRINGS, CALIFORNIA

1999

I feel weaker today.

I wish I had a *balut*.

I close my eyes and see the street vendors at night in the Philippines. A bamboo pole hangs across their shoulder and bends from the weight of a metal pot full of baluts on both ends of the pole as they shout, "Baloooot, baloooot."

Balut (ballot, which means "wrapped") is a fertilized duck egg with a nearly developed embryo inside that is boiled and eaten in the shell and is believed to be an aphrodisiac. It is said to be a completely packaged meal with the beak used to pick feathers from your teeth!

My mouth waters.

Or maybe I should send for a Filipino faith healer. An egg is probably not enough.

Filipino faith healers are known around the world. They perform operations with their bare hands without any trace or scarring after their psychic surgery. They are called espiritists.

There are two other types of traditional healers in the Philippines. The Albularyos, or herb doctors, use herbs and *oraciones* (prayers) to drive out evil sprits that cause diseases. The Baylan does mediumistic healing to cure sickness, to exorcise evil spirits from the rice fields or out of the human body, and to intercede with good spirits for the petitions of the people.

I remember the warning of the apostle Paul: "And no wonder, for Satan himself masquerades as an angel of light" (2 Corinthians 11:14, NIV). The evil one can come in very appealing forms. Spiritualistic healings have nothing to do with the gifts and the fruit of the Spirit.

My sister, Lina Barretto, went to an espiritist in Baguio City for removal of a growth in her wrist. The healer massaged the swollen area. Blood flowed when the tumor was removed even without a scalpel, displayed for everyone to see. The site was immediately bandaged. Lina said it looked like a piece of chicken meat to her. The next day, she removed the dressing. No wound was visible on her skin, but the tumor was still there.

She had the growth removed by a surgeon. The pathological report disclosed it to be a benign cyst. She had an incision that healed. The tumor did not reoccur.

No. I won't want a Filipino faith healer. I should just eat a big meal tonight, full of protein.

No. I might have *bangungot.*

Bangungot is a disease said to be peculiar to Filipino men aged twenty-five to forty. They go to sleep and are found dead the next morning after an apparent violent nightmare. Filipinos blame it on a heavy meal before bedtime or a demon that sits on the chest.

My mouth continues to water.

No. I should just get a balut.

Maybe by DHL.

Anyway, God must be mad at me.

I have prayed, yet he does not answer.

He doesn't care about me.

It is worthless for me to try and receive the power of his healings.

If he really wanted to, he could do it right in my bedroom.

He doesn't care.

"Yes, he does," Buddy interrupts.

"No, he doesn't!" I yell.

19

MANILA, PHILIPPINES

1975

I immersed myself in my studies. My clinical rotations were ending. The *revalida* (to validate again) examination was fast approaching. My medical school was distinct from other medical schools in the Philippines in its policy of requiring graduating students to undergo a series of written and oral exams known as the revalida. In the oral exams, groups of three students each are questioned by panels composed of three professors on basic, clinical, and emergency medical sciences. Passing the revalida was a prerequisite to graduation.

I had to pass the revalida and graduate. My parents from the States would be at my graduation. I should not disappoint him. My years of diligent study and my devoted attention in clinical training were to be tested. I reviewed hard for the revalida. My experience from the medical missionary work gave me confidence. My performance was exemplary.

"Jay, you must be excited that your mom and dad are coming to your graduation," Tatay remarked. "It has been four years since you last saw them."

"You're right, it has been a long time," I replied to avoid a lie.

"Don't worry. Everything will be fine," reassured Nanay with a mother's touch.

"Thanks. I'm not worried."

Not worried. But not excited to see him.

My parents arrived and stayed at the Barrettos' home.

I wanted to spare Beverly from my father.

But I couldn't.

I opened up to her about my father but did not tell her all. I did not disclose all of the abuse or the gory details. She felt my father was wrong to do what he did. That he must have had a bad childhood and was a troubled and sad man. But she was firm in her belief that I should show him respect. He was an elder and my father. "We must pray for your father." She spoke softly with tears, "Jay, he is your father. Don't hate."

Beverly was my saving angel from the beginning of our courtship. She gave me the strength I needed to finish medical school, both spiritually and nutritionally. Brownies, pies, and the local favorite, Food for the Gods pastries, were delivered to me by her driver for my *meriendas* (snacks). She learned to bake from the most respected pastry chefs on the island. She also kept me grounded and focused on my studies. She was sent to me from God.

"I am nervous to meet your parents. I hope they like me. Do I look okay?" Beverly readjusted her seating to help prevent wrinkles on her dress. I had fetched her with Tatay's driver and Mercedes.

"You look beautiful. My parents will adore you. So don't be nervous."

"Then why are you so nervous?"

"I just pray that my father has not been drinking," I whispered.

We pulled up to the gate. The driver honked the horn four times and then a houseboy ran to open the gate. I took a deep breath as we pulled into the driveway. "I love you, Beverly."

"I love you too, Jay."

We entered the home. My mother was sitting with Nanay on a couch. My father was with Tatay at the bar.

My throat tightened.

"Mom and Dad, this is Beverly." My eyes were on my mother. I avoided my father's stare.

"Beverly, you look beautiful," whispered Nanay as they kissed each other on the cheek.

"As always," added Tatay with a kiss to the cheek.

"Thank you," replied Beverly in a soft voice.

"Beverly, this is my mom and dad." I glanced at Beverly.

"Nice to meet you." Beverly smiled and shook my parents' hands. "I have looked forward to this day. You have a fine son."

"Thank you. We think so," confirmed my mother.

My father smiled and stared.

There was a long pause and then he added, "Yes. Thank you very much."

"So Beverly, tell me a little about yourself. I understand that you're in medical school too." My mother gestured for Beverly to sit next to her.

"Mom."

"Oh Jay, it's okay. You know how mothers are. Don't worry. I won't embarrass you."

My mother laughed.

I did not.

My father stared.

"Dinner will be ready in a few minutes," announced Nanay.

"Jay, would you like a scotch?" asked Tatay. He knew I did not usually drink but occasionally sipped a bit of his favorite single malt scotch.

"No, thank you."

"I'll have another." My father handed his glass to the houseboy.

"Good. I will too." Tatay handed his glass over to another servant.

My throat constricted until the end of the evening.

The rest of the evening's conversation was cordial, no secrets exposed.

My father uttered a few words but mainly stared. My mother was kind but a bit forward for the Philippines. She was determined to find out all she could about Beverly. Tatay and Nanay were gracious. I am sure they felt the tension, but they never let on that they did.

As I brought Beverly back to her home, I looked out the window of the car and wanted my father gone. To be rid of him forever.

I locked my bedroom door that night, the first time in four years.

Graduation day, once a dream, was now here. I stood out at graduation for two reasons. I was taller than anyone, and I had two sets of parents. My mom and father adored Beverly as I expected they would. They grasped the depth of our love and knew Beverly would be my wife.

The next night, we sat at a long rectangular table at the Elegant Supper Club, atop the twenty-second floor of the Manila Hilton Hotel. It was my parents' wedding anniversary. Nanay and Tatay were hosting the dinner and sat next to my parents. Beverly and I sat next to Tito Jack and Tita Berta (dear friends of the Barrettos).

The view of Manila Bay was spectacular. We witnessed one of the famous sunsets, with the sun changing from vibrant yellow to orange to red, as it faded into the mountain and reflected on the water.

My mother was happy and talkative. Nanay, Tita Berta, and Beverly were more reserved. Tito Jack was a bit loud, as was Tatay. They had consumed several glasses of scotch at the Barrettos' and were telling some old secrets and war stories. My father drank and smiled at first. With more scotch, he quieted. My mother chatted all the more.

"Roy, tell us a secret. I know you must have some," challenged Tito Jack.

"Yeah, buddy, tell one," nudged Tatay.

My father smirked and stared at me.

My throat constricted.

"I think we ladies should excuse ourselves," Nanay stated and glared at Tatay.

"Never mind, Roy. I was just kidding." Tatay patted my father on his back.

"Mr. and Mrs. Roberts, look at the sunset," stated Beverly as she discreetly patted my knee, covered by the long white tablecloth.

"Yeah. Isn't it beautiful," I replied.

"It is breathtaking," declared my mother.

My father stared at the sunset, but I felt his eyes reflected on me. The rest of the evening, he spoke to Tatay and Tito Jack. The women, including Beverly, listened, smiled, and talked amongst themselves.

I avoided my father's glare. He was leaving soon.

"You're doing great. Keep strong," whispered Buddy.

My throat loosened.

I never had a father-to-son talk about marriage during my parents' visit. I had it with Tatay. My father was too busy. His priority was drinking San Miguel Beer and talking about the good old days. My mom watched the lack of interaction between us. It stressed her. She wanted everything to be perfect. She wanted control but could not get it. She desired that perfect family but did not have it. I loved my mom and wished she could stay. I despised my father and was relieved it was time for him to return to the States.

"Have a safe flight," I recited as if I was a ticket agent at the airport. I stood erect and shook my father's hand. The bones in my right hand crushed from the force of the grasp. He had to show me, again, his strength and power. He succeeded. I felt weak. I glanced down to abort the impact of his eyes and nose on me.

Get out of here. Just leave.

My mom cried, kissed, and hugged me.

My dad did not, would not, or could not.

I turned, stepped into my car, and signaled my driver to go.

"Take me home," I commanded. This was now my home.

The original plan was for me to return to the States after graduation with my parents. My sister expected me to be on the flight and would be disappointed. I didn't think my brother would care. Instead of leaving, I had decided to do a medical-surgical internship at the University of Santo Tomas Hospital. An internship was a requirement for licensure in the States, and it gave me another year to be with Beverly. I was afraid I would lose her if I left.

"I want to marry Beverly," I confided to Edwin as we entered the charity hospital.

"What? Now?" Edwin staggered, mouth wide-open.

"Well, not this minute. But soon."

"Have you asked her?" His mouth closed.

"Yes, of course."

"And?" He grinned.

"She said yes. I knew that pizza was a winner."

"Good luck, pare, in getting permission from her parents, especially her mother."

He shook his head. Edwin knew that her stepmother was not keen on us being together. She felt I was not good enough for Beverly.

"It is a disgrace that you are being seen with that American. You should stay with our own kind, a Filipino. He is just a lonely boy away from home and will ruin your reputation." Her stepmother's staccato articulation had pierced Beverly's ears many times.

Beverly's biological mother died when she was nine years old. Beverly and her sister, Alice, were sent to a nearby island to a Catholic convent and school run by Belgian nuns. Their father felt it was best for their upbringing, a proper environment for two sisters without a mother to nurture them.

Beverly's respect for her stepmother was tested. She remained respectful despite her inner anger. She passed. In fact, she passed many verbal assaults. She had splendid schooling.

Two of Beverly's brothers detested me. They agreed with their stepmother's opinion and wanted to harm me. I was not hurt because I was a son of Tatay. Reprisal for my harm would be costly.

I was accused of wanting Beverly for her family's wealth. As a proud American, I vowed never to touch her money; a vow I realized, years later, was immature and unwise. I prayed that someday they would realize my genuine love for Beverly.

I might have been lonely, but I was in love.

Beverly failed a test of respect one night. Her stepmother and two brothers were relentless with their rage over Beverly and me. She was forbidden to ever see me again.

Beverly broke. She walked out of her home and hailed a taxi. Her family did not know where she was for two days. I did not know she was missing.

Her brothers drove by the Barrettos' home to see if they could spot Beverly. They never stopped to ask if she was there. That would have disrespected the Barrettos and embarrassed her family. They looked everywhere for her. She could not be found.

Beverly's father was alerted and flew up to Manila. Prayers for her safe return were offered. She was a single girl out alone. Her honor and life were at stake.

After two days, she returned home from her female classmate's shack in the poorest area of Greater Manila. There was no phone to tempt Beverly to call.

Beverly's father overruled her stepmother and announced that I could continue to see Beverly.

Beverly never bragged about her first act of defiance. She was sorry for worrying her family but happy with the result of her transgression.

To request Beverly's hand in marriage was a formal affair. First, I had to ask her father, then her mother. By Filipino culture, they could make me wait a year for their answers. Beverly would not marry without their blessings. Running away to Las Vegas was out of the question. A trip to Iligan City was in order.

"Are you ready?" asked Rody Borja, a light brown *pogi* (handsome) Mestizo and cousin of Beverly.

"Yes." I sucked hard on my cigarette, exhaled smoke through my mouth and nose, tossed the butt to the ground, and crushed it with my shoe. "Let's go."

"Dr. Cuyugan is at his medical clinic. I will take you there," chuckled Rody.

Rody had met me at the airport in Iligan City. He smiled and shook his head several times as he drove me to Beverly's father.

"Hi, Jay. I did not know you were coming. Are you on another mission?" Dr. Cuyugan glanced around as he looked for members of my team.

"Yeah, mission impossible!" Rody uttered from behind my back.

"No, sir. I came to ask you something." I bit my lip to avoid laughing at Rody's remark.

"Oh. Well, please come in." The tone of his voice lowered. His smile stretched.

Filipinos were big on smiles. They smiled when praised, criticized, embarrassed, made to feel happy, or for any other reason. An awkward situation invited a smile because of potential conflict. You were expected to smile in return to diffuse the situation.

I smiled back at Dr. Cuyugan and entered the clinic.

After several hours of questions including how I would provide for Beverly, how our children would be raised, and if I was truly in love with his daughter, I received his blessing.

I wanted to jump for joy.

I did not.

I smiled, kept eye contact, and shook his hand.

"Salamat po." My voice cracked, my eyes watered.

"I will pray for you and Beverly and for many *apo* (grandchildren)." His smile now included laughter.

We were off to the relatives' estates in Iligan. After we entered each home and announced his blessings for our marriage, a feast ensued. To show favorable respect, I consumed large portions of food at each home. By the end of the day, my stomach was stuffed with sinigang, *batchoy* (noodle soup with pork, shrimp, chicken, and vegetables), adobo, lumpia (spring roll), bangus, tilapia, prawns, *lechon* (roasted pig), pancit, rice, *buko* (coconut) pie, leche flan (caramel custard), mango, and papaya. I wanted to purge but did not. I could not waste all that delicious food. And there was the matter of respect and watchful eyes. I just gave thanks and smiled.

During the course of the meals, relatives commented on "how cute your apos will be" to Dr. Cuyugan. He smiled, actually, beamed. I squirmed a bit but smiled.

I was given a quick tour of Iligan, which means "fortress of defense." The city's history is rich in defending attacks by pirates and hostile Mindanao tribes. Iligan is known as the "City of Majestic Waterfalls" because there are around twenty-three waterfalls in and around the area. Among them are the Maria Cristina Falls, Limunsudan Falls, and Tinago (hidden) Falls.

On the tour of Iligan, I was shown a safer swimming location in Iligan and one of Beverly's favorites, the Timoga Springs, well-known for the ice-cold, crystal-clear natural springs that flow freely all the way to the numerous swimming pools at each of the five resorts in the area. The cold water eased the hotness of the tropical heat. Then I viewed Bucana beach, another favorite of Beverly's. I tried to envision little Beverly and her friends as they made sandcastles on the pristine beach, swam in the aqua-blue water, and drank milk from fresh coconuts. My picture had no time to develop as our car left the treasured area for "the large house on the hill," Dr. Cuyugan's home.

I was not to stay in a hotel that night. After all, I was now the future son-in-law of the doctor. It was proper for me to stay with him. It did feel strange to be shown to Beverly's room. I was gun-shy about the "no touch" rule and felt, in a weird way, that I would be breaking the rule being in her bedroom. I accepted the invitation and did my best to hide my apprehension.

The next morning, I flew back to Manila to ask Beverly's stepmother for her blessings. It was not that easy. It was difficult to concentrate on my planned speech that sounded more like a dissertation. Her perfectly groomed fingernails clicked on the table top in rapid succession while I pled my case.

"I cannot give you my blessings today," she declared, her finger tapping replaced by firm pressure of open hands on the table.

"But…" My response halted as her right hand raised, palm toward me.

"My request is for Beverly and you to attend early morning mass for thirty days. You are to pray for insight into your desire and God's guidance. When you have completed this, come back to me, and I will consider your appeal."

She stood.

I stood.

She left the room and went upstairs to the master bedroom.

Her request sounded to me like a command, her sentences like a declaration. I knew why some relatives called her the "commander." I thought she was just hard and cruel. After the thirty days of prayer, I went back to Beverly's stepmother. Her blessings were given with a smile.

Mission accomplished.

Smile returned and lip bitten.

Our marriage date was set.

Beverly's father, mother, and stepmother graduated from the same medical school that we were attending. Most of our professors were prior classmates and friends of her parents. Beverly knew that her father wanted her to go to medical school. She obeyed his wishes. But her true love was fashion design and business.

Beverly was God-centered. She walked with the Lord, gave thanks to the Lord, and saw the poor and rich alike as loving children of God. She prayed for the oppressed and the oppressors. She cared for the poor and the rich. She did not discriminate. People loved Beverly.

There were many professors and students, who like her stepmother, thought that Beverly should court and marry a Filipino. They were the spies for her stepmother who scrutinized us at school and in the hospital. Their mission was to report any indiscretion, a break in the "no touch" rule. They could soon rest their eyes and terminate their duty.

One gossiper at school was the son of the dean of the College of Medicine. The dean was also my swimming coach. My barkada heard him spread malicious, vicious rumors about Beverly and me. His mother was a close friend of Beverly's mother, a professor at our school and an adamant supporter of "no touch." I had just been informed of the rumors when Edwin told me the son was at the front of the school. I ran; my barkada in pursuit behind me. I slammed him up against the wall. "You little punk. You bastard. If I ever hear you slander us again, I will kill you." My eyes bulged, my neck veins engorged, my words sputtered with spit.

He remained mute and coiled in a corner. His barkada stood still. My eyes dared them to move. My barkada moved closer.

"You are going to be expelled for this!" Edwin shouted at me. "Jay, let's get out of here."

"Believe me, pare ko, I will not be expelled. Do you remember the swimming incident with Rene?" I hissed.

"I do." Edwin grabbed my arm, pulled, and pleaded, "We have to go now."

"Believe me, I will not be expelled or even disciplined."

I conceded to his pull.

I was right. Nothing happened except for quieting one set of loose lips.

Our marriage day, August 9, 1975, was near.

It was expected that men in the Philippines were sexually experienced before marriage. There were "pleasure girls" for them.

Beverly's youngest brother, Guzzie, took me a few weeks before our marriage to a high-class massage parlor to relieve me of my tension and protect his sister's virtue. I was bathed, received a special massage, bathed again, dressed, and went home relieved of my stress and tension.

"Jay, let me know if you need to come back here again. I will be happy to arrange it and accompany you," said Guzzie.

"Or I could take you to a nice one I know," I blurted.

Guzzie beamed and slapped me on my back.

"Did one of the Barretto boys take you there?" he asked.

I smiled and shrugged my shoulders.

He laughed.

We left.

On the day of our marriage, Nanay insisted that I have a manicure. She wanted my hands to look good for the traditional close-up wedding picture of Beverly's and my hands united. I had never had a manicure. I had always resisted. But I agreed to please Nanay; after all, it was a special day and a legitimate request. A driver was sent to fetch Diding, the manicurist who came regularly to our home for her services. By mid-morning, my manicure was done. By mid-afternoon, typhoon Diding hit the island. What were the odds that Diding would be the same name of my first manicurist and the typhoon that struck on our special day?

Typhoons, *bagyos*, in the Philippines were tropical cyclones. An average of six to seven hit the Philippines per year. They accounted for at least thirty percent of the annual rainfall in northern Philippines and less than ten percent in the southern islands. They occurred between July and October, with September being the most active month. Typhoons entering the Philippines were given a local name.

Typhoons achieved maximum sustained winds of 120 to 185 kilometers per hour. Super typhoons had maximum winds exceeding 185 kilometers per hour. The deadliest typhoon in the Philippines was Uring in 1991, which caused floods and killed thousands of people. The wettest typhoon in 1911 dropped over forty-six inches of rainfall within a twenty-four-hour period in Baguio City in Northern Luzon.

"Jay, be happy. Each raindrop is a blessing from heaven that will bring you prosperity and happiness in your marriage. It is a good sign," encouraged Nanay as we watched the downpour, a massive waterfall-like stream of rain.

"Well, then we sure are getting an enormous amount of blessings," I exclaimed.

I was not completely convinced of that belief. I was more positive of the association between the two Didings.

But just in case the raindrop belief proved valid, I thanked God.

Early that morning, Beverly's parents had their driver deliver eggs to the Monasterio de Sta. Clara for an offering to St. Clare. It was a popular monastery in Manila where nuns of the order of Saint Clare of Assisi lead a life of prayer and poverty. The cream-colored church was where people came with egg offerings and asked the saintly nuns to pray for good weather. A famous legend states that if you want to have great weather at your wedding, you must bring some eggs to a Clarisse monastery. A long time ago, it rained hard for days. People fell ill and died. To stop the rain, the locals called a nun, Sister Claire, for help. She told the people to bring eggs to her chapel where she laid them on the altar. All of a sudden, the sun started shining again. The sick people healed.

With typhoon Diding on our wedding day, I think too few eggs were offered!

Floods devastated Metro Manila and encumbered our wedding. Many of our guests were stranded as they attempted to get to the Old Paco Church in Manila, where the ceremony was held, and the Hotel del Rico for the formal reception dinner. Their cars were halted by the torrential downpour and flooded streets. Beverly's wedding dress was dampened from floodwater that seeped into their Mercedes. The unrelenting determination of her driver delivered her to the church almost on time. By Philippine standards, a bride must not appear too eager by appearing too early at her wedding.

Paco Church, also known as the Saint Pancratius Chapel, was a domed Romanesque architecture, constructed under the Spanish regime, and stood majestically inside Paco Park in Manila.

Beverly was luminous. She glowed underneath her veil. The pearls on her gown sparkled. She was angelic, the most beautiful bride in the world.

Our formal Filipino Catholic wedding was beautiful despite the torrential rain. The wedding party included principal sponsors (Tatay, Beverly's stepmother, Beverly's Tita Maling, and my Tito Jack) who acted as witnesses to the marriage.

Secondary sponsors handled the candles, the cord, and the veil parts of the ceremony. Candle sponsors lighted two candles, which Beverly and I used to light a single candle to symbolize the joining of our two families and to invoke the light of Christ in our married life. Veil sponsors placed a white veil over Beverly's head and my shoulders, a symbol of two people clothed as one. Cord sponsors draped the *yugal* (a decorative silk cord) in a figure-eight shape to symbolize everlasting fidelity over Beverly and my shoulders.

Beverly wore a long white wedding gown she designed. It was made of white organza material (sheer fabric similar to silk) over the white sateen material with embroidered tiny white flowers attached with white pearls that formed her long sheath gown with its squared-scoop neck. Her neck and arms showed through the organza. Her long black hair was pulled back to expose her face. She wore white gloves and held a cascading bouquet of white orchids with white ribbon.

I wore a newly tailored dark blue-gray suit. Beverly wanted me in a suit, not a *barong*, the traditional hand-embroidered formal shirt made from specially hand-loomed *pinya jusi* (pineapple fiber) cloth.

My family in the States was not able to attend our wedding. I like to think we had all of their best wishes, and they were present in spirit.

The length of the wedding, coupled with the heat, humidity, and no air conditioning in the church, stifled Beverly. A standing large fan, on full blast, revitalized her. The short interruption in the service was over.

An arras of thirteen silver coins from WWII era, one side Filipino and the other side American, were dropped from my hands into Beverly's hands. It was a symbolic act of me as the provider and Beverly as the receiver in our marriage. The coins were a special gift to us from Beverly's father.

The symbolic rituals seemed endless.

Finally, vows completed!

I lifted her veil. Her eyes expressed love. I paused for a brief moment, sighed, and went for the kiss. Her cheek was offered. I accepted. I knew planting a big one on her lips was not going to happen. I had been warned before the ceremony. Still, I tried. No luck. A big smack on her cheek produced applause from our guests. I was most thankful the "no touch" was gone, vaporized.

The reception included a sit-down dinner of lobster, steak, some vegetable that I cannot remember, and rice instead of potato. We danced with a small orchestra that played classical music during dinner and '70s music for dancing while the floor spun 360 degrees. Beverly's pearl-laden "money bag" was filled with money from our guests as we performed the "money dance." There were speeches, toasts, and songs sung—some in tune, some not—but all appreciated. Our wedding cake was a tower of elegance and beauty. It was the cake Beverly wanted and designed, the wedding cake she dreamed of as a child. Beverly and I pulled a long white cord of a white bell that hung from the ceiling and released two white doves. If the doves flew away, our marriage would be successful; if not, doomed. Our doves flew strong and hard. Believe me, if they did not fly away, I would have thrown them out the window myself. This was the final ritual. Then Beverly and I and the bridal entourage were escorted to an adjoining room for a photography session.

It was after one in the morning when I opened the door to the honeymoon suite. I carried Beverly across the threshold and tried to close the door with my right foot. I had seen this move countless times in the movies and planned to do it on our wedding night. The door did not close. I pulled again with my foot. The door did not budge. I let Beverly down. I turned and saw one of her maids at the door, a live doorstopper. "What are you doing?" I asked in a calm tone. I did not want anything to ruin the atmosphere of our special night, actually early morning.

"Sir, I am here to assist Beverly out of her wedding gown and to help in her preparations," the maid answered as her head bowed.

"Absolutely not. I've waited three years. I'll help Beverly undress," I replied with restraint.

"Jay, please." Beverly touched my arm. "Let me dismiss her, please."

"Okay, but please, Beverly, enough is enough," I pled, actually begged.

"*Manang* (a respectful title for a female servant), I will not be requiring your help. You may leave us. *Salamat ho*," Beverly spoke softly.

"Okay, but Sir Jay, please be gentle with Beverly. Do not hurt her," the maid begged.

"Beverly, please, that's too much," I said, my voice raised.

Beverly's gentle hand moved and her head nod gave the final dismissal to that intrusive maid. She finally left. I actually think I heard her cry.

Beverly's touch quieted me, refocused me, pleasured me. Our wedding night was magical.

We were united as one.

But I don't kiss and tell!

Typhoon Diding destroyed our honeymoon plans. All planes were grounded. We decided to stay in the suite and pretend we were at our intended honeymoon site. It was fantastic just to be alone with Beverly. The next day, we decided to go to the US Embassy to start on Beverly's paperwork. As we crossed Roxas Boulevard, one of her shoes lost a heel. Traffic was horrendous as usual. I grabbed her heel and helped her across the street. I pounded the heel back into place with the aid of a stone. Beverly kept her grace and composure as she carefully walked into the US Embassy. She showed no sign of embarrassment, fear, or shame. She had excellent *amor proprio* (self-esteem).

I admired her. I loved her. I adored her.

We were blessed that year.

Maybe there was something to that raindrop belief.

We vowed to live on our own, moving out of our homes despite our families' wishes.

It is customary for newlyweds to live with the parents of the husband or wife for at least a year until they get settled. Breaking off from the parents too soon can cause emotional distress in the family. The parents will regard the desire of the married children to leave as a sign of unhappiness with the family.

We pleased our families when we agreed to bring a trusted servant with us.

We were happy, busy but happy. Beverly was in her last year of medical school. My internship demanded long hours away from my bride. We cherished our nights together. We dreaded the coming end of the year when I would have to leave for the States for my residency program.

But the end came. I had to go.

We cried and cried some more.

We ignored the crowd at the airport. We ignored their stares and whispers.

"Take care of yourself, Jay. I love you," sobbed Nanay.

"I am so proud of you, son. Don't worry about Beverly. She has her family and our family. We will take good care of her," Tatay added as he cried.

My Tatay cried and was still a man, a strong man.

"Beverly, *mahal kita* (I love you)." I had to let her go. I had to. I had to go.

I was the last to enter the plane. I sat down, cried, and did not hide my face. I looked out the window but could not see Beverly. Condensation was on the window.

I looked deeper into the fog-like screen that blurred my view through the window and saw myself as a child.

I have a smile across my little face as I trade my new Tonka truck, which was made in the USA, for a homemade slingshot from a native boy. I feel I made the better deal.

I catch lizards and paint their backs with different-colored spots. The color is provided by my mother's nail polishes. A chart has their names next to their spots and allows for easy identification of my pets. Their suction feet keep them attached to the walls and ceilings.

I run to the dining room during an earthquake. At home, we measure the intensity of an earthquake on how hard the large dining room chandelier moves. A little sway causes no concern, and we return to our playing. Larger movements alert danger, and we take cover under the sturdy wood table. If we are outside during an earthquake, we quickly move away from any coconut tree. Falling coconuts can be deadly.

Faster and faster images of more recent events flashed on the blurred window.

The flashes burst into one blaze that covered the window as the plane moved away from the gate and past an outdoor floodlight. I stared harder out the window into the darkness of the night.

No sign of Beverly.

I shed tears and did not hide my face.

As the plane departed the Philippines, I was leaving behind another family; but now, it included my wife. I also left wounds that needed to be healed and missions to be performed. But there were wounds for me to heal in the States. And there might be missions for me to accomplish.

As the plane leveled at its cruising altitude, I looked out the window and stared into a formation of clouds. I looked closer and saw a nose, his nose.

I feared that one day I might kill him.

I prayed to God to take that thought out of me.

Buddy told me not to kill. He had said it to me when I was a child with a knife in my hand and my father asleep, drunk on the couch.

20

PALM SPRINGS, CALIFORNIA

1999

The TV is on but not watched. The Bible is next to me but not read. I stare out the window, into the backyard, at the palm trees.

There is a knock at the door of my prison, and Ryan and Derek enter. They have just finished playing basketball outside, and they wear their usual at-home basketball gear: untucked, extra large white T-shirts, long, baggy, black basketball shorts, black basketball shoes, low-ankle black socks, and sweatbands over their right wrists. Thin, white sweat towels drape their necks and sweat beads dot their foreheads as they gulp from large bottles of Gatorade drinks.

I sit on the bed, my back supported with pillows. I have on a pair of long, lounging pants, a long-sleeve T-shirt, and white athletic socks. I do not want them to see the atrophy in my arms and legs.

"Dad, how did you and mom do it? Most of my friends' parents are divorced. What's the secret?" Ryan asks with a serious look.

"Yeah, Dad, what's the secret?" Derek asks.

"Well, sit down and I'll tell." I smile as they sit on the couch. "Do you really want to know? This is important. I feel it is my duty as your father to tell you the truth. Are you prepared to hear it?" I ask in a low tone.

They both lean closer.

"Okay. The secret is in two words. The two most important words any married man must know and say from the get-go." My voice remains low.

"What are they?" Ryan inquires.

"Well, the two most important words are 'Yes, dear.'" I smile.

"Really? Come on, Dad. Are you serious?" doubts Derek.

"Yep. Really," I affirm. "Every happily married man knows the importance and power of those two words. I do not care what you do for work, from a laborer to president and CEO of any company or president of the United States. When a happily married man goes home, we all say 'Yes, dear.'"

Derek and Ryan look at each other, shrug their shoulders, and nod in agreement.

"Sons. Another thing. A truism," I add.

"What?" they ask in unison.

"A happily married man means there is a happy wife." I beam.

"What was that I heard?" asks Beverly, entering our bedroom.

"Nothing. I was just talking to the boys," I reply in haste.

"Okay," Beverly responds with a doubtful look.

My eye contact with Ryan and Derek solidifies the silent agreement of "keeping this information between us."

"Jay, I really want you to try the homemade chicken soup I just made. It will be good for you," says Beverly as she leaves the room.

"Yes, dear," I reply.

I glance at my boys and smile.

They smile back at me, chuckle, and settle into the couch.

"Sons, you have to show honor and respect to each other, to like each other, not just love each other. You must let your wife grow through the years of your marriage. She won't be the exact person you dated and married. And neither will you."

"Okay. What else?" Ryan asks.

"Try not to go to bed angry."

"Hmmm."

"What else, boys? What do you want to talk about now?"

They look at each other with intent and nod in agreement.

Oh, Lord. Help me to say the right words. I think I am in for it now.

"Dad, we want to thank you for the way you and Mom raised us," says Ryan.

Derek nods.

"You're welcome, but what brought this on?"

"Well, Dad, we see the difference at school. Kids that were not raised with rules and consequences are really going wild. We're glad we're not part of that group." Their eyes fill.

"So, I wasn't too strict after all? You always said we were the strictest parents. That you were the only ones who had curfews and had to keep your bedroom doors open when you had female friends over."

"Yeah, but you were right," Ryan says as Derek places an arm around Ryan's shoulder.

"Sons, thank you for saying that. Please remember that when you have children, you are their father, not their best friend. They can have many friends but only one father. It is your responsibility and honor to be their father. They might not like your rules, but you must do what you think is right. You can only do your best and pray that you are doing the right thing."

"We know, Dad. Thank you for being our father." Ryan stands and gives me a hug.

"Me too, Dad. Thank you." Derek joins the hug.

"I love you, sons."

"I love you too, Dad."

"Me too, Dad."

"Sons, make sure your children know that you love them. Show them and tell them. Don't let them wonder."

"Okay."

"And talk to your kids. Try your best to keep the line of communication open."

"Okay."

"Dad, we want to go play some more basketball now. Is that alright?" Ryan asks as Derek nudges his side.

"Sure. Have fun."

I smile long after they leave my bedroom. Later, I lie in bed thinking about my talk with my sons. I feel like a hypocrite. I've been mad at Beverly for months. I have not shown her honor and respect. I have not shown her love. I've gone to sleep angry. Suddenly, I begin to cry.

"Buddy, I do love Beverly. I don't want to be mean to her."

"I know."

"Help me."

"I will."

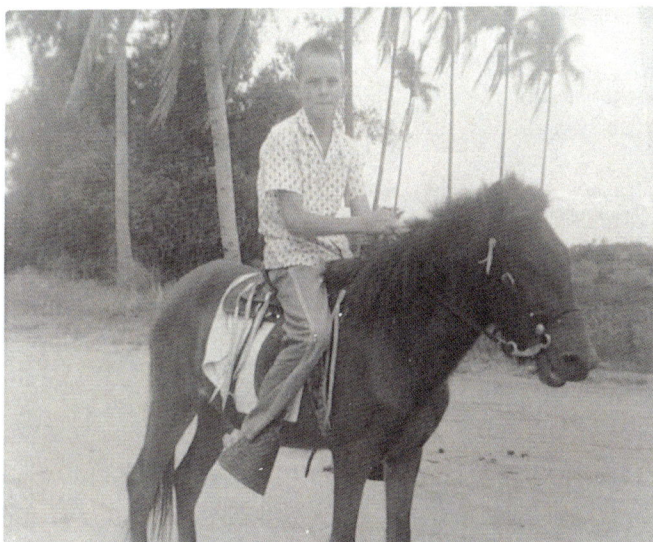

Me on my horse, Tioga, in Zambales.

Standing in front of bronze statue of Fr. Miguel de Benavides,
founder of the University of Santo Tomas (UST).

On top of tower of Main Building at UST.

A typical rice field in Mindanao. Atypical person in front of it!

Sitting on bangka in Mindanao.

Walking on wall of Banaue Rice Terraces.

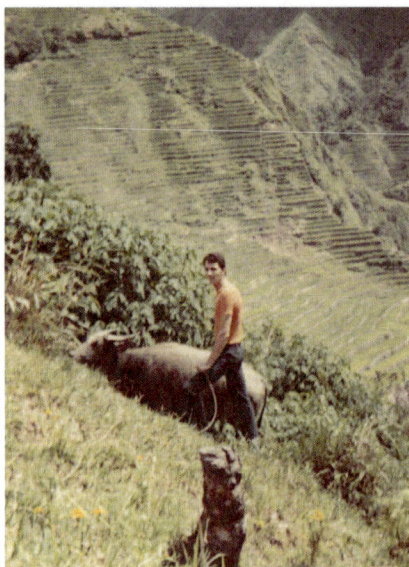

Carabao and me at Banaue Rice Terraces. If I were younger I would have ridden him instead of walked.

Local Ifugao man wondering what this white man is doing so deep into the Banaue Rice Terraces.

Helping a sick man in bangka get back to
his home on an island near Jolo.

Sister in Iligan with local woman. Removed
her enlarged goiter later that day.

Sister with locals preparing bibingka for our medical team's merienda.

En route to Jolo from Zamboanga. Inside the smaller military plane with opened windows and no door. That's why I'm holding on tight with both hands to the ceiling bar across from the door.

Some members of the "bad ass" army in Jolo. The guy to the right of me is not happy. I took his rifle for the picture.

Downtown Jolo. Mosque remains standing.

Downtown Jolo. Catholic Church's tower remains standing.

Inspecting our drug supply from the back of a truck in Jolo.

Surrounded by kids as we disembark from
a boat onto an island near Jolo.

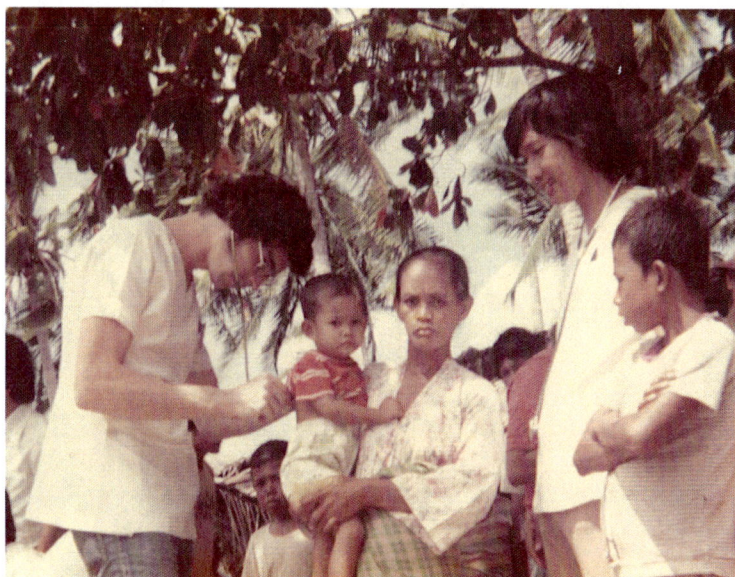

Examining kids at the same island near Jolo.

Disembarking on another island near Jolo.

Arriving at another island near Jolo.

My shower in Jolo!

Beverly and me in Iligan, during our first year of marriage.

Tatay, Nanay, and me on my medical school graduation day.

Beverly, me, Mom, and Dad on the same day.

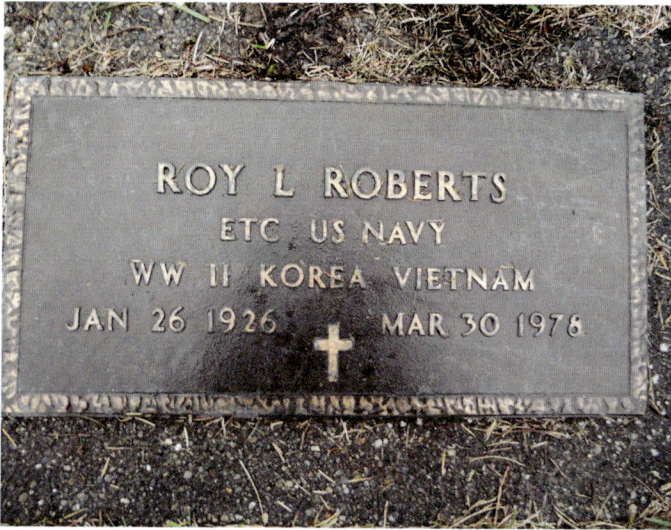

My dad's headstone, Onalaska, Washington.

Recent family picture, taken in Palm Springs, CA. From left to right: back row, Ryan, me, Derek; middle row, Emily, Grant, Beverly, Anna (baby Sofia resting inside); front row, Maxwell, Kate

21

PHILADELPHIA, PENNSYLVANIA

1976

I yearned for Beverly. I shivered from the cold weather and actually missed the tropical heat. And it was not even winter yet. I also missed the maids, my driver, Edwin and the rest of my barkada, and my family in the Philippines.

I lived in a small apartment.

I craved Filipino food. There were no Filipino restaurants in Philadelphia.

I was distressed to witness disrespect to elders.

I was a first-year resident physician at Thomas Jefferson University Hospital in the Department of Physical Medicine and Rehabilitation (PM&R). During my last months in the Philippines, I completed an elective rotation with Drs. Ofelia and Tyrone Reyes. They were new diplomats in this specialty of medicine that provided quality of life for impaired people.

They were bright, energetic, and compassionate physicians.

They healed wounds.

I wanted to heal wounds.

They had trained in Philadelphia, and with their strong recommendation, I was accepted at Jefferson, one of the top residency-training programs in the States for PM&R.

I was the first FMG (foreign medical graduate) ever accepted in my department. Dr. John Ditunno, Jr. MD, chairman of the Department of PM&R, boasted that he only had American residents from American medical schools. He made the exception for me because I was an American and I had strong recommendations from Doctors Reyes. He knew the Reyes from Temple University Hospital in Philadelphia when they were fellow residents. There were about twelve FMGs dispersed in the rest of the departments at Jefferson.

I did not tell my fellow residents that I was a foreign medical graduate. One of the residents had commented, "Boy, those FMGs are ignorant." The other physicians agreed. I kept silent but vowed to prove them wrong.

I'll outperform all of them and then inform them that I am a foreign medical graduate, one of those FMGs!

My shame for my silence was replaced by anticipation in their reaction to my declaration.

"What do I do with these?" I held the ends of my surgical gloves between my right hand's thumb and index finger at a patient's bedside. His wounds sutured with precision, the work of a skilled missionary physician.

"Throw it in there. What do you think? I don't want them," the nurse smirked and her eyebrows drew together in the middle of her forehead as she pointed to the plastic lined trashcan. She held unused gauze from a dressing tray between her right thumb and index finger, dropped them into the trash can, tilted her head toward the can as if to say, "That's what you do with them, now do what I did."

I grinned as I dropped the gloves and walked away. I began to think of patients on the unit that might be seriously constipated, maybe impacted, and in need of high colonic enemas by this most charming nurse. My smile widened. I did not order any enemas. Just the thought had eased my humiliation.

As I left the unit and nurse Nightingale, I was struck with the waste of medical supplies in the States. Sterile gloves, suture needles, syringes and needles discarded after one use. Opened but unused dressings and suture threads were tossed in trashcans. These were precious items that could heal wounds at our missionary work and at hospitals for the indigent in the Philippines. On the island, we cleansed, sterilized, and reused these items until they were worn beyond repair.

I never looked for another container to recycle my gloves. I tossed them into the trashcan, the stateside technique.

I stayed up nights learning the modern equipment used and the latest medical tests performed routinely in the States. I was cautious about this lack of knowledge; it might give away my secret.

My fellow residents asked me where I was from because of my accent. My homegrown-in-the-USA persona was not perfect. I pronounced words differently, like mediastinum, inventory, conduit, as well as others. I told them I was a mixture of east and west, which was true. They assumed a continental compass while I used a global one. I just smiled.

My accent was a result of being a "true Filipino." The inability among many Filipinos to pronounce *f*, which is substituted by *p* (an example is the national language which is spelled and pronounced Pilipino), is due to the absence of the letter *f* in Philippine languages. And there is little distinction between the short *i* and long *e* sound. Filipinos use vowel sounds like Spanish, five vowel sounds without the complex and illogical phonetic variation English gives these vowels.

The quality of medical care at the university hospital was excellent. Physicians were dressed in white lab coats devoid of sweat stains. The rooms were appointed with the latest equipment, including electric adjustable beds. The hospital had a centrally controlled temperature and was devoid of mosquitoes. What a treat. What a difference from the hospital environment in a third-world country. Another treat was free food for twenty-four hours when a resident physician was on duty. I soon learned what the oversized pockets in the lab coats were really for. I had assumed their design was to have at hand the latest medical reference pocket book or to hold a stethoscope. No. They were containers for your food supply, sandwiches, and snacks wrapped in cellophane to be eaten the next day. Bananas and apples were stuffed into the hidden inner pockets.

The food I placed into my lab coat could feed a whole family on a mission on the island for two days. Except there was no rice.

I have a scientifically unproven theory about Filipinos and rice. I believe Filipinos have two stomachs. I have never seen two stomachs on an autopsy, but they must have two stomachs. One stomach is for their *ulam* (viand), and one stomach is for their rice. The basis for my theory: if a Filipino eats a lot of ulam and little rice, he is still hungry. If that same Filipino eats little ulam and a lot of rice, he is full. They are not satisfied until their rice stomach is full. Living on the islands, I had two stomachs. Another reason I was considered a "true Filipino."

My clinical eye, the essence of my training, was my salvation. My diagnostic skills were sharp as a knife. My reputation for inserting IVs in arms without visible veins spread throughout the hospital. I was called to help with a difficult IV insertion and avoid an unnecessary cut down for an infusion. I studied and trained extra hard. I had to be the best. I had to get the respect of my fellow residents and help prove the worth of us FMGs.

"Jay, you are really good at inserting IVs in difficult patients. What medical school did you go to?" asked a fellow intern as I placed an IV in a dehydrated infant one day.

"Oh. I did medical mission work in the Philippines. I learned a lot of useful skills there."

"Really?"

"Yeah." I glanced at my beeper as if it had vibrated. "Let's talk more later. I have to run. They need me in the ICU."

"Okay. Bye."

"Bye."

A week later, I evaluated a seriously ill patient with another physician.

"Jay, how did you get the correct diagnosis from the history and physical exam of the patient? The lab studies and X-ray results weren't back yet. You must have been at the top of your class. What medical school was it?" asked a resident in my department.

"Thanks. I did okay. By the way, tell me about the latest article on insulin shock you mentioned earlier," I replied as I quickened my walk down the corridor of the hospital.

"Sure. In fact, I have a copy of it in my locker. Let me get it for you."

"Okay, but I'll get it from you later. I have to run. I'm needed at the spinal cord unit," I remarked as I looked at my beeper.

A page on a beeper to an intern and resident physician usually required a quick response.

The tactic worked on many occasions for different needs.

I had succeeded. I was a respected resident physician by my fellow residents and attending physicians. My commitment to excellence was fueled every time I overheard, or was told, disparaging remarks about those FMGs. It powered my drive to perfection in medicine. But I was not satisfied. I needed confirmation of excellence to demonstrate the validity of us FMGs. My goal was to be chosen chief resident in my final year of my training.

A chief resident is a senior resident physician who acts as the clinical and administrative director of the house staff in a department of the hospital. The criterion for this distinguished position is excellence in patient care and leadership. It would validate my merit and redeem us FMGs. It would also help to alleviate my hiya for non-disclosure of my FMG status.

I longed for Beverly. We had written many letters. We talked only twice on the telephone. It was too expensive and painful to hear her voice and her crying.

But after six months, I went to the Philippines to see Beverly for one week.

I took a week's vacation from my residency training. Beverly was also granted a week off from her internship at Baguio Hospital in Northern Luzon.

Beverly met me at Manila International Airport. I spotted her as I exited immigration. We embraced amid tears of joy.

"Jay, the driver can see," whispered Beverly in the backseat of the car.

"I know."

I stopped pawing at her. But never let go of her hand.

We stayed in my room at the Barrettos' home.

We stayed in the room a lot.

Beverly had never been in my bedroom, and it had been six months since we last touched. We did not want to leave the room, but we had to visit the Barrettos and her family.

The visits with family and friends are a bit blurred. My mind was elsewhere.

I thought of not leaving or taking Beverly back with me.

Leaving the second time was harder than the first.

We said our intimate good-byes in the room. We wanted no eyes on us. We wanted to be alone. We were one.

We cried.

Five months later, my heart palpitated while I waited for Beverly's arrival. It had been almost a year since I first left her behind. I was surprised when she called me two weeks earlier with the great news that she was coming for a visit. I was ecstatic but shocked that her father allowed her to come. She was not finished with her medical requirements in the Philippines.

I finally saw her as she walked out of U.S. Customs and up a ramp, pulling a suitcase. Her face was aglow with her radiant smile. Our embrace was magical. I felt the warmth of her body, the softness of her face, and tenderness over her lips. Her sweet smell overwhelmed my senses. Energy flowed between us. My American blood boiled.

"Jay, people are staring," whispered Beverly in my ear as we continued our hug.

"Let them," I whispered back.

"Jay, I am embarrassed."

"Okay, let's go." I was reluctant to end our treasured embrace. Her hug loosened. I released my hold and grabbed her suitcase.

"I'm amazed that you have only one suitcase, although it is heavy." I struggled with the luggage to my car.

Beverly smiled and walked in her slow, refined style then posed. "I did not bring a lot, but isn't that what stores are for?"

I tried to smile but was focused on getting the large international-size luggage into the trunk of my car, wondering if it would fit.

"I sure miss Temiong," I blurted out struggling.

Temiong was her devoted driver in the Philippines. He was always smiling and laughing. He had my respect by withstanding the demands from the "commander."

"I bet you do. He misses you too. You were always so kind to him." Beverly patted my bent back as I gave a final push to the luggage.

"Okay, we can go. But please don't sit in the back or else you'll have to call me Temiong."

"I know. When in Rome, do as the Romans do." Beverly grinned.

"Yep. Now this Roman wants to take you to his villa, his domus, where I can pleasure you." I closed the trunk, proud of my triumph with the luggage, and stood erect.

"Jay, we are not alone." Beverly's sense of hiya interfered with my playacting in the public parking lot. It was a proper restraint from Beverly, a memory of "no touch" to me. Anyway, our ride to my apartment was not too long. My right foot pulled the front door closed. I beamed with Beverly in my arms. The door maneuver that failed in Manila was a success. It was the start of our second honeymoon, without the downpour of Diding or the intrusion of a maid.

The days flew by. The nights cherished. I found it hard to concentrate at the hospital. I wanted time to stand still. We played tourist a little, shopped for things for Beverly and pasalubongs (gifts) for her family and servants, but mostly nested at home.

"No, absolutely not." I was adamant. Our romance stifled.

"Jay, I promised my father," Beverly said with her head bowed.

"That is not what we agreed to. We agreed to be separated for one year, not two. I was shocked your father sent you here for one month, but I'm grateful. I did not understand why you came for a visit when you were to finish your internship then join me for our life here. But now I get it, and I don't like it. It is not fair. It is just not fair."

I now knew why Beverly had traveled with only one suitcase. She had graduated from medical school and was doing her internship as planned. But now, she needed to stay in the Philippines for another year to complete her internship and fulfill a new six-month rural medical service mandated by President Marcos. The rural service was to be performed after completion of internship and was a requirement for licensure. The purpose of the new law was to provide more medical care in the provinces. The plan felt to be admirable by the Filipinos was a disaster to me. Her father knew that our separation was difficult and decided to send her to me for a visit.

"I know. I do not want to go either. But I promised my father I would go back."

"Then you must break your promise. Another year is unthinkable. Please, stay. Don't go," I begged with gut-wrenching pain.

I was more consumed with my needs than the respect for her father's wishes.

I did fear that Beverly might resent me later when the heat of the passion died down and she reflected more on disobeying her father. I worried that her father would never forgive us. But I was selfish. I wanted Beverly to stay. And she wanted to stay.

"I love you, Jay. But I promised my father that I would return."

I pulled out all the pathetic lines I knew, like, "If you really loved me, you would stay. I thought you loved me more than your father."

I felt ashamed of myself when I said those things, but I did it anyway.

Buddy told me not to let her go.

I loved Buddy.

He was a true friend.

Beverly and I embraced and sobbed.

"Jay, I do love you. I'll stay. I will not leave you. I hope my father will forgive me."

"He will. He is a good and reasonable man. He will. He will."

"I pray he will. I have never disobeyed my father like this before."

We cried tears of happiness and sadness, pleasure and pain, innocence and guilt. We cried ourselves to sleep. It was a monumental decision for her. She would break her father's heart and mend mine. We would never be divided again.

One month later, we found out she was pregnant. We knew she had made the right decision.

Buddy knew too.

It was a career-changing decision for Beverly. By not returning to the Philippines to complete her requirements, she could not be admitted to a resident training program in the States. Her medical career would come to an end. Her future was planned before we met. She would graduate from UST medical school, complete an OB-GYN residency training program in the States, return to the island, and join her father's practice.

I had derailed the plan.

But Beverly never regretted staying. We were family, and we needed to be together. We hoped and prayed her father would forgive us, but he did not.

We still hoped and prayed.

Guzzie, Beverly's younger brother, will tell me thirty-four years later that his father had told him, "It is not healthy for a husband and wife to be apart for one year early in their married life. It is not healthy, and it is not wise. I am going to send Beverly to Jay for a one-month visit. I will not send her with a lot of money. She needs to come back after one month."

On the day Beverly left, her father told Guzzie, "Go to Beverly's bedroom, and see if she left behind most of her clothes and things."

He complied, went back to his father, and informed him she had. Her father then said, "Good, she will be back."

Guzzie laughed as he told me this story. He was the storyteller and jokester of the family. He was a tall Mestizo with dark hair and eyes, light milk chocolate skin, and a thin, trimmed mustache. His animation and enthusiasm produced laughter irrespective of his story or joke.

In our first year together in Philadelphia, we lived in a small two-bedroom apartment across the street from the hospital. The apartment complex was for medical students, interns, and residents. Beverly's bedroom on the island was as big as our entire apartment. It was tight, but we were happy. We were like two kids exploring a novel way of life in our new world. She learned to live without servants. She never complained and was determined to adapt to her new world.

"If your mother and sister can do this, so can I," Beverly stated in more of an affirmation than a proclamation as she learned to cook, to clean and vacuum, to wash dishes, to launder clothes, and to shop without a servant to carry her bags.

She beamed the day she gave herself her first manicure and wiggled her fingers in the air to display her achievement. "What would my friends back home say to this?" Beverly asked as she giggled and then blushed.

"They would be shocked for sure. Some would think I was *kuripot* (stingy). Others would just wonder why," I replied with a shoulder shrug, "but I'm proud of you." I gave her a big hug and avoided damaging the damp nail polish.

She also learned to buy ready-made clothes. She had always designed her clothes and had them made for her on the island. The store attendants were shocked and gave her strange looks when she did not know her sizes.

She had nosebleeds and dry skin from the lack of humidity in the air. She tried many moisturizers. I bought a humidifier for our bedroom.

Beverly also experienced some ugly things that first year. She was saddened by the disrespect that some children blatantly showed to their elders, shocked to see teenagers in public fondle and kiss, tongues down throats.

She had an accent and oriental eyes. Store clerks asked her slowly, "Caaan I heeelp yooou?" I answered, "Sure. When you speak proper English to her. Or would you rather converse in another language? She speaks four." To which Beverly replied, "Jay, never mind. It's okay."

One afternoon, while walking alone to a nearby store, a man confronted her and tried to snatch her purse. From then on, rain or shine, Beverly carried an umbrella on the streets of Philadelphia. It was the only weapon she thought of taking outside. A bolo was out of the question! In the Philippines, women used umbrellas to shelter themselves from the rain and the sun. For Beverly, it was natural to take an umbrella. She could be feisty and fight if she or her family were in danger. She had the primal instinct of a mother. She was pregnant.

"Jay, it's snowing." Beverly's excitement was infectious. She had called me at the hospital with the big news.

"I never thought it would be this beautiful. I'm going outside. Do you use an umbrella when it snows?"

"Beverly, promise me that you will not use an umbrella. Just go outside and have fun. But please, no umbrella."

"Okay, bye. Wish you were going with me."

"Me too. See you later tonight. Enjoy."

She enjoyed. She still glowed from her newly found winter wonderland at the late hour of the night when I got home to my angel.

"Did you make snow angels?" I asked with a baby's voice.

"What's that?" Beverly asked as she tried to block my attempt to tickle her stomach.

"Never mind. I'll show you later. I have something else I want to show you now." I winked.

Beverly smiled and followed me.

She slept in winter with socks and a bathrobe under mounds of blankets and a comforter. I said, "Socks are grounds for divorce in the States!" She smiled and kept wearing them. Beverly knew her father would be disappointed in her giving up her medical career. Her older brother had failed in his first year in medical school. She was the family's last hope to carry on the medical tradition. She was supposed to become an obstetrician.

We heard no word from him.

The silence was painful.

I knew her stepmother would say to her father, "I told you so. That white boy was just a lonely boy away from home. He was no good for her. He has ruined Beverly's future."

But Beverly was taught by her father and the nuns at school to honor her husband. "When a woman marries, she leaves her family and goes with her husband. Your husband is now your family."

I respected Beverly's father and admired their father-daughter loving relationship. I did not care what her stepmother thought, though Beverly did. Through it all, Beverly prayed daily. She went to church weekly and read her Bible.

I did not.

She was a good listener.

I was not.

Beverly was trained not to show emotions. But as time passed and she became more Americanized, her anger became vividly displayed. Not often. But when it was, it was like a volcano erupting.

There was the incident of the pancake. Beverly decided to surprise me one weekend morning and make me pancakes. She had never made them before. I did not know that she was in the kitchen for quite a while, trying to make me "the perfect pancake." I walked into the kitchen and saw this super-sized thick pancake and blurted out, "I wish you could make thin pancakes like my mother." She tossed the pancake, frying pan, and spatula in the garbage can and threw her apron at me, yelling, "Then go to your mother's." She didn't make pancakes again for two years. I never compared Beverly's cooking to my mother's again.

Beverly could be stubborn, which she attributed to being a Borja, her mother's maiden name. "Borjas are from Spain and are known to be hardheaded."

She was modest about herself and her family.

One night in Philadelphia, we were at Dr. Naso's home for dinner. Dr. Naso, my attending physician, and I were talking in the living room when I heard someone playing the piano. A beautiful classical song stopped us from speaking. At the end of the first piece, I said, "Your wife is quite accomplished on the piano." He shook his head and informed me, "My wife can't even play chopsticks."

We went to the family room, and I saw Beverly sitting at the piano and playing another classical song. There was no sheet music. Her eyes were closed. She glowed as she struck the keys.

"Jay, I didn't know your wife could play," whispered Dr. Naso.

"I didn't either." I could feel my face redden.

At the end of the performance, I approached Beverly. At that instant, I felt I did not really know her.

"Beverly, you never told me you could play the piano."

She smiled. "You never asked."

Later that night, I wondered what else I had not asked!

❧

It was a narrow Philadelphia street. Sidewalk vendors at each intersection boasted they had the best hotdogs and pretzels. I could not resist. I devoured the large, warm, soft, salted, twisted pretzel smothered with yellow mustard as I continued my walk down a cobblestone alleyway. I was exhausted from the stressful day at the hospital but compelled to stroll on this unknown trail. My mind was devoid of thought. I had finished my pretzel, stopped, wiped some mustard from my mouth, turned to throw the yellow-stained napkin in a trashcan, and was about to light up a cigarette.

And there it was, right in front of me. Tears swelled in my eyes as I stared at the painting in the small storefront's window; it was of a patient lying in bed, a doctor and nurse in attendance, and Christ watching over them. The light in the window shined on him and enlightened me.

In my medical missions, I had seen God's work. I knew God was real and loving, and I wanted a better relationship with him. I believed in him, in his power of healing. And if it was his will, I could heal wounds. The picture reinforced my belief that Christ was in charge. I was his servant. It humbled me.

I had to have that painting.

The store was closed. My heart sank. That night was the first time I prayed for a work of art.

"How much for this painting?" I asked the storekeeper the next day.

"I'm sorry. It's not for sale," he answered.

"Oh no." My eyes watered and my head hung as I turned to walk out.

"Wait a minute. Are you a doctor?" he asked with a thick, deep Italian accent.

I turned and attempted a smile. I had rushed to the store during lunchtime while wearing my white lab coat.

"Yes, I am." My voice cracked. I tried to hold back my tears.

"I want you to have it. I can tell it is very important to you," the shopkeeper almost whispered, although there were no other customers in his small shop. Or maybe his wife was in the back room.

"Really?"

"Yes. Please take good care of it. It has been in my family for years."

"But I only have thirty dollars."

"No. No money, please. It's a gift." His raised hand stopped me from getting my wallet.

"I will. I will. Salamat po." I bowed my head.

"What? I didn't understand that," he said and scratched his head.

"Oh, I'm sorry. I'll take good of it. Thank you very much." In my excitement, I had forgotten where I was.

"Good. May it guide and protect you." His voice was louder, his smile large, as he handed me the wrapped painting.

"Thank you." I shook his hand and looked deep into his eyes.

His eyes seemed to look into my soul.

I opened the door to leave and heard a short ring of the bell over the door as if to announce the start of a new life for the treasured picture. I looked back and saw the storekeeper and his wife, who wore a white apron, with their arms around each other, smiling and waving. Maybe the wife knew more than I thought.

Beverly smiled and cried when I showed her the painting. No words spoken, she knew the meaning of the scene. I hung my treasured painting in our small living room. I shared an office at the hospital with other resident physicians and did not want to take the risk of it being damaged or lost. I vowed to display it in my private office after completing my training.

Those were happy times. We had a tight budget, living off my small annual resident stipend of $10,000. Beverly's father had not forgiven us, and I did not want to ask my father for any help.

"It's beautiful, Jay. I love it." Beverly cried. We stood in the doorway of the nursery for our expected little one.

"I'm glad. I'm very pleased too. I think it is perfect." I gave her a hug from the side. Front hugs had been difficult for a while.

"I love you. Thank you for being my husband. I know you'll be a wonderful father," sobbed Beverly.

"I love you more. And you'll be the best mother. Now, if the little one would just get with the program and join our family." I cried and laughed as I rubbed her stomach.

We remained at the doorway and stared into the once-tiny hospital-white extra room, now our little one's yellow and green room. There was no blue or pink since we did not know the sex of our baby. The walls, we painted a pale yellow. A green and yellow cushion was positioned on the used rocking chair that we painted white. Green and yellow crib bumper pads and yellow sheets were in the secondhand crib that we also painted white. Beverly crocheted blankets for the baby throughout her pregnancy. One blanket was draped across an end of the crib and one across the back of the rocking chair. Beverly also sewed a yellow skirt, adorned with yellow bows, for the white basinet that stood next to the crib; but it would be moved to our bedroom once the baby came home.

We were happy and at peace. We had completed the Lamaze training at Thomas Jefferson University Hospital. Our bags were packed, her personal things and my coaching items. We were ready.

I arrived at the apartment late that night. Beverly was in her eighth month. The phone rang. I learned to hate the sound of the phone ringing. It usually meant I had to rush back to the hospital, an interruption to whatever I was doing. It had control over me. It made me feel like a trained rat. It rang, and I responded in the same way each time.

"Hello, Jay." My mother's cracked voice was replaced by sobbing.

"Yes. What's wrong?"

"Your father is dead. They want to do an autopsy. Should I let them?"

That's it. Your father is dead. You want my medical opinion on whether to do an autopsy or not. Not, I'm sorry. Just medical advice.

"Sure, let them do an autopsy," I replied as if talking about a stranger.

The autopsy proved to be negative. No cause of death. He just fell over in their countryside front lawn in Onalaska, Washington, and died. A friend stood by. No resuscitation attempted. An ambulance arrived without oxygen in the tanks.

He was meant to die.

22

SOMEWHERE BETWEEN PHILADELPHIA AND SEATTLE, WASHINGTON

1978

Beverly closed her eyes, held my hand, and prayed as the plane took off. I gave her fingers a gentle squeeze. She smiled and then frowned as the plane bounced. Beverly was in her third trimester, and her obstetrician had cleared her to fly.

I wondered how the ride felt to our precious one inside of her. I leaned close, placed my other hand on her belly, rubbed with tenderness, and whispered, "Hey little one. Everything is fine. You're safe. Mommy and Daddy love you. You'll know we love you. You'll never have to wonder. I promise to be a good daddy, a loving daddy. You rest well now."

Beverly glowed.

My lower lip trembled, and I closed my eyes quickly.

Beverly knew my father was abusive, physically and mentally, to me when he was drunk. She knew he showed me no love. She knew of the circle and my nose punishment.

I peeked at Beverly. I never had doubts about falling in love with her. From the first time I saw her, as she descended the stairs, I knew she was the one for me.

Initially, I had doubts that I would be the one for her. Her family did not think I was good enough, and maybe I wasn't.

She was a kind and lovable person, pure and selfless, an angel. She became a guiding influence for my trust in love, love that does not hurt, and she taught me patience and the meaning of obedience to God. She helped me to understand that God loves all of us equally. She felt God sent me to her.

But I believe she was sent to me.

23

ONALASKA, WASHINGTON

1978

I stood at the graveside. The honor guards' rifles cracked the still air as tears flowed and sobs echoed around the cemetery.

My eyes were dry. I was mute. As I stared down at his casket, saliva collected in my mouth. I wanted to spit on him.

The folded American flag was presented to my mother. She wept.

I clenched my teeth and swallowed.

A bugler sounded the Taps, a declaration that the "day is done."

My insides twisted. I heard the Taps nightly as a child to indicate "lights out," the time of danger for me.

My fists tightened, and my eyes remained fixed. My saliva accumulated.

"Don't do it," Buddy warned.

I swallowed and stared at the casket. My hands clutched. My jaw tightened.

"Be strong," encouraged Buddy.

I turned my back on my father and walked away with a smirk I didn't try to hide. He could not hurt me anymore. At the reception, which is really a blur to me, my father's friends raved about how resilient and strong I was not to cry. Others said how lucky I was to have had such a wonderful and loving father. Some offered prayers that I would turn out to be just like my father.

Obviously, our family secret was intact.

I did not care to see or talk to anyone. I was only concerned about Beverly. She stood by me during my duty as a good son and never complained. She did cry. She respected elders; she even thought my father should be respected. She felt sorry for the hidden child inside of him that was abused by his father. I just hated him and wanted to get back to our life in Philadelphia.

I was glad the funeral was not held in the Philippines. The wake before the funeral lasts for days on the island, too many days for me to be tempted to spit.

The next day, we flew back to the City of Brotherly Love. I looked out the window of the plane and saw Robbie's reflection. I did not always show brotherly love. I was supposed to protect my brother but was then beaten for not being like him.

"Sir, would you care for a wet towel for your hands," asked a flight attendant.

"Sure."

I took the towel and looked out the window.

Robbie was still there.

I remembered another towel, his towel.

We were in Spokane, Washington, visiting my father's sister and her family. Dona, Robbie, two female cousins, one male cousin, and I were going to swim in the neighborhood pool.

"Jay, watch your brother. You're responsible for him," ordered my father.

"Yes, sir." I answered.

I was in sixth grade, Robbie in second.

I jumped off the diving board several times and swam to exhaustion. Then I remembered Robbie. I looked around the pool and in the pool. He wasn't there. I found him in the bathroom, behind a locked stall door. His swimming suit string was in a knot. He could not get it undone in time and had messed himself.

I ran back outside to the pool area, grabbed our towels, and returned to the stall where Robbie was crying and trembling. I untied the knot, placed his trunks in one towel, took him to the showers, helped him clean up, and wrapped the other towel around him.

We walked back our aunt's home. Along the way, I teased Robbie, saying, "I'm going to pull off your towel."

He cried. My cousins laughed, but Dona got mad. My sister, then my cousins, told me to stop it. I did, but that night, my father hit me. I did not cry.

I blinked and looked back out the airplane window.

Robbie was gone.

I threw my towel down.

24

SOMEWHERE BETWEEN
SEATTLE AND PHILADELPHIA

1978

I felt numb as I looked out the plane's window into cloud formations.

I blinked and stared back into space. I was a child on the island. I was in fourth grade. My fungus nail infection would not heal despite home remedies and professed local cures. My mother took me to the military base outpatient clinic. My father was not around. My mother said he was off the base on a military special mission. I was just glad he was gone.

A corpsman at the clinic acted as a doctor. He tied me down with white straps, like a straitjacket, atop white sheets that covered an examination table. I glanced at the surgical tray with cotton balls, gauze, vials with clear liquid, syringes and needles, and forceps. The snap of the surgical gloves caused my eyes to widen.

"Mom, make him stop," I begged.

"Hush, you'll be fine. Be strong and brave." She smiled and patted my head.

The corpsman injected my fingers with a solution from one of the vials. It was meant to numb my fingers, but it did not. Looking back, I think his blurred eyes mistook saline for lidocaine. With his first yank of my fingernail, I screamed for him to stop. My mother cried out and was ordered to leave the room. It was a military clinic and she was an obedient military wife, so she obeyed. He proceeded to pull off my fingernails with those surgical pliers. I passed out after the fourth fingernail was ripped from its bed and awoke to more torture. A scalpel, which appeared to be a small bolo in my gaze, was used to scrape my ten exposed nail beds. Drops of blood drenched the white sheets.

The corpsman stumbled out of the room. My mother returned, cried, and cradled me. I looked at my hands wrapped in white gauze. The dressings were blood-soaked at my fingers.

"Mom, look what he did to me," I sobbed and shivered.

"It's okay. It's okay. Good boy. Be strong."

It was her usual response after I was punished or harmed. I think she did not know how to react any differently. I think she feared my father and the military. I think she was horrified. I saw it in her eyes and felt it in her touch. I heard it in her voice despite her automatic words.

When my father returned to the base, he "interacted" with the corpsman. My father was a Golden Gloves boxer and good at beatings. After a surgical repair of his face, the corpsman was sent back to the States. My father never consoled me. Never spoke to me of my torture. And my father was never disciplined for pulverizing the corpsman.

At the time, I was so consumed with pain that I didn't feel much about my father's reaction. Afterwards, I wanted to think he fought for me. But in my heart, I knew he fought for his honor, not my pain.

After all, pain toughened me.

I looked back out the plane's window.

I stared at my hands.

"Buddy, medical care should not hurt, especially for kids,"

"You're right," Buddy answered.

25

PHILADELPHIA, PENNSYLVANIA

1978

"It's a boy. Oh my God, it's a boy," I cried to Beverly through my face mask.

No response from Beverly.

"She's crashing. No blood pressure. No pulse. Paddles!" shouted her obstetrician. He pushed away from the delivery table. Beverly was blue. An endotracheal tube was inserted. IV site established.

Beverly's body rose with the shock of the paddles.

"Code blue on the baby. Code blue," screeched a nurse.

I wanted to take our precious little one in my arms and protect him. He was blue and limp. A nurse prepared an IV tube for him.

"Get out of here," ordered the obstetrician, his finger pointed at me. "Now!"

"My God. No...please no...not my family..." I stammered.

"Get him out of here!"

I was pushed out and thrown into a waiting room.

Beverly was born with a heart problem, a conduction deficit. Her obstetrician wanted Beverly to have a "perfect vaginal delivery," but after four hours of hard labor, she told the doctor that it was okay to do a C-section. After eight hours more, I told the doctor it was okay to do a section. Each time he replied, "No. Let's wait a few more hours."

After twelve hours of hard labor, her heart gave out.

Ryan had suffered from the hard labor and delivery. He was forcefully delivered with forceps. He was a blue baby with markings of the forceps on his face.

There were others in the small waiting room. I did not look at them.

I stayed in the stiff chair, my eyes closed, and tears seeping between my lids and down my cheeks. I prayed, first, several Lord's Prayers. As I repeated "Thy will be done," my head bowed further and my heart pounded. Then I recited multiple Hail Mary's. Later, I began talking, not praying, to God. I spoke like a son to a father. I asked him for his love and mercy. I begged him for forgiveness and cried and pleaded for mercy to save Beverly and our baby. I promised to be a better person, a good husband, father, and servant of God.

I swore to stop smoking.

I beseeched him for his compassion and power of healing. I reminded him that I had witnessed his power in the medical missions. I believed in him. I trusted him.

But I did want his will to be my will.

Two hours dragged. When the doctor finally entered the waiting room, I didn't even notice him.

"Jay, they'll be fine," said the obstetrician. His mask hung in front of his neck, surgical scrub suits soaked around the V-necked collar and armpits. "Did you hear me? Your wife and baby are going to be okay."

"Yes, thank you. Thank you. Thank you." I grabbed him in a two-handed handshake. My body was drenched with sweat, as if I were on the island.

My prayers were answered. Beverly and little Ryan Lester were alive.

I vowed to be the best father and husband, to be worthy of their love.

"Buddy, you must help me keep my promises."

"I will," he emphatically answered.

I stopped smoking cigarettes on that day, September 15, 1978. I had tried many times before without success. This time, there was no doubt that I would ever smoke again. It was on my list of promises. Besides, I wanted no cigarette smoke around or ashes from a cigarette held between my lips to drop on our little one.

We received good news from abroad. With the birth of his first American-born grandson, Beverly's father forgave us. Beverly and I hugged, cried, and smiled after that cherished phone call. Our spirits soared.

❧

The next year, we bought our first home. It was a beautiful two-story brick house in Haddonfield, New Jersey, across the Benjamin Franklin Bridge from Philadelphia. I took a high-speed train to and from the hospital, a bit different than my car and driver on the island.

When we moved into our home, the neighbor across the street boasted, "You'll like it here. There are no blacks, Mexicans, or Orientals."

"You obviously haven't met my wife yet," I replied.

He looked confused.

"Buddy, I want to punch him."

"Behave."

I turned and went back inside and told Beverly.

"Jay, it's okay. Let's pray for him."

She did.

I didn't.

Our neighbor and his wife, Mr. and Mrs. Cawley, became our friends. They adored my family, especially Beverly.

We knew that Beverly's father had forgiven us when he visited us and held his first "American-born" grandson. He beamed. He did not hide his emotions that day. Tears flowed down his cheeks.

He was a man of few but profound words. "Beverly, you did the right thing. I love you."

Beverly cried, kissed her father's cheek, turned, and embraced me.

We both stared at *Lolo* (Grandpa) as he held the precious little one.

Later that evening, her father came to me, placed his hand on my shoulder, and said, "Thank you for loving Beverly."

I choked.

Tears fell.

Years later, her stepmother forgave us.

I had two good friends, my new pares, Dr. Geno Merli and Dr. Paul Cerza. They were senior residents in my training program at Jefferson. They were Italians and both married to "good Italian girls." Geno and his wife, Char, lived around the corner from our home and helped us find our house. Geno was the godfather of our son, Ryan. Paul and his wife, Anna Marie, lived in the apartment across the street from the hospital. Geno and Paul had pakikisama but not as much as my Filipino barkada.

Those were happy years.

A year after Ryan's birth, all of the resident physicians were gathered in the largest conference room at the hospital for the announcement of the next chief resident. I stood next to Paul. Geno, our current chief resident, was with Dr. Ditunno.

Dr. Ditunno scanned the room, looking for his chosen one.

I laughed inside.

Dr. Ditunno reminded me of myself when I looked around a pen of cocks to select the best one for the next cockfight.

"Excuse me, can you all hear me?" Dr. Ditunno tapped on the microphone over the podium. His voice was strong. The microphone was not needed.

"Thank you for all coming," he continued and motioned for me to come forward.

I went to the front of the room and tried not to walk like a cocky rooster.

"I am pleased to announce that Dr. Roberts will be our next chief resident." He patted, actually slapped, me on my back. Dr. Ditunno was a large Italian with more power than he realized.

"Thank you. It is an honor to be the next chief resident, for me and for all my fellow foreign medical graduates. Thank you." I was the winner. But I did not puff out my chest, and I did not crow.

After my speech, two resident physicians came up to me.

"I knew you were an FMG. I can't believe you just didn't say it before," said one resident.

"Yeah, I did too," chimed the other resident. "I bet it was in the Philippines."

"Yep. You went to school there. Makes sense. That's were you lived and did your mission work. Why didn't you just tell us?" added the other resident.

"I heard too many horrible remarks about 'those ignorant FMGs' to tell you I was one," I conceded.

"But you're an American. We weren't talking about Americans."

"Yes, I'm an American, but I'm also an FMG."

"And a damn good one," confirmed the first resident as he slapped me on my back.

"Come on, let's celebrate, Jay."

"Sure."

"Oh, by the way, Jay. It is customary for the newly elected chief resident to pay. You might not know that being an FMG." The first resident laughed.

"Not funny. But I know I have to pay. Even in the third world, a celebrant pays," I added with a smile.

"Ouch."

"So let's go," I ordered then gave an exaggerated bow.

Jason Derek Roberts was born on October 17, 1981, completing our family. I saw God's work with the birth of our precious babies, our gifts from him. I wondered how you could not believe in God if you've witnessed the birth of your baby. We were also blessed not to have complications with the arrival of Derek. No code blues. I called my son both Derek and Jason, but usually Derek. Family calls him Derek. Classmates call him Jason or Derek depending on when they knew him: Jason in grade school, Jason in high school, Derek in college, Derek in professional basketball in the Philippines, Derek in his MBA program, and currently, Derek in his profession of senior consultant in communications, media and entertainment for Hitachi Consulting. Ryan, on the other hand, has always been Ryan, in grade school, high school, college, economics master's program, law school, and in his corporate law firm for start-up companies, securities, and mergers and acquisitions. People have at times thought I had three sons, Ryan, Jason, and Derek. But they always knew I had only one wife, my *mahal* (love), Beverly.

I completed my residency program as chief resident for the entire year. Dr. Ditunno demanded an enormous amount out of me in academics, clinical skills, and leadership. It was difficult, but it paid off. I was offered, and I accepted, an academic position at Thomas Jefferson University Hospital.

"That's a nice picture, Dr. Roberts." My secretary watched as I hung my painting.

"Thank you. It means a lot to me." I adjusted it.

There. Keep me focused on being his servant.

❧

My hospital was chosen to be one of the first thirteen federally designated spinal cord centers for the United States. We were responsible for the states of Pennsylvania, Delaware, and New Jersey. Dr. Ditunno was the executive medical director for the center. I was medical director for the rehabilitation care of the patients, an enormous task for a new attending physician, but I was up to the challenge. I plunged into the charge and developed a high quadriplegic ventilator-dependent program for the center.

It was a typical admission to our Spinal Cord Injury Center. Or so I thought. Teddy Pendergrass lay in the trauma center unable to move his arms and legs. He had just been extricated from his mangled Rolls-Royce, which crashed against a tree. The news media wasted no time with their descent toward the hospital. His lawyers and agents were not far behind.

Teddy Pendergrass was an American R&B/soul singer and songwriter, the reigning sex symbol in 1970s and 1980s. He was known for sold-out "panty-throwing, women-only" concerts. He was tall, fit, with rich dark chocolate skin, a huge smile, and brilliant white teeth.

I never listened to Teddy's music before he became my patient. I did soon after he was admitted. I found his baritone voice soulful. I was surprised at how many people loved him in Philadelphia and around the world. It was common for chocolate teddy bears, as well as panties, to be thrown at him during the concerts.

I finished a family conference and informed them of Teddy's grave condition. The barrage commenced after my last word was spoken.

"Dr. Roberts, you can't say that he is paralyzed," said a lawyer.

"Dr. Roberts, you can't say he won't recover," said an agent.

"Dr. Roberts. Dr. Roberts."

Demands and requests were fired at me from his entourage. His lawyers dressed in suits I could not afford. His managers were clothed in sportier attire. His mother, Ida, was calm, eyes closed in prayer.

"Dr. Roberts. About his women," an agent whispered as he tried to pull me aside.

"I am sorry, gentlemen and Mrs. Pendergrass, but I have to get back to the intensive care unit." I tried to sound stern but compassionate. I attempted to stand a little straighter in my long white lab coat as I shook their hands. My maneuver to be "higher" than his lawyers and agents felt like those of my professors on the island, whose heads had to be higher than us seated students to command authority and control.

"I understand your concerns." I shook each of their hands.

They stared into my eyes. No blinking.

"Mrs. Pendergrass, give me a moment with Teddy, then you can come in."

She smiled.

There were daily media conferences. A multitude of microphones were thrust in my face and provided a barrier from the reporters. They pursued me for information. For weeks, I resorted to entering and exiting the hospital at the back, through the supply loading dock.

Celebrities descended upon the spinal cord center and posed logistical problems. But it was the wave of flowers that flooded the hospital that caused a colossal challenge. The solution was to send truckloads of flowers to nearby nursing homes.

The women, his women, were a challenge in timing of visitation. "Discreet. Need to be discreet," repeated one of his agents. "I heard there have been some conflicts. No sense in having two or more at a time, now, is there?" another agent smirked.

"No sense." My extreme smile caused my eyes to squint. "Excuse me, but I have to get back to my patients." I ditched the irritants.

"Dr. Roberts. I'm scared," mouthed Teddy. I was about to remove his tracheal tube. He was concerned about his voice. He was terrified that he might not sing again.

I removed the tube.

"Okay. How are you?" I asked with a smile.

"Fine," Teddy whispered.

"Good. Now try it again."

"Fine." A louder response. His infectious broad smile displayed those incredible white teeth.

"How fine?" I asked.

"Real fine." Teddy's tears flowed, lips quivered.

Teddy's desire to improve and his commitment to the tiring exercises were admirable. He persevered and fought infections and setbacks with dignity. He commanded respect. He had my respect.

Weeks later, I stood next to him. My motivation speech was over. Reassurances were given. It was now time for him to try to sing.

"Okay, impress me," I said with a gentle laugh.

His voice was soft and tentative at first, a distinct soulful sound on the subsequent tries. That voice was pure and divine.

Tears flowed.

"I told you, Dr. Roberts. I had a voice inside me."

"Yeah. I believe you. But I won't be throwing chocolates at you. Sorry. But I do have something for you." I snapped on my examination gloves.

"Oh no. It's not time for that again, is it?"

"I'm afraid so. It's now time for me to perform."

"More like upstaging me." He laughed. "Oh well, it happens to the best of us."

Teddy took to the harsh reality of his situation like a champion. He lost some rounds but remained focused on the big fight. I knew that he would perform on stage again. He had that "it" factor, standing or sitting. He would have it even lying down. Well, according to the women, he did have it in any position. He was a man on a mission.

As I was about to leave his room, I saw a large chocolate teddy bear on his bedside stand. I smiled and looked over at Teddy. He beamed and nodded his head.

"I will perform and record again. I promise you that, Dr. Roberts." Teddy spoke in a soft and deep tone.

"I believe you. You're a man of your word."

"Dr. Roberts, we're alike in a lot of ways. We're best at what we do. We're strong men." He grinned and winked.

I turned and walked away. I did not want him to see the tears in my eyes. He had lost the use of his arms, legs, and voice in a second. His voice was his life, the expression of his soul, his being. He faced his worst fear head on with courage. He didn't quit.

We had nothing in common.

❧

I began to feel uneasy living on the East Coast. Ever since the difficult delivery of Ryan, Beverly's heart suffered. She never complained. She appeared healthy. Her cardiologist approved of our wish for a second baby. But her health deteriorated with the demands of the new baby, a toddler, and a husband.

"Beverly, I'm home," I announced, as usual.

It had been a long day at the hospital. Ryan and Derek were already asleep.

"Beverly. Where are you?"

"I'm over here," she responded. Her voice sounded like she was miles away.

She was on her side on the floor in the living room, her skin whiter than mine. "What's wrong?" I asked and knelt beside her.

"I'm just so tired. Please help me up."

"I'm taking you to the hospital."

"No, Jay. Please, just help me to bed. I'll be better after I get some sleep."

"Beverly, we should go."

"No. Please."

We prayed. She recovered. Her cardiologist prescribed some drugs and advised rest, but she reacted poorly to the medication, and it was hard to rest with two little ones.

I was concerned about her heart. Her biological mother died from a heart condition. She was forty-one years young. Beverly and I had vowed to get old together "gracefully." We had friends in the Philadelphia area but no family.

My mother had moved to California to be close to my sister and brother soon after my father died. I was fortunate that my wife and my mother were friends. Beverly showed the same respect to my mother that she would to her mother. Beverly loved my mother. She told her, "Mom, you'll never live in a nursing home as long as I am alive."

A home in California, with its more pleasant year-round climate and my doting mother nearby, would be our new sanctuary.

Beverly agreed with the plan. Her smile and eyes told me she was also happy and relieved.

"Hi, Jay. Come on in." Dr. Ditunno smiled and gestured. "Marie, hold my calls," he added to his executive secretary.

"Thanks." I sat down in a side chair next to his desk.

He leaned back in his chair, put his feet on the desk, then said, "I needed a break. What's on your mind?"

Dr. Ditunno and I had become close through the past six years. We respected each other. Some said he was like a father figure to me. It felt good.

"I have to tell you something." My eyes filled.

His feet fell from the desk as he sat up in his chair.

"What's wrong, Jay?"

"You know how much I like it here. How much I think of you."

"Yes." He leaned forward.

"Dr. Ditunno, Beverly's not doing well. She needs help. We have to move to California."

"What?"

"I have to resign and move to be near my family."

"What the hell?"

"She needs help."

"Then get her some."

"Dr. Ditunno, I need to be near my family."

"I thought you were committed here. I put so much faith into you. I can't believe you're doing this to me."

"Dr. Ditunno, I'm not doing this to you. I have to do what's best for my family."

"By leaving?"

"Yes."

"What hospital are you going to? How long have you planned this?"

"I don't know yet. I haven't planned this. I agonized over this for a few weeks but decided yesterday. I wanted to tell you right away."

"I can't believe this. I thought you would never leave." Dr. Ditunno was a native Philadelphian who could not comprehend leaving Philadelphia.

"I didn't think so either."

"I've invested a lot of energy in you. I had plans for your future."

"I know."

"What do you plan to do?"

"To start with, I'll do private practice."

"What? You'll be a professional whore in the land of the weird. I can't believe you, Jay. How can you throw all of this away?"

"I have to."

"No, you don't."

"I do."

I stood.

He glared. His face reddened.

"Jay, stay strong. You're doing the right thing," I heard Buddy say.

"I'm sorry, Dr. Ditunno."

No response. He just stared.

I left his office.

26

SOMEWHERE BETWEEN PHILADELPHIA AND SAN FRANCISCO

1982

Another plane, another window, more cloud formations and mystical reflections. I saw myself as a child in the Philippines.

I danced the *Tinikling*, the national folk dance, with the same skill as my young native friends.

The dance traditionally involved two boys and two girls hopping between bamboo poles held just above ground and struck together in time to music. It symbolized the Filipino prancing in and out between clashing Western and Asian cultures. To be offbeat meant bruises or fracture to our little ankles. We learned to keep the beat.

Maybe that was why this white boy could dance.

A sudden thunderstorm transformed the bamboo poles into whips that struck and slashed me like a bolo. The pungent odor of beer polluted the air. A bolt of lighting cracked the reflection and dispersed the clouds. I turned away from the window and toward the stale stench. A grimy man with greasy hair, slumped in the seat next to me, ordered another beer from the flight attendant.

I looked back out the window.

Clouds were an important part of the earth's weather. They carried water that fell to the earth's surface as rain and snow to support all forms of life. Clouds could also bring destruction in the form of hail or tornadoes. Bolos were used to build shelter and cut down fruit for food. Bolos could also be a brutal weapon for beheading. Bullwhips directed cattle out of danger. Bullwhips could be brutal and brand a young boy's body. Knives helped heal wounds. Knives could cause wounds. A nose helped you smell the sweetness of *sampaguita* flowers. A nose could be evil. Hands gently hold a baby and caress a loved one. Hands could hurt. Eyes let you see the wonders of the world. Eyes could pierce you like a knife and inflict deep wounds.

I touched my eyes and nose. I thought of my scars. I looked at my hands.

There were a lot of wounds to heal.

I knew God healed. I didn't always know him or even want to know him. I turned to the window and felt the light shine on me, and I imagined it was God's light. Then I closed my eyes and felt at peace. My mind spun and the plane soared.

I saw my windy and broken path with God.

As a child, I occasionally attended bible school on Sundays, rarely church with my parents. My parents were Protestants. I never knew what church they belonged to or if they did. My mother said my father taught Sunday school when I was younger, but I have no memory of this. My maternal grandmother went to a Presbyterian church. My paternal grandmother did not go to church.

We had a large, dark brown leather bound "family Bible" in the living room that functioned as a centerpiece on the wooden coffee table, but it was never read.

My father invoked the name of Jesus and God a lot when he was drunk.

I remember asking God once if the devil was in my father whenever he was drunk. He was only mean to me when he reeked of beer or liquor. I never got an answer.

In junior high, I felt the need to belong to a church. I told my mother of my wish and she said, "Fine. But remember your manners." I asked if I should get permission from my father and was relieved when she quickly answered no.

I went alone to different churches around our city and the next town. Most of the churches felt like the one I had just visited. But one stood out, or should I say the congregation stood, jumped, crawled, and wailed out. I prayed hard for Jesus to protect me at that church. I never returned there.

The last church I planned to attend was the Catholic church. Our neighbors across the street went to that church. They had a lot of pain in their lives and still had steadfast faith. I was not sure I really wanted to go to the Catholic church. After all, Catholics could not eat meat on Fridays and were always doing penance for something. I had enough of my own punishment at home. And they confessed all their sins and secrets to a priest on Saturdays. I could never tell my secret.

I went to the Catholic church. There were lots of empty places in the front pews, but I squeezed between two adults in the back pew. I did not know when to stand, sit, or kneel. I was always a little behind the congregation. They all recited prayers from memory. I did not. I was confused during the Mass. I did not know Latin. I focused on the beautiful statues around the church. My eyes stopped on the Bleeding Heart of Jesus.

Tears flowed down my cheeks. It was the first time I saw his heart hurt. A warm feeling permeated my body. I stayed seated while everyone else stood. I bowed my head and prayed my prayer. Not in Latin.

I had found my church.

My mother said, "It's fine if you go to the Catholic church. Anyway, there are good people there."

I never heard a word from my father, which I knew meant it was okay by him. If not, I would have felt his opinion.

I attended weekly Mass throughout high school. I learned the prayers, though I didn't read the Bible. I didn't know any Catholic who read the Bible. But I knew when to kneel, sit, and stand. I could not take Communion. I was not a real Catholic. I did want to share the body of Christ. Someday, I told myself.

Not being a real Catholic also meant I did not have to go to confession. I did not mind. Never, I assured myself.

In college, I went to Mass less frequently. I prayed less. I didn't read the Bible. In medical school, I went to Mass weekly. I prayed at home, in school, in the hospital, and on medical missions. I didn't read the Bible.

I was baptized and confirmed in the Catholic church with Beverly at my side.

I didn't read the Bible.

In Philadelphia, I went to Mass most Sundays. I prayed most nights. I didn't read the Bible. The births of our two sons were gifts from God.

My road had often been tortuous.

I felt I was on the right path now.

I did not know where it would lead.

"Lord, help me," I prayed in silence. "Be my rock of safety, the stronghold that saves me. Heal me. Guide me."

"He will," Buddy answered.

I opened my eyes.

The clouds were gone.

The plane began a descent.

California was near.

27

CHICO, CALIFORNIA

1982

I was in conflict, torn between academic medicine and private practice.

I developed the medical rehabilitation center at Chico Community Hospital, the first in the area. I was the medical director. I fought for the standard of academic medicine in a community hospital environment. I refused to accept less than the best. But my insecurities from being a foreign medical graduate intensified in a setting without prior foreign graduates.

"Welcome, Jay. You're going to really like it here. Although we're a community hospital, our standards are very high. And we don't have any of those foreign doctors here," remarked a neurosurgeon as he showed me around the operating room on my first day at the hospital.

I had been so excited to begin the day.

"What do you mean, 'those foreign doctors'?" I asked and felt like I had been punched in the stomach.

"You know. They're really not good doctors. They're not well-educated. Hell, most of them can't even speak English properly. But don't worry, we don't allow them here."

"But you know I graduated from the Philippines."

The neurosurgeon had been part of the search team to find a physician in my specialty for the hospital.

"Yeah, I know. But you are an American."

"Yes, but still an FMG."

"Jay, I wouldn't broadcast that around. Some doctors here are very closed-minded."

"Be quiet," Buddy said. "Be strong, be good, and prove them wrong."

I did.

My standard of excellence and sharp clinical eye gained me respect. My specialty training focused on treating the cause of my patients' problems, not the symptoms. I promoted adding quality of life for my patients.

But I remained the only foreign graduated doctor on the hospital staff.

I was overwhelmed with the paperwork in private practice. Viability of the practice demanded operation as a business. Patients demanded compassion and quality.

I was expected to know just about everything but not to act like it. If I did not know the answer to something, even not related to medicine, I heard, "You're a doctor, and you don't know that?"

I was busy at work and had little time for my family.

My quality of life was reduced.

❧

"You should have seen it, Dad. It was great. It went really far," exclaimed Ryan one day. "I did like this, Dad," he added as he swung in the air as if holding his bat and hitting the baseball out of the park.

He was still wearing his Little League uniform, with dirt stains on his left side from sliding into a base, cap tilting down a bit, and shirt hanging out of the back of his pants. His shoes had been placed in the garage hours before, when he got home from the Saturday afternoon post-game ice cream celebration. He was seven at the time but looked older than his age.

"I wish I'd been there too. I'm so proud of you. Way to go, Ryan." I smiled and hugged him.

I looked at Beverly.

I had missed his first home run.

Too busy for my son.

My heart hurt and my head hung as I continued to keep him close to me.

I wanted to slow down, but I became even more consumed by my work. I felt I was in a speeding car without brakes. It had a power of its own, its own speed. And I was going further away from my family.

"Jay, Derek stayed awake as long as he could. He wanted to show you the good citizenship certificate he received at school today," explained Beverly when I got home late one night from the hospital.

I looked and saw Derek asleep on the family room sofa. He was in first grade.

"He's so proud of that certificate," added Beverly.

She smiled, put her arm around my waist, and squeezed.

"He loves you so much, Jay."

I looked down at Derek. He was asleep but still held onto his award.

I picked him up, carried him to bed, gave him several forehead kisses, and whispered, "I love you, son. I'm so proud of you. I'll see you tomorrow."

His eyes remained closed. He never let go of his prize.

It was difficult for me to go to sleep.

I felt I was a failure that night.

❧

I prayed to be an instrument of God, a healing servant. I was consumed with a desire to heal wounds. I was taught not to talk politics or religion with patients. I gave advice and made decisions for my patients' health, even life and death issues. Why could I not include God's healing power in the discussions with my patients and their families? I was entrusted with their well-being. I was accountable but frivolous lawsuits tainted the practice of medicine. Why call it my practice? In the beginning of my career, I was practicing but not for years. I wanted to change the title to "my service of medicine" to better denote the meaning of my medical profession of servanthood. I wanted to be his servant, an instrument for him.

I began to pray in silence at the hospital and in my office. I prayed but did not talk to God.

We were about to leave for a party at our friend's home one evening when my beeper buzzed.

"Jay, do you have to go back to the hospital?" Beverly asked, but she already knew the answer.

"Yes, I do. I'm sorry. But you go ahead, and I'll catch up."

"Jay, you work so hard. Can't it wait until tomorrow?"

"No, I'm sorry." My eyes pleaded for understanding.

"Okay, but please hurry."

"I'll do my best."

"You always do your best," affirmed Beverly, then she kissed me. "I love you."

"I love you too."

We both left that night in separate cars.

We learned the two-car routine early on in my practice. If I was late to go to an event, Beverly could go ahead. If I had to leave early, she could stay.

❧

Our home telephone rang one evening later that month, the intrusive signal.

"Jay, Tatay is not well," Nanay whimpered.

"What do you mean?"

"He is in the emergency room at the Kaiser Hospital in Walnut Creek." Her voice faded.

"What?"

"Please come!" Nanay wailed.

Nanay and Tatay were on vacation. They had just arrived at the home of their daughter, Nida, in Lafayette, California. I had planned to visit the next weekend.

"Of course. Right away."

I packed my bag in haste and jumped into my car.

I sped south.

My black Mercedes 190, with its sixteen valves and low side door aprons and spoiler, took the back-curved roads through Durham and Willows and onto I-5 South like a speedway.

I focused on the roads and watched for anticipated traffic. But there was none. No obstacles. I smiled, thinking of the usual obstacles and traffic on the island and the time we drove from Zambales to Manila for Vicky's dengue fever treatment: cars with aggressive feint-and-jab-style drivers, buses and jeepneys that stopped for passengers anywhere on the road, motorized tricycles and bikes with multiple passengers, kalesas with slow horses, carabaos that stop to defecate or stare you down, dogs everywhere, street hawkers who dodge between vehicles, and poorly maintained roads.

Red lights flashed and reflected in my rear view mirror. A siren blazed. I pulled over. An ambulance passed. My heart pounded. I settled back into my seat as I realized that no speeding ticket would be issued, astonished that I was in Walnut Creek, near the hospital. I had been focused on the roads but did not remember all of the drive. The normal two-and-a-half-hour drive had taken one-and-a-half hours.

I closed my eyes, took a deep breath, and remembered the time I was pulled over in Pleasant Hill, California.

The sirens shrieked. The red lights shined. My heart sped.

"Young man, do you know how fast you were going?" A policeman peered down at me through the rolled down window on the driver's side of my timeworn blue Pontiac.

"No, sir." My voice cracked, throat tightened, and breath deepened.

"Give me your driver's license."

"Yes, sir."

My hand shook as I gave it to him.

"Young man, shame on you. You just turned sixteen and drive like you're on a race track."

"Sir." Tears flowed down both cheeks. "I beg you. Please don't give me a ticket. I'll have to send my license to Vietnam."

"What did you say?" The police officer removed his dark eyeglasses and stared into my wet eyes.

"My father is fighting in Vietnam. He told me that if I ever got a ticket, I would have to send my license to him. Please don't give me a ticket."

More tears and sobs.

"Calm down, calm down." His strong hand rested on my left shoulder.

"Yes, sir." I wiped some tears.

"I won't give you a ticket. Count this as your first and last warning from me."

"Yes, sir."

I bit my lip so as not to say "No, sir."

"Now, get on your way. Be good, and obey the rules. Stay alive and grow up to be like your dad."

"Yes, sir. Thank you, sir."

Another sore produced on my lip.

❧

I opened my eyes and checked my lip in the rearview mirror. No sores. I eased back onto the road and observed the speed limit the rest of the short distance to Kaiser Hospital.

Nida and Nanay stood as I entered the emergency room.

"How is Tatay?"

"Not good," Nida cried as she hugged me.

Nanay cried.

I hugged and kissed her on both cheeks.

"Let me see his doctor. I'll be right back."

"Jay, help him," pleaded Nanay.

"I'll be right back."

I approached the doctor in haste. He uttered a statement I had hoped I misunderstood. "What are you talking about?" I asked in disbelief.

"I said, we told him to go to the county hospital since he had no insurance," he stated in a matter-of-fact tone.

"What?" I screamed in absolute disgust.

"That's right. You're a doctor. You should know how expensive his cardiac care would be here," the doctor answered.

"You pompous idiot. Did you ask him if he had any money?"

"I told you, he said he had no insurance."

"I didn't say insurance, I said money." The veins on my neck were visible.

"No. I assumed he had no money. He looked like he couldn't afford to pay cash for his needed care," answered the bewildered doctor with wide eyes. "He looked poor."

"You fool. He can buy this entire hospital. You assumed a Filipino without insurance is poor. Because he rushed here without his Rolex and designer clothes, he was poor."

No response.

"For your information he is Govenor Barretto from the Philippines. He has a meeting with the president of the Philippines in two weeks. You idiot. Money is not an issue."

No response.

"You are an idiot. Where is he?"

"Be...behind those curtains...over there...," stammered the doctor.

"Stay calm, be in control," warned Buddy.

"I will," I replied, pulling open the curtains.

Tatay looked smaller on the hospital gurney, the hospital gown barely covering his torso. I wondered if he was given a pediatric gown or the cheapest gown they had. I grabbed a sheet on the adjacent vacant gurney and covered Tatay.

The vision of Tatay, alone in that hospital, was a sharp contrast to the image in the Philippines, where it is customary for the patient to have relatives keeping him company at all times. A relative, and particularly an elder, is never left alone. The rooms are designed with a sitting room and a kitchen. Food and drinks are offered to visitors. Relatives and friends keep vigil and strive to keep the spirits up.

"Tatay, I'm here. Everything is going to be okay."

"Thank you, Jay. I feel better now that you are here. I am sorry to be such a bother."

"You're not a bother. Don't be silly. I'll be right back."

I had to get back immediately to that doctor without seeming alarmed to Tatay. He did not look good. He was not receiving appropriate care.

He was warehoused, deposited, and stored without further attention or treatment in his stall.

"I demand the best care for my father. You better pray that he'll be okay. How dare you ignore him," I exploded at the doctor.

Buddy told me to be calm.

I wasn't.

I was disgusted. Doctors and hospitals should treat emergencies regardless of money. But they didn't. Not in the Philippines without cash. Not in the States without insurance.

I was an angry son who hated prejudice.

I did not want to listen to Buddy.

Orders flew, nurses ran. The doctor was finally in motion. I heard "STAT, STAT, STAT." After all these hours, things were actually "stat."

I returned to Nanay and Nida. "Tatay is being taken cared of. Don't worry."

They tried to smile and stared into my eyes.

I looked away. I prayed as I sat, stood, and paced in the room. I watched Nanay pray the rosary many times. I talked with Nanay and Nida, just superficial conversation. I drank coffee. I tried to sleep in the chair but couldn't, so I stared at the TV with its poor reception, low volume, and no remote control. But it didn't really matter.

I had time to realize the pain of waiting in a waiting room—the uncomfortable seats, no recliner, no windows, no fresh air, and lousy coffee. I watched other people in the room come and go. We waited. For hours. Every time a nurse or doctor would enter the room, I would start to stand up. The nurse would call out a name that wasn't mine.

Nida and I left to get something to eat and drink from the basement cafeteria. Nanay stayed in case they came for us. I was an expert at getting hospital food. We were back in a short time. We barely ate.

"Doctor Roberts, may I please speak with you?" the doctor asked in a soft and compassionate tone. He stood with two cardiac surgeons.

"Your father needs immediate cardiac surgery. Should we proceed?" The doctor seemed timid.

"Of course you should. Whatever he needs." I didn't shout.

"Well, he should have had a drug infusion when he arrived at the emergency, but it's too late now. It's a shame because the drug company reimburses the hospital if the patient cannot pay for the infusion. We get better outcomes with patients who had the infusion," one of the surgeons declared like a robot. He was stopped in his dissertation by an elbow in the side by the emergency room doctor.

"What did you say? Look. We need to focus on the best care for my father now. Please. Do not withhold any treatment out of monetary concerns." My eyes pierced into the doctors' eyes like poisonous darts. If I had my father's whip, I would have carved their bodies.

More STAT orders spouted from the doctors.

I was now scared.

God, I beg of you, please help.

I returned to Tatay.

"Everything is okay. You'll be fine, I promise," I assured Tatay as I kissed his forehead.

"I know. I believe. I love you, Jay."

Tatay's eyes watered.

"I love you too."

My eyes watered.

More tortuous hours passed.

A nurse approached the waiting room and asked me to follow her. She showed me to the doctors' locker room for the operating suites.

"Shame about the case you just lost. Should have started treatment earlier. Poor soul. Oh well, better luck next time. Are you the coroner?" a physician asked me in the doctors' locker room.

I had heard "shame about the case" before. It is common to hear "shame" instead of "sorry to hear" in the medical environment between physicians. It is used to state regret or disappointment, combined with disgrace and dishonor. Physicians are supposed to heal and save lives. To lose a life could discredit the physician. A physician's nightmare is to face the family of a patient they lost for the pain and possible anger the family will show, and the fear of lawsuits even if the physician did nothing wrong.

But I had never heard "shame about the case" when my father was the patient.

The question was aimed at me. I was changing into surgical scrubs to enter the operating room. The cardiac surgeon stood next to me and informed me that Tatay was dead. I did not believe him. I had told Tatay everything would be okay. I promised him that as he was rolled into the surgical suite. He told me he believed me. He trusted me. I had prayed to God for help.

I knew he was not dead. I knew it.

"Stupid. He's his son," shouted the surgeon as he slammed the ignorant doctor into his locker.

"I'm so sorry. Please forgive me." His hand offered for a shake. I stared at the hand, then into his eyes, turned, adjusted my mask, and walked into the operating room.

I just stood there frozen.

Tatay's heart was exposed and still.

I was stunned. I kept waiting for the heart to start beating.

My heart pounded. My senses dulled.

"Doctor Roberts. Doctor Roberts."

"Yes."

"As you can see, your father is gone. I'm going to let my team back off, break sterilization, and state the official time of death as now."

"Okay." My throat closed after the one word utterance.

I must go to Nanay. Oh my God. I also promised Nanay.

"Be strong. It's not your fault," Buddy assured me as I left the operating room.

My legs seemed heavy, my walk to the waiting room was in slow motion. Nida rose form her chair as I entered. Nanay stayed seated.

"I am so sorry. I tried. I should have been here earlier for Tatay. I failed," I cried as I bent over and hugged Nanay.

"Jay. Jay. Tatay loved you. You did your best. He was so proud of you. I love you. It is not your fault." Nanay consoled me as a mother would.

"Jay, it's not your fault," Nida sobbed.

No more words spoken.

We all collapsed and cried.

❧

Tatay lay in wake for three days in Walnut Creek before his body was flown to the Philippines to his final resting place in Zambales.

Hundreds of Filipino viewers came from across the United States to show their last respects to him. Condolence cards, letters, and flowers were sent from around the world. Telephone calls from American and foreign politicians, dignitaries, relatives, and friends flooded the lines.

This was the man ignored and warehoused in the emergency room.

"Jay, this if for you," Nanay said before she returned to the Philippines.

Nanay handed me one of Tatay's neckties.

"Tatay would want you to have it. Something to remember him by," Nanay said with a quiet and gracious voice.

It was a thin brown silk tie, made in the USA. It was new. I never saw Tatay wear it. It had no value to me other than it had been in his closet and suitcase. I would have treasured a ring or one of the gold cross necklaces that he wore. I wanted something tangible.

I felt like a stray dog being thrown a bone. That was how I ranked in the family? It was the first time I felt adopted and not a blood son. I felt a piece of my heart die.

I said thank you to Nanay and fought to keep back my tears and not show my feelings.

Buddy said, "It's okay, be strong, you know Tatay loved you. Nanay loves you too. She is in pain and not thinking right. Forgive her."

Thousands lined the streets in Zambales as his casket went by to the cemetery. For three days before the procession, Filipinos prayed and viewed his body in the Zambales home.

A Filipino wake is anything but solemn, though less noisy than a normal gathering. The family stood vigil day and night, taking turns, until the burial. Flowers upon flowers surrounded the casket. Nightly prayers were given. Because all the kin and friends were expected to come, food and drinks were always provided, sometimes appearing as a feast rather than just refreshments. To the Filipinos, food was an important social element and part of the hospitality given to any visitor. A *novena* or nine days of prayer was held after the burial.

After Tatay's death, I struggled to practice. I felt a huge loss. I needed something to fill the void. I thought of other things I missed, like my academic practice in Philadelphia. I missed teaching interns and resident physicians. I applied and was accepted as a clinical assistant professor in the Department of Rehabilitation Medicine at Davis School of Medicine in Sacramento, California. Once a week, I conducted outpatient clinics with resident physicians. I had my academic position in Davis and my private practice in Chico. I was content for two years. It felt good and right to donate my salary at Davis to the residency program. But the weekly ninety-minute drive south to Sacramento, the two-hour clinic, and then the ninety-minute drive back north to Chico, and the demands of my private practice, quenched my academic desire.

I needed to be busy, to overload my mind and abort images of a whip that sliced the chest of Tatay and exposed his heart. These images had intruded on my thoughts for months.

I had nightmares of his open chest and still heart.

I awoke in a sweat.

Beverly comforted me each time and prayed for my peace.

"Jay, it's not your fault Tatay died. You did all you could. You were a good son to Tatay."

"I promised him he would be okay. He believed in me."

"But Jay, what else could you have done?"

"I don't know. But I promised."

I also had random visions of his opened chest while I examined and treated patients. Wounds, irregular heartbeats, labored breathing, or any sign of distress could trigger the visions.

I would blink my eyes and shake my head to erase the image and refocus.

I was determined to be the best doctor.

Tatay would be proud of me.

It felt good to please Tatay.

Instead of my weekly academic rounds at Davis, I developed rehabilitation centers for hospital chains, including National Medical Enterprises, Rehabilitation Hospital Services Corporation, and Paracelsus Healthcare. I also established multiple private practice centers in Chico, Lodi, Los Gatos, and San Jose, California. My demands required the purchase of a plane and a full-time pilot. I traveled every other day by plane and worked aboard with my administrative assistant. Private cars were kept at airports for our use. My career skyrocketed and seemed fulfilling, but my family time plummeted and suffered.

My sons worried about my absence and thought I was leaving them and their mother. They both began to stutter and needed speech therapy. I was devastated, full of shame and guilt. I caused them pain. I had vowed never to hurt my sons. But I did.

I spun out of control and was about to crash. I needed a change. My family deserved better.

God help us.

He did.

Out of nowhere, I was offered the medical directorship for the Rehabilitation Center at Desert Hospital in Palm Springs, California. I had never been to Palm Springs. I went for the interview. At worst, I would see Palm Springs.

Billie Baldini, a rehab nurse, was part of my administrative staff at Chico Community Hospital. She was a dedicated and loyal person. She resigned to devote full time to a rehabilitation company and was sent to Desert Hospital in Palm Springs to assess their rehab needs. She determined they needed a different medical director and recommended me.

I accepted the position.

My sons' stuttering stopped.

Our life in Chico had been great for seven years. It was a perfect place to raise our sons. Outdoor activities were plentiful. Bidwell Park was massive and impressive. It was the production setting for Sherwood Forest in *Robin Hood*. Picnic tables discreetly placed along Bidwell Creek provided for many memorable lunches and rests. My mother lived a few streets from our home. She was a daily part of our sons' lives. Everything was good, except for my regular absences and my impending crash. It would be difficult, but I knew we had to leave.

The closeness of our friends made it harder. Beverly was tearful to leave her best friend, Madeline Nolta. I admired Madeline's strength despite her physical challenge. She had been treated for multiple sclerosis for years when in fact she had Lyme disease. Beverly and Madeline shared the same love of God and family. Madeline, her daughter Lisa, and husband Ray, would be missed, but not forgotten. A kinship had grown between us. Ryan and Derek did not want to leave their friends and grandma. Chico was home to them.

"I'm leaving today for Palm Springs," I gently told our sons. "You and your mom will come in a few weeks. I don't know the exact time." A "few weeks" seemed better than "someday."

"Do we really have to move?" Ryan asked, knowing what the answer would be.

"Yes. It'll be for the best. You'll see. We'll be together more. We are family. Our home is where we are."

"That's right. We're a family and our home is where we live. No matter where," reinforced Beverly with a calm and reassuring effect.

"I love you, Dad," said Derek. His lower jaw trembled.

"Me too, Dad," Ryan added with a stiff upper lip.

"I love both of you so much. I'm proud to be your father. Come on, group hug."

Beverly and I circled the boys, and we all hugged and cried.

It was okay to cry.

My family knew I loved them.

28

PALM SPRINGS, CALIFORNIA

1999

I awake. It is late at night. Beverly is asleep next to me.

I find myself remembering a hot summer night in Pleasant Hill. I am in seventh grade. My bed is under the open window, without a screen. Robbie has left the room. He had heard our mother cry out. My sister is already with her in the living room.

I am slow to get up. I have fresh wounds from a spanking earlier that night. When I turn over to my side and sit up, it hurts.

I hear a loud grunt and deep breathing. I turn. A man is trying to climb through the window. I stare.

He stares. His eyes freeze me. He pulls his leg back and runs around our backyard to the other side of the house. I stand and limp into the living room.

My father is telling my mother, "A man has been seen trying to break into homes around us."

"Oh my God," my mother gasps and places her hand over her mouth.

Dona, Robbie, and I stand still, with our eyes and mouths opened wide.

"You all stay here. I am going out to find him," commands my father.

"I saw him," I say, my voice cracking.

"What? How in the hell could you?" asks my father with a glare.

"He just tried to come through my bedroom window."

"Why in the hell didn't say so earlier?" He runs out the front door.

My father catches the man hiding in our garage. He pulverizes him. The police arrive and pat my father's back. The neighbors tell me my father is a hero and that I must be so proud of him. I just smile at them. I want to show the police my wounds. I want my father beaten and arrested, but Buddy tells me to be quiet.

My father never thanks me for telling him about the intruder.

I no longer sleep with the window open.

The next night I cannot sleep, even with the window closed. My father says I am weak, that he beats me for my own good.

He falls asleep, drunk, on the couch. A cigarette with a long piece of bent ash is still lit in his ashtray. I take the cigarette, walk to the bathroom, and close the door. I blow on the cigarette and press the burning end into my left forearm.

I do not wince.

I do not cry.

I stare into the mirror. A strong, brave boy stares back, without blinking. I smell burnt flesh, remove the cigarette, and flush it down the toilet. I bandage my arm.

I turn out the light and go back to bed.

"You are strong and brave," consoles my Buddy. "You didn't have to do that."

"Better than what I was thinking earlier," I retort.

I visualize my father over my casket, crying and saying he is sorry and that he loves me. I look at him and spit. He can't hurt me anymore. I am dead.

❧

I raise my hand at my father once in junior high school to protect my mother and myself from a beating. I ran into the living room that night when I heard my mother scream. My father was slapping her face. The sounds of the slaps echoed through the room. I tried to hit him, but I failed.

I felt the power of his punch for days.

I never raised my hand against him again.

I did shout at him that night, "I wish you would die."

My mother told me my father beats me because he loves me, and slaps her because she deserves it. She forced me to apologize to him for my hateful words. I did, but he rejected the apology. I hated him even more.

❧

"Do not harm yourself," says Buddy.

"I won't anymore. I know it is wrong. Good night, Buddy."

"Good night. Sleep well."

I do, despite my new arm wound.

29

PALM SPRINGS, CALIFORNIA

1989

The hand with its thick, stubby digits, broken dirty nails, black wiry hair between enlarged joints, and brownish-yellow stain inside the long and middle finger, scratches and crawls across the old, splintered, wooden window seal. There is no screen. The middle finger stretches to grasp the inner edge of the window. The hand stands alone against the blackness of the night.

I jump out of bed alert despite the lack of sleep from the previous nights. My heart pounds like an overbeaten drum. My throat tightens. I lunge at the window. Slam. Latch. The middle finger curls back. The hand retreats.

I glance over to the bed. My younger brother, Robbie, is safe, lying in a fetal position, a pillow scrunched in his arms. The queen size bed we share barely fits in our bedroom. An oversized desk competes for the limited space. He sleeps next to the wall, always next to the wall. I must be near the window.

I run to the next room, barefoot, pulling on my sagging pajama bottoms.

Slam. Latch. Just in time. My sister is safe.

The next room.

Slam. Latch. My mother is safe.

Deep breathing competes with my pounding heart. Sweat rolls down my bare chest.

Scratching, relentless scratching against all the windows of our house slowly intensifies. I turn and turn to hear where the loudest scratch is coming from. I run and pound my open hand against the window. The pulsating hand dwarfs my hand. I pound again. No effect.

I run back to my room and pound. No effect.

My sister's room. No effect.

My mother's room. No effect.

The hands now move from side to side in a rhythm, like an orchestra. The sound heightens. It is deafening. I no longer hear the scratching.

I stare at the pulsating hands. I stand erect. I must not move.

The hand inches downwards and off the window, leaving behind five wet streak marks.

I crawl back into bed. The slower pounding of my heart lulls me to sleep like a sound machine.

That dream started when my father went to fight in Vietnam for two years. I was fifteen, my sister sixteen, and my brother eleven.

Before he left, he summoned me. "Jay, you're now the man of the house. It is your responsibility to protect your mother, sister, and brother. If anything happens to them, it will be your fault. You must be strong. Do you understand?" My father shouted, as if I was on a military combat mission.

"Yes, sir."

"Do you understand?"

"Yes, sir."

"Then say it like a man and stand up straighter."

"Yes, sir!" My eyes fixed forward on his nose, not on his eyes.

"Yes, sir!"

The nightly dreams stopped when my father returned from Vietnam, and I went off to college. I awoke a few times during my first year in college, drenched in sweat from running to latch the windows. I would inspect my hands to make sure there were no wounds from the glass.

For years the dream did not return, until that night in Palm Springs; my first night, alone, in my hotel room.

I must protect my family.

We had to be together. They needed me, and I needed them.

I had to hear Beverly's voice.

"Hi, honey. Sorry for the lateness of this call, but I miss you guys so much." Sweat from the dream still dripped off my face.

"We miss you, too. Is everything okay?" Beverly asked in a sleepy voice.

"Yes. I just wanted to talk."

"Okay. How is it there?"

"It's hot. Beautiful, but hot."

It was the start of summer season. I was staying at the Hotel de Paris on Palm Canyon Drive in Palm Springs. My family would join me once our home in Chico was sold.

"They tell me it's warm but dry. First, it's not warm. One hundred and twenty degrees Fahrenheit is hot. Second, our stove is dry. After a certain temperature, hot is hot," I said as I looked out my hotel suite window toward the San Jacinto Mountain.

I'd taken a good look at the mountain earlier in the day. At first glance, it looked like barren, brown dirt. At closer look, there was scattered color from desert plants and wild flowers, including light green and brown *Carex Senta* and sedge plants, darker green and brown fan palms and *piñon* pine trees, *Sonora Creocote* cacti and other stem succulents, and Pratt's dark aurora-blue butterfly species. Rock and sand formations anchored the scenery. Endangered animals added life to the mountains. There were southern rubber boas, Peninsular bighorn sheep, desert tortoises, Coachella Valley fringe-toed lizards, and Southwestern willow flycatchers. The non-endangered coyotes frolicked and hunted on and off the mountains.

"Yeah, but remember the humidity in the Philippines. It's better dry than humid," Beverly tried to comfort me.

She succeeded.

"You're right. I didn't have to change my clothes several times today. Remember all the changes of clothes in the Philippines?" I felt cooler as we talked.

The next morning, I looked out the window at the desert mountain that appeared devoid of any rain and vegetation from that distance. It was a sharp contrast to the tropical weather and lush landscape in the Philippines.

On the island, there were the daily late afternoon rains with thumbnail-size rain drops that balanced on wide leaves of mango and papaya trees and slid down the bent, swaying coconut palms. I saw my friends and myself, as children, our bodies painted with mud from a rice field, bamboo poles in hand, shouting as we performed a war dance in the rain. Local ancestors used mud paint to give their bodies a supernatural or nonhuman form to intimidate their enemy. We used it to frighten our enemy, the carabaos and dogs, to the laughter of our elders. At the defeat of the enemy, we showered in the strong torrential downpour that blurred nearby trees and huts. The outdoor shower was our treasured reward and welcomed by our parents. The rains also provided us a respite from annoying flying pests like mosquitoes and flies. After the rains, the bent trees and plants stood tall, energized with the returned sunlight. They appeared stronger. The air was crisp and sweet. The symphony of the tropics returned with chirping birds and cricking crickets. A sudden halt in the music alerted us to a predator, animal or man. We grabbed our bamboo sticks. Danger was gone, with the resumption of the music. We continued our victory celebration with fresh coconut milk and fried bananas.

❧

Three months later, my family joined me in the hotel. Ryan and Derek loved the chauffeured rides in the Rolls-Royce to and from school. It was a service provided by the hotel for long-staying guests in a suite. To help compensate for the sadness of leaving Chico, their routine included a snack at the hotel restaurant upon their arrival from school each afternoon. My sons were troopers. Once in Palm Springs, they never complained about leaving Chico. They knew our family was together, as we should be.

For three more months, our life at the hotel was tolerable. But I knew it was time to leave the hotel when a receptionist complimented me one morning on my new tie.

My God, they know my wardrobe.

Before the next new tie comment, we were out. Anyway, it was time to move into our new home.

"Nice dog," I stated to a man as he bent over to pick up his dog's ball. My sons and I stood in the front yard of our new home in Las Palmas in Palm Springs.

"Thanks. He is a good dog," the man answered with a distinct voice, one I had heard before.

He turned around and I froze for a second.

"E...enjoy your day. It sure is nice here." I partially stammered my reply.

"We like it here. Have a good day." He turned and walked toward his driveway. The dog jumped at the ball in the man's outstretched hand.

"Boys, do you know who that was?" I asked with a smile.

"No," answered Ryan.

"No," echoed Derek.

"Well, that was Kirk Douglas," I announced.

Blank stares were the responses.

"You know, the actor, Kirk Douglas," I added.

More stares with shoulder shrugs.

"That man is the father of Michael Douglas," I further added.

"Oh really. I know who Michael Douglas is. He's an actor," Ryan answered with a nod.

"Me too," Derek said.

"That's right, and his father is an actor too."

No responses.

My mother later said, "Poor Sparticus. These kids do not know who you are."

My mother moved to Palm Springs. Ryan and Derek had their grandma back. We had a wonderful new home with family nearby.

It felt right.

Our neighborhood was on the celebrity tour route. Kirk Douglas, Harold Robbins, Jeannette Rockefeller, Sidney Sheldon, and Mike and Bob Pollack (writers for *Dynasty*) lived in the same area. Elvis and Priscilla Presley's honeymoon house was a stone's throw away. The tour buses slowed down in front of their homes but never slowed in front of ours, except for once. That bus driver must have been confused.

We saw Loretta Young and Bob and Dolores Hope in church. It was surreal.

Crystal ashtrays next to cigarettes in crystal containers, and silver lighters throughout the home of Jeannette Rockefeller astonished me. It felt like I was in a classic Hollywood movie set.

Palatial estates, fancy cars, and butlers were the usual in our neighborhood. This was Palm Springs and the lifestyles of the rich and famous. Their fortunes did not spare them of aches and pains. Diseases and disorders did not discriminate. But their notoriety and money helped with access and care not covered by insurances. Most of the famous were kind and appreciative, some demanding and rude, which could also be said of non-celebrity patients.

❧

I had a business meeting to attend in Chico. We had a small almond orchard on the west side of Chico that we wanted to sell. I was on a United Airlines thirty-two-seater plane that would get me back in time for Ryan's soccer game the next day.

I heard a loud noise and looked out the window.

The plane's right engine was on fire.

Another loud noise blasted the cabin.

The left engine was on fire.

"This is the captain. We will be making an emergency landing. Secure you seat belts."

"Buddy, this can't be happening."

"Stay calm," he answered.

"This is the captain. We will be circling as long as possible to empty fuel."

The plane jolted and dived.

"Assume crash positions," shouted the captain without announcing who he was.

"Remove all sharp objects from your person," yelled a female co-pilot.

I threw my Cartier gold eyeglasses and Montblanc pen to the floor. I was not afraid. I was sad. I could not say good-bye to my family.

I heard screams about the cabin.

An elderly lady next to me sat up straight. I had helped to secure her seat belt before take off. She was confused and disoriented, and spoke few words, mainly smiled.

"You have to lean forward," I told her.

"What?"

"You have to lean forward and lock your arms under your legs."

"What?"

"Like me. See?"

No response.

I sat up and pushed on her back. She bent at the waist.

"That's right. Now stay like that." I bent forward and hooked my arms.

"Why? I never had to do this before. Is this something new?" She smiled, as if we were on an amusement park ride.

"Yeah. It's new."

The plane rattled. She sat up.

"No. Get back down."

No response.

I sat up, released my seat belt, and kept my left arm on her back and pressed down. I did not have time to fasten my seat belt. I placed my right arm under my leg and braced myself.

The landing was hard. Items flew about the cabin.

I was not strong enough to hold my position and slammed into the seat in front of me. It felt like a sledge hammer had struck my gut.

"Are we there yet?" the woman asked as she sat up.

"Yeah, were here," I gasped in pain.

"That was fun."

We had landed somewhere between San Francisco and Chico and were rescued shortly. She smiled as I helped her out of the plane.

I was flown back to Palm Springs in a smaller plane. I was in too much pain to be afraid. I just wanted to get home in a hurry.

Other passengers refused and took a bus back.

"Dr. Roberts, you're going right to surgery," announced Dr. Ercoli, a head trauma surgeon at Desert Hospital.

"No. Wait. I have over thirty patients in here. Get me a nurse. I must give some orders first," I barked.

"You're not doing anything but going to sleep," answered Dr. Ercoli.

I tried to grab his arm as he pushed on the syringe attached to my intravenous line.

It was like slow motion. My hand never reached his.

❧

"Dr. Roberts. Dr. Roberts. Take some deep breaths. The surgery went fine. You're in recovery now. Take some deep breaths," instructed a nurse.

I was confused and disoriented, like the elderly lady.

But I did not smile.

An exploration of my abdomen revealed my gallbladder took the brunt of the impact. It had been removed.

At home, I attended to my new wound.

This one I did not have to hide.

It scarred just the same.

Later, I had Dr. Scott Aaronson, a plastic surgeon, redo my incision.

"Scott, pretend that my abdomen is the face of a beautiful woman. Make this nasty railroad track scar go away." I laughed, but I meant it.

"I will," he assured me.

He did.

A wound hidden.

I smiled. Later, I missed my Cartier eyeglasses and Montblanc pen.

"I sure wish I had gone back into the wreckage and retrieved my glasses and pen," I said to Buddy,

"Never mind. They probably were destroyed. You're alive. You can always get some more."

"You're right."

I did. Rather, Beverly did and surprised me with them.

❧

I immersed myself in my private practice and medical directorship at the hospital. I worked long hours but was home for dinners and weekends. I had more time with my family. That was what they wanted and deserved.

"Are you ready to see your mother?" I asked Sonny Bono.

We stood at the nurses' station at the rehabilitation center at Desert Hospital. His mother was recently admitted under my service for her stroke care. They had not spoken to each other for years.

"Yes, I am. Thank you," replied Sonny with a nervous smile.

Their reunion was short but heartwarming.

"Thanks, Dr. Roberts. This meant a lot to me." Sonny was sincere and humble. He was a grateful son at that moment, not a performer.

Our friendship grew from that day. Two unlikely men became comrades, sharing interests, concerns, and dreams.

We talked about medical care in the States, many political issues, and God.

He talked of happy times with Cher, their painful divorce, and his struggle with Chastity. He spoke about his happiness with his beloved wife Mary, their daughter Chianna, and son Chesare.

I talked about my happiness with Beverly, Ryan, and Derek.

He explained his strained relationship with his mother.

I disclosed facts about my abusive father, but not all the details.

He told me of his younger years, when he struggled and delivered meat for a butcher.

I shared about my younger years in the Philippines, how I struggled to be as good as the local boys.

He spoke of his inner desire to succeed, to be the best.

I revealed my inner desire to be the best, but not of my inner friend.

Buddy told me I could trust Sonny. But I kept Buddy hidden.

We planned to build a medical spa facility, including bungalows for the guests, at the old Biltmore Hotel site in Palm Springs. But I was busy being a doctor, and he was busy being a politician. The buildings never materialized beyond the drawing plans.

I encouraged him on several occasions to spend as much time with his kids as he could. That our children would remember things we did with them, that we were there for them at important times, and not the fancy things we gave them.

He listened and agreed.

He presented me a gold cross ring as a sign of our everlasting friendship.

"Jay, you and Beverly will sit at our table at the gala," Sonny stated with a strong voice.

"Great. Are you excited about the festival?" I asked.

The Palm Springs International Film Festival was to start in a few days, kicked off by the celebrity dinner.

"Yeah. A bit nervous but excited."

"Well, as you guys say, the show must go on." My attempt at humor.

"Right. And the beat must go on," Sonny sang.

Sophia Loren was to be the honored celebrity for the film festival. A small group of close friends were at Sonny and Mary's home for lunch before the evening gala celebration at the Palm Springs Convention Center. Sophia Loren was in the kitchen making her favorite pasta. Peter Coyote surveyed the food and scenery. It felt like a movie set. I was waiting for a movie director to shout "cut, take, it's a wrap."

"She is more beautiful in person than on screen," I whispered to Mary and added, "Boy, that sounded like a worn-out cliché."

"Yeah, but true. She is stunning," Mary replied without hesitation.

"Jay, your mouth is open," Beverly commented with a gentle grasp of my arm. Beverly frequently kept me out of trouble. She was my protector, my angel, and at that moment, my director. Her eyes spoke "take, cut, you're wrapped."

I stopped gawking at Sophia.

❧

"Come on, Dad. This will be the last house," Derek pleaded. It was Halloween night. Our neighbors' estates were hidden behind walls and large gates. I felt uncomfortable if I could not see Derek at their front doors. I would walk with him at least partway up the pathways. But at this last estate, the front gate was propped open, and I could see the front door from my car.

"Okay. Go ahead. I can see you from here."

Derek rang the door. "Trick or treat?"

"Well, hello there. What a great costume. Kurt, come and look at this cutie."

Kurt Russell joined Goldie Hawn as she handed Derek a bag of goodies.

"Thank you," answered Derek as he looked at the goodies and not at Goldie.

When we got home, I told Beverly of Goldie Hawn passing out treats and my thought of putting on a costume and ringing Goldie's doorbell.

"Jay, get over it. You would have been tricked and not treated."

Beverly refocused me and brought me back to reality again.

❧

My private practice flourished. I never knew what to expect. I was always eager for a challenge.

"This is Harold Robbins," introduced Jann, his devoted partner and wife-to-be.

"Glad to meet you." I extended my hand to him in my waiting room. Harold had come for a consultation.

"Are you any good?" Harold went right to his concern.

"Well, if you ask my mom or wife, I'm the best," I blurted.

"That's good enough for me. Now, can you help me with my damn pain and get me out of this wheelchair. I don't mind pain with sex but not sitting in this chair."

Jann shook her head and gave a nervous laugh. Her blonde hair and large mammary glands bounced.

Dr. Pierre, a physician and friend of Harold's from France, hid his face in his hands and then uttered, "That's Harold."

"Being famous does not preclude you from pain and suffering. They have their own wounds," Buddy reminded me.

"I know," I whispered.

I never sought fame.

As a young man, I dreamt of being famous, admired, and respected, even by my father. It felt good until I woke up and felt my fresh wounds.

"Can I examine you first then give you my opinion?" I said to Harold. "It's the usual method."

"Great. Let's get on with it. Right here is fine," Harold barked.

"I think in the examination room would be better. Nurse, prepare my gloves and lubricant," I ordered.

"What?" Harold lunged backward into his chair.

Jann and Dr. Pierre's eyes widened.

"Just kidding about the gloves. But not about the examination room."

"Jann, I like this one." Harold flashed a grin and tipped the brim of his brown Stetson hat.

"How tall are you, Mr. Robbins?" asked my medical assistant.

"Six-two."

I looked over at Harold with raised eyebrows.

"Well, I was that tall before I broke my hips." A smirk covered his face.

I knew I was in trouble.

Harold was generous and liked parties, those were the good times. Beverly and I were fortunate to meet several friends of Harold and Jann's, including Quincy Jones, Jerry Vale, Mike and Bob Pollack, and Jeannette Rockefeller. He loved Jann and cherished their dogs, two gray and white Schnauzers and one white Pekingese. His dogs ate Russian caviar and flew a few times on the Concorde. Jann loved Harold. She was devoted to him.

One night, Beverly and I were at Harold and Jann's home for dinner. Their cook got sick. Harold asked us if we would like to eat at the Palms. We said yes. It was already late, and I had to be in the hospital early the next morning. Since we were in Palm Springs, I assumed the restaurant would be near and we would get home before eleven.

The four of us got into their new Rolls-Royce, opened the gates to the estate, and left. I knew I was in trouble when we were heading west on Interstate 10. The Palms was in Los Angeles. Silly me, thinking the Palms was in Palm Springs.

That night, I ate the largest lobster in my life and got home at one in the morning. I also learned to ask for the zip code of any restaurant that Harold ever suggested.

Harold loved to barbecue. He had style. He would sit in his wheelchair, next to his Weber, with his white apron and tilted chef's hat, douse the charcoals with half a container of lighter fluid, and throw the meat on the large flames. His cook stood close with vigilant eyes.

"The secret is to just sear both sides of the meat and keep the meat red and moist," Harold would instruct.

He delighted in adding lighter fluid to the flames and watching our alarmed reactions. I was surprised he had any eyebrows. The heat was intense, and he was close enough to kiss the flames.

"I use a gas barbecue and like my meat medium well, not red," I announced to Harold as he squirted more fluid.

"You have a lot to learn, my fine doctor." Harold squirted some more.

I stood back.

A few days later, our phone rang as we were about to leave for church. Beverly and the boys were already in the car.

"Jay, what are you doing?" asked Harold.

"We're leaving for church."

"Wait a minute. My driver will be at your house shortly."

"Harold, we have to go."

"Please, just wait a minute. God will be there when you get there."

"Harold, God is always with us."

"Whatever you say but just wait."

The driver pulled up in Harold's convertible Rolls-Royce Cornishe with a new Weber grill in the backseat.

"Harold, why the Weber?" I asked in bewilderment.

"I can't believe that you barbecue with a gas grill at your home. It is not healthy for you and your family. Use the Weber," ordered Harold.

"Okay. But only if you bring your cook and staff to clean the Weber after it is used."

"Deal," Harold chuckled.

"Too bad it was my barbecue that displeased you. It could have been my car."

"You are good," roared Harold.

"Okay, I have got to go. I'll say a prayer for you."

"If that's what you want to do."

"It is."

Harold perfected his portrayal of toughness, harshness, and even crudeness. But he was a puppy inside. He told me he learned to be tough as a kid at Hell's Kitchen in New York. He insisted he was the leading man in his books. He told me many stories that I preferred not to believe. But he was convincing in his tales. After all, he was the master storyteller.

I learned courage and determination from Harold. He was not a quitter. For months, I spent nights at his bedside and treated him while he finished his book, *The Piranhas*. He had intractable back pain and severe respiratory distress from years of smoking. I injected pain medications slowly, monitoring for feared breathing failure, and adjusted his continuous oxygen flow. A few nights, I thought he would die. My hand was on the phone to call 911, but he would rally and continue to work.

I prayed to God for strength and guidance.

I talked to Buddy for advice and reassurance.

I did not hear God.

I heard Buddy. "Keep strong, you're doing good," he said.

Harold would curse God, and I would object. He would ask me to pray for him and I did. I told him he should pray, but he never did, at least not in front of me.

Harold was proud of me. He praised and encouraged me like a father to a son. He knew my story, not all of the abuse, and wanted me to write it. "It will make for a hell of a story and get some of that crap out of you."

I told him I was not a writer.

He said he was not one before a friend bet him $200 he couldn't write a book. He accepted the wager and wrote his first book, *Never Love a Stranger*.

"Are you betting me $200, Harold?" I asked.

"Hell no. I'd lose." He laughed and hammered on his typewriter.

"Harold, why don't you get a computer?" I shouted over the noise of the key strikes.

"I don't trust those damn things."

"What's that saying about old dogs and new tricks?" I laughed.

Harold chuckled and kept typing.

He became frail later, yet remained strong-willed and focused on completing his next book. He could no longer use his favorite typewriter and began to dictate while Jann transcribed. He may not have been six-foot in stature, but he was large in spirit.

When Harold passed away, it felt like I had lost a father who loved me and was proud of me. And I loved him. Just like Tatay.

❧

My practice continued to flourish. There were a lot of wounds to heal. I remained focused, usually. At times I would stare, as in a trance, at a new male patient's nose, as if my father's nose was in front of me.

I would start to feel pain from old wounds.

"Jay, snap out of it. Stop staring at the nose."

"Help me. I want to go away," I pleaded.

"Stop it. You are strong. He is not your father," Buddy advised.

"Dr. Roberts. Dr. Roberts. Are you okay?" asked a perplexed patient.

I blinked.

"Yes, I'm fine. Sorry. A thought just crossed my mind. Now let me explain my findings. I know where your pain is coming from. I should be able to help you," I continued after a few seconds.

"Hi. I'm Sidney Sheldon, and this is my wife, Alexandra. We've heard good things about you." He sat on the examination table, she on a side chair.

"You must have been talking to my wife." I smiled as I closed my examination room door.

"Actually, to our neighbors," Sidney clarified.

"Well, some of them have questionable taste."

"True," replied Alexandra as she smiled and nodded her head.

The first bighorn sheep given to Beverly and me by the Sheldons was Sasha. We were named the official adoptive parents on her papers and name tag. Kimberly joined our extended family the next year, and then it was Walter the subsequent year.

The "kids" were a wonderful and heartfelt gift of appreciation for the medical care Sidney and Alexandra received at my office. Sasha, Kimberly, and Walter were released to roam the hillside next to Palm Springs. We were proud parents.

❧

I entered an examination room.

Mrs. Apfelbaum sat on the table. Her husband, Murray, slouched on a chair. They were in their late sixties.

"Good morning. I understand you have neck pain," I said to Mrs. Apfelbaum as I sat on my rolling stool.

"Yes. It's horrible. I wouldn't wish it on my worst enemy," she responded.

Buddy interrupted me and implored, "You better look at her right leg."

"I'm sorry you are in pain. But let me see your right leg first."

"What? I'm here for my neck."

"I understand. But please, let me see your leg."

She pulled up her right pant leg.

Her leg was swollen, hot, and tender when I squeezed her calf muscle.

"Better send her right now," warned Buddy.

"Mrs. Apfelbaum, you must go to the hospital right now. My medical assistant will push you in one of our wheelchairs. You cannot walk, not even to your car."

"No. I don't want to go. I came here to see you for my neck."

"I know, but I'm very concerned about your leg. Please, sit in the chair," I commanded as I pointed to the wheelchair my assistant had brought to the room.

"Listen to the doctor. He's a fine doctor. Sit in the chair," asserted Mr. Apfelbaum.

She did but with a look that could have stopped a train.

My diagnosis was correct. She had a severe blood clot in her leg. A large fragment of the clot was dangling and could have broken off on her next step. It could have been fatal.

"Dr. Roberts, the vascular specialist said you saved my life," she said a few weeks later in my office.

"You're now responsible for Edith for the rest of her years," added Mr. Apfelbaum.

She smiled.

He laughed then said, "Good luck."

She shot him a displeased look, grinned at me, then said, "But you still need to help me with my neck pain."

The Apfelbaums and Beverly and I became dear friends.

❧

Happy years passed. Blessed years.

There were two times though that I wanted to cause wounds, not heal them.

Derek and I went to Hamburger Hamlet restaurant on Palm Canyon. He was in sixth grade, and it was one of our father-and-son lunches. After ordering, Derek excused himself to go the bathroom.

Four men, sitting at the adjacent table, turned and stared at his rear as he walked by. They turned to each other, raised their eyebrows up and down, and smiled.

Derek kept walking and never saw what happened.

I pounced to their table.

"How dare you do that to my son. He is a child. You sick bastards," I hollered.

The men remained mute, eyes wide.

"I swear to God if you even look at him when he returns, I'll bust this chair over your damn heads." My voice exploded with spit.

I stared at each one of them. They remained speechless and motionless. I returned to our booth, prayed, and called upon my friend.

"Buddy, help."

"I'm here. Calm down. Derek is coming back."

I watched as Derek returned.

The men looked deep into their menus. No eye contact with Derek.

"Dad, what's wrong?" Derek asked as he sat down.

"Nothing, son."

"You look so red. Are you okay?"

"Yes, don't worry. Now tell me about your day so far." I smiled and looked at him.

During our lunch, I glanced over at the other table. The men ate fast and left before us. They never looked at Derek again.

The chair remained intact.

Derek's pelvis did not a year later.

He was playing in a championship soccer game in Palm Springs, having a great game against a team from Los Angeles.

My friend and fellow physician arrived late and went to the wrong side of the field, next to the coaches of the other team. Then I saw him running toward me.

As I turned back to the field, Derek was on a fast run and about to kick for a goal when he was viciously tripped.

He writhed in pain and couldn't get up.

I ran to him, picked him up, and carried him to my car.

My friend caught up with us. "Jay, I was running to tell you Derek was in trouble," he announced winded.

"What?"

"Yeah. I heard the coach say to take out number eighteen, to take him out hard, to hurt him bad, or they would not win."

Derek's number was eighteen.

I rushed him to the Desert Regional Medical Center. Beverly and Ryan followed in her car, and my friend behind them.

Derek had a fractured pelvis.

As soon as I knew he was being cared for and would be in good hands, I turned to Beverly. "You stay here. I have something to do."

"No, Jay. Don't go."

I ran out to my car, opened the trunk, and took out one of Ryan's baseball bats.

I sped back to the soccer field.

"Don't do it, Jay," Buddy shouted.

"I'm going to. I'm going to bust that coach's head in."

"Don't. You'll go to prison."

"I don't care. Hurt me but not my family." I screamed and pounded the steering wheel.

The parking lot was empty. The soccer field was cleared of players and coaches, including my target.

My legs weakened, and I fell to the ground.

God, help me.

He already had. The coach was gone.

Derek sat in a wheelchair for months.

We all prayed for him.

He healed.

30

PALM SPRINGS, CALIFORNIA

1999

My eyes are irritated. The ceiling fan may have blown dust in my eyes.

I adjust the pillows behind me and look into a hand mirror. My eyes are fine. I lay down the mirror and close my eyes.

I begin to sleep when I see his eyes. Peace flows through his opaque scarred corneas.

Father Peter Mary Rookey seemed to look into my soul as I sat alone with him in a small, dim lit room in his Chicago home.

Father Rookey was once blind from a firecracker blast near his eyes when he was seven. The doctors said there was no treatment. He would be blind forever. With constant prayers by his mother and family, his sight gradually returned. He became a priest.

Fr. Rookey is known as the healing priest from his first healing in Benburb, County Tyrone (where he helped found the Servite order in Ireland in 1948) to thousands of healings worldwide. Witness letters, some with medical consensus, have been submitted to the International Compassion Ministry.

He is a great and humble man who says of the healings: "It's God's work, not mine. I just do what he told us to do and the people are delivered and healed. We are answering the last command of Jesus, 'They shall lay hands upon the sick, and they shall recover' (Mark 16:18, NKJV). He does all the healing, I just pray."

Beverly and a younger sister of my mother-in-law, Sylvia (Paquita), brought me to him six months ago. Paquita had witnessed healings on several pilgrimages with Fr. Rookey. I initially objected to seeing him. My resistance to Beverly was weak. I surrendered.

At first we just sat face-to-face. His eyes comforted me. "Do you want Jesus to heal you?" he asked in a soft, compassionate voice. "Is Jesus your Lord and Savior?"

"Yes." My eyes watered.

"Do you ask forgiveness of your sins?"

"Yes."

"You are a child of God. He loves you. He wants to heal you."

I cried.

"Now say the Miracle Prayer."

He handed me piece of paper and I prayed:

> Lord Jesus, I come before you just as I am. I am sorry for my sins. I repent of my sins, please forgive me. In your name, I forgive all others for what they have done against me. I renounce Satan, the evil spirits, and all their works. I give you my entire self, Lord Jesus, now and forever. I invite you into my life, Jesus. I accept you as my Lord, God, and Savior. Heal me, change me, and strengthen me in body, soul, and spirit. Come, Lord Jesus, cover me with your precious blood and fill me with your Holy Spirit. I love you, Lord Jesus. I praise you, Jesus. I thank you, Jesus. I shall follow you every day of my life. Amen. Mary, my mother, Queen of Peace, all the angels and saints, please help me. Amen.

I felt a warm blast through my body.

Fr. Rookey said, "Say this prayer faithfully, no matter how you feel. When you come to the point where you sincerely mean each word with all your heart, something good spiritually will happen to you. You will experience Jesus, and he will change your whole life in a very special way. You will see."

I was comforted but not changed.

I did not mean each word with all my heart.

31

WASHINGTON, DC

1997

"Dad. Thanks for bringing me to Washington, DC," Ryan said as he gave me a hug.

"I am so happy to be with you. I am very proud of you," I replied. "It's an honor for you to be Sonny Bono's congressional intern for the summer. I'm sure he will take good care of you."

"I know. But I really do thank you, Dad."

"You're welcome. Now let's hurry. We have dinner tonight with Sonny and Mary and then a private tour of Capitol Hill."

We hurried, placed our luggage in the hotel room, showered, changed clothes, stopped for a quick hug and high-five, and made it to the restaurant late, quite late. I took the wrong exit off of one of the roundabouts and ended up in Virginia. I thought it was the right monument and exit, but I could not see the statue up close, and there was no posted sign with the name of the statue. It was at least twenty minutes to the first exit to turn around.

It was a fashionable and traditional Italian restaurant with rich, dark wood, Italian tapestry and landscape frescoes on the walls, and background Italian guitar music.

It was warm and alive like Sonny.

As Ryan and I were shown to the large, black leather booth with white linens, I saw Sonny signing autographs for some customers. His infectious smile was visible from the other side of the room. Mary talked, smiled, and nodded to the people as they waited for their autographs.

Mary was gracious as ever when we arrived. After all, the beat must go on! "Jay. Ryan. You're here. Sit down. I was getting worried about you," stated Sonny as he finished an autograph.

"I took a wrong turn and ended up somewhere in Virginia."

"I've done that too, Jay." Mary laughed.

We mainly talked about family that night and also about Ryan's internship.

"Ryan, are you ready for some hard work and long hours?" asked Sonny.

"Yes, sir."

"Good. Now let's order some food. Eat well, Ryan. Your first day on the Hill starts early tomorrow," said Sonny. He gestured for our waiter and winked at me.

"No problem," answered Ryan with a grin.

"Good answer," chuckled Mary.

"Sonny, what's your favorite here? I'll order it. I am sure I won't be disappointed," I commented.

"Do you trust me that much?"

"I do."

"Me too," added Ryan.

"Me too," echoed Mary as she tapped him on his hand.

"Okay. Let me order." Sonny pushed aside his menu and spoke to the waiter.

Pasta, fish, and chicken, all with their special family secret sauces, were set before us.

We ate and laughed through dinner with a few interruptions by more customers wanting autographs and pictures with Sonny.

Then Sonny drove all of us to the Capital. We would get my car at the restaurant on the way back. He knew the monuments, and he named each one as we passed. He had a special pass for parking. But we were delayed from entering the U.S. Capitol Building. Tourists requested pictures with Sonny. Multiple cameras flashed. Yeah, the beat went on.

"Jay, this is exciting for me too," Mary said as we entered the chamber room. "Spouses of congressmen and congresswomen do not get to be in this room very often."

"Ryan, sit in the speaker's chair," Sonny directed with a head nod.

"It looks like you belong there," I said while Ryan sat in the chair.

"Okay, Ryan, it's my turn to see if I fit," teased Mary.

"Mary, you look pretty darn good," shouted Sonny from his congressional seat.

"Think so? It does feel comfortable," Mary affirmed with a flushed face.

"Yeah. You do fit in this room, Mary. Or should I say congresswoman?" I teased.

"Only in a dream," Mary whispered.

I was sure we all had our own special dreams that night.

I did.

❧

Months passed.

I began to feel a periodic sharp pain and weakness in my legs. I dismissed it in my mind and told myself that I was just overworked and tired.

I prescribed rest but did not follow.

I knew it would just go away. But it did not stop. My gait became unsteady with the pain and weakness increasing.

I trembled inside. My heart knew my mind was wrong.

Intense flashes of my beatings momentarily stunned me. The images appeared more frequent with passing weeks. I began to dream of the hand as it tried to enter our windows.

I could not predict when the pain, weakness, and old wounds would surface. I felt vulnerable. The pain and weakness receded and flowed through me like tidal water. Then it disappeared for weeks, only to reappear with stronger waves.

I told no one, not even Beverly. I did not want her to worry. And I would not accept that it was permanent.

I could keep things to myself.

I talked to Buddy more and more.

I prayed to him less and less.

❧

"Jay, come on, go skiing with us," insisted Sonny as we sat at his dining room table. Our families were having Christmas dinner at Mary and Sonny's home in Palm Springs.

"Sonny, I can't. Maybe next time."

"Are you okay? You look tired," Sonny said as he placed his hand on my shoulder.

"I'm fine." I tapped my hand on his hand.

"Jay, tell Sonny the importance of wearing a helmet while skiing," instructed Mary.

"I know, I know. I know you are going to remind me about the poor Kennedy kid," chimed Sonny with his hand raised to stop the feared lecture.

"Okay, then are you going to wear one?" I asked.

"Yes, I will."

"Promise?" Mary and I posed in unison.

"Yes."

"We all heard that promise," said Beverly.

Ryan and Derek nodded.

Chesare and Chianna looked up from their plates of pasta and nodded with synchronized affirmative headshakes.

Sonny rolled his eyes, hummed, and entertained us for the rest of the evening.

I thought of Sonny skiing several times on the succeeding days. Then our home telephone rang.

"Jay. Oh my God. Sonny is dead." The distress in Mary's voice was palpable.

"What? What happened? I can't believe it. My God, what happened?"

"He didn't wear his helmet. Well, he did wear it the first day but not after that. He crashed into a tree." Mary's voice faded.

"I just can't believe it. He promised," I blurted. As the words came out, I wished I had not spoken of the broken promise.

"I know, Jay. He did," Mary whimpered.

"What can I do?" I asked, not expecting an answer.

"Please come over to the house when we get back to Palm Springs."

"I will. Of course I will."

The subsequent days were a blur. I was planning to meet Sonny when he returned from the skiing trip. I never imagined that he would be in his coffin.

I stood next to his open casket at Our Lady of Solitude Church in Palm Springs. It was the evening before the televised funeral at Saint Theresa's church. I poured my heart out about Sonny in front of the closely guarded group of family and friends.

I turned to his open casket and cried.

Mary and Cher sobbed. Others moaned, wept, or sniveled. Some shed quiet tears.

No cameras, no press. Just us.

"Jay and Beverly, I need your opinion," Mary said later as she grabbed our arms and guided us to a private area of her home. "They want me to take over Sonny's congressional seat."

We were at the Bonos' home with other invited guests after Sonny's graveside funeral the next day. Members of Congress wasted no time to persuade her to accept the proposal. Mary was concerned about her children. She knew what it meant. She would be away from them more than she wanted.

"Mary, you'll figure it out. You'll do the right thing. We're here for you," Beverly reassured her and gave her a warm hug.

"I agree. Pray and do what you feel is right," I added and joined in the hug.

Congresswoman Mary Bono did step up to the challenge and won. She sat duly in her seat in Congress, once thought of only as a dream. Mary was a devoted mother, loyal wife, stellar congresswoman, and good person.

She carried the beat.

❧

Months later, I was faced with a nightmare. The medical rehabilitation center at Desert Hospital suddenly closed, by decision of the CEO of the hospital. I had to make a change in my practice. I joined an orthopedic surgery group on the campus of Eisenhower Medical Center in Rancho Mirage, California, near Palm Springs. I was only allowed to provide non-surgical care for neck and back pain. I felt restricted and stifled by this limitation.

Doctors at the orthopedic center were assigned to a pod. Mine was on the third floor. Examination rooms faced the nursing station, where my medical assistant was based. A small dictation room was behind the nursing area.

"There. A perfect place. I think it looks great," I announced to my medical assistant as I stepped back to look at my painting of Christ.

"I think so too, Dr. Roberts," confirmed my assistant.

My painting hung on the wall outside of my dictation room, behind my assistant.

I had seen God's work at medical missions on the island. The picture reminded me of his presence, his healing power, and focused me to serve him to heal wounds. I looked at it several times a day.

One week later, a physician member of the board of the orthopedic group approached me. "Jay, you must remove that," stated the physician as he pointed to the painting.

"Why?"

"The board met yesterday. We feel that the painting is offensive to some of our patients. You must remove it now."

"You're joking."

"Jay, please remove it now."

I did.

My heart hurt as I lowered the painting and brought it to my car. I walked wounded. I was forsaking him.

At the next monthly physician meeting, a senior board member announced that religion should not be a part of the practice at the center.

All eyes were focused on me. I wanted to stand and leave but did not. Buddy told me to stay. I remained in the chair but did not hear the rest of the discussions.

My mind wandered to my medical school training and mission work in the Philippines, where his guidance and healing powers were wanted, a time when prayers and thanksgiving to God were voiced and shouted.

Several physicians smirked at me from that day forward. I tried, as Beverly suggested, praying for them. But my heart was not in it.

I focused on my practice, to be the best. My patients appreciated their care; the physician board, the revenue I brought to the center. I was asked to join the orthopedic group as a partner. It was the first time a non-orthopedic surgeon was offered partnership.

I declined.

The smirks increased.

For months, I prayed for God to give me strength, but felt weaker. I prayed for a better attitude and to remain loyal, but was discouraged. I tried to remain strong, but felt vulnerable. I tried to remain loyal, but was apathetic.

I no longer smiled. I stumbled more, and my pain deepened. I could no longer hide my wounds. I quit practicing and retreated to my bedroom.

Buddy told me I did the right thing, but I felt awful, a failure.

The burning pain in my feet blazed and felt like I walked on hot coals. My balance and endurance deteriorated. My legs could fold without warning. My grip strength diminished, shoulders weakened.

I had abdominal fullness and relentless diarrhea.

I was angry and desperate.

I was dying a slow death.

32

PALM SPRINGS, CALIFORNIA

1999

It is late at night. My mind spins like the fan blade. Beverly lies asleep next to me. An owl screeches a melody. My eyes widen. More hoots. My heart races.

I have known, since I was a child on the island, what that owl means. An owl resting on the roof of a house signals death for any of its residents.

Many Filipinos try to foretell the future by observing natural things. Although organized religion discourages superstition, some Filipinos adhere to unique beliefs that have developed over centuries.

"Buddy, do you hear that owl?" I ask in a low voice.

"Yes," he answers.

"An owl is an owl, whether on the island or here," I whisper.

"Everything will be fine. Don't worry."

"Are you sure?" I ask as I hear another hoot.

"Yes. Go to sleep. You need your rest."

"Okay. But watch that owl for me."

"I will. Good night."

"Good night."

❧

I thought the discussion about a pilgrimage to Europe was over. Beverly has other thoughts. She sits on our bed and holds my hand. "We're going. Please do not argue with me." Her voice cracks, eyes water as she tries to be stern and compassionate.

"No. No. No." My voice fades after each attempt of defiance.

I do not want any help from anyone, including my wife. The thought of going to Lourdes and Fatima for a religious healing repulses me.

I am mad at God. I have prayed and he did not answer.

I am convinced he does not care about me. It will be worthless for me to go and try to receive the power of his healings. If he really wants to, he can do it right in my bedroom. He doesn't care about me.

Buddy tells me he does. But I don't think so.

"Jay, please. Please go."

"No."

"Dad, just go," pleads Ryan.

Derek nods in agreement.

Despair marks their faces and weakens my defense.

I also remember the owl. "Alright. Now will you leave me alone?" Smiles on my sons' faces divert the flow of tears down their cheeks. They quickly leave the room, pat each other on the backs, and nudge each other on the sides. It was their relief that caused me to cry inside. They are strong college students trying to motivate a pathetic dad.

"Thank you. God bless you," Beverly whispers in my ear with a soft kiss.

My eyes close.

Beverly wastes no time. She enlists the assistance of our dear friend, Peachy. The three of us are to go on the pilgrimage to Fatima and Lourdes.

Peachy and Beverly have been friends since high school. She was instrumental in introducing me to Beverly.

For that, I have an undying *utang*.

33

FATIMA, PORTUGAL

2000

"Isn't it beautiful?" whispers Beverly.

"Yes." Tears flow down my face.

A sea of white handkerchiefs waves overhead at the passing statue of Our Lady of Fatima. Tens of thousands of the white cloths flutter in the warm breeze in rhythmic waveform. My white cloth waves at my side. My arms are weak and unable to extend overhead. But I feel connected to the tide of white fabric.

Fatima is famous for the sighting of the Virgin of the Rosary by three peasant children in 1917. Today, pilgrimages to the site go on all year round. The largest crowds gather on May 13 and October 13, the days of the apparitions of the Virgin Mary to the children, when millions of pilgrims attend to pray and witness the processions. Heartfelt songs fill the air in the square of Our Lady of Fatima Basilica. People stand, crawl, and kneel. Praises to God echo about as if riding on the waves of white handkerchiefs. Hours pass. People remain transfixed in a peaceful state.

We pray until nightfall and then witness a procession of tens of thousands of lit candles for the statue of Our Lady of the Rosary of Fatima.

I am entranced. My thoughts flow like a stream of water.

Look at all of those flickering candles. Look at all those people, worse off than me. Some crawl. Some can't even stand.

They are in more pain than I am. No wonder I'm not important enough to be healed. They need to be healed first. They're probably better believers than me.

But I want to be healed too. I really do want to believe.

I can't believe how long I have been standing here. My feet don't burn as much right now. Could something be happening? It's probably just my endorphins decreasing my pain right now. Just enjoy the moment.

Look at those candles. It's like we are all flickering to him, sending our flames as Morse code to God to get his attention.

Maybe I should have a bigger candle. Maybe he would see me better that way.

I need to listen to him better. I keep praying, but he does not answer. Maybe he does, but I just don't hear. Maybe he had to smack me on my head and knock me down to listen. Crap. I feel like a Mack truck hit me.

I don't want to leave. I should stand right where I am. Maybe this is where I'm supposed to be for him to see me. I'm going to stay here longer just in case.

I really like all the candles. I wonder if this is what heaven looks like. If so, there will be millions and millions of candles flickering. Hope I get to see that.

Oh heavenly Father, please heal me. I beg of you. I'm really not that bad. I thought you loved all sinners. Besides, we are all sinners. Hey, I am one. Love me. Love this one.

God, please heal me.

The flow of thoughts that floods my mind stops with a gentle tap on my shoulder.

"We better get you back to the hotel and get something to eat." Beverly whispers and breaks the silence. "We leave tomorrow for Lourdes."

"Sure."

I'm not tired or hungry.

I'm at peace.

The next day, we travel to Lourdes, France, by private motor coach, through Portugal, Spain and the Pyrenees Mountains. The bus is packed with pilgrims seeking a healing at Fatima and Lourdes. A Catholic priest, Father Roy Henderson from Wilton, Connecticut, leads us miracle seekers while a short male Portuguese tour guide keeps us on the right path. I wonder if the guide will seek healing for the guttural sounds that emit from his throat.

It takes two days to Lourdes from Fatima. The motor coach has reclining seats and foot rests. I tolerate the ride well, changing my position often.

All of our fellow passengers worship with Father Roy at Our Lady of Fatima Church except for the priest's mother and sister who are Protestants. Most seek spiritual and physical healing. Some are friends and relatives of the desperate ones. All are dressed in very casual attire and tennis shoes except the three of us. We have a different idea of what the brochure means as casual. We wear silk, fine cottons, and leather shoes fit for sightseeing in Paris.

The priest wears his collar.

I spend a lot of time praying, looking out the window, and talking to Beverly and Peachy. My attitude since Fatima has changed. I laugh and joke with them.

I am annoyed at some of our fellow passengers when they give us displeased looks as we talk and they recite the rosary.

"I hope they brought extra rosary beads. They're going to wear out the ones they're using," I remark to Beverly and Peachy as I stare back at one of the passengers who looks like an old spinster.

"Jay, behave," whispers Beverly as she nudges my side.

"I have an extra one for you, Jay," chuckles Peachy.

"You two, behave. They might hear you. I'll pray for both of you," whispers Beverly.

"Thanks. I could use all the prayers I can get."

Beverly does not laugh, just shakes her head and gives me that look.

I stop then grin at Peachy. She bows her head and hides her face. I see her body jerking from her self-contained laughing. I slowly turn to Beverly. She smiles and shakes her head. I shrug my shoulders and mouth, "Okay, I'll behave." I turn and stare out the window.

I know God can heal. I have witnessed his healings in the Philippines, and I have now felt his presence in Fatima.

We stop in towns and villages to visit churches, including in Lisbon, Salamanca, Avila, Burgos, and Loyola. We have stopped to see and pray in another church in Loyola.

I have finished my prayers and am seated on a bench outside of the church.

"My sister is in a lot pain. I understand that you're a doctor, a specialist in pain. Maybe you can help her. She cannot bear the pain," says the priest.

Wait a minute. We're on a religious pilgrimage, and you're the priest. Can't she wait until the baths in Lourdes? Isn't that what we are here for?

I look at Beverly and Peachy.

They smile.

My God, can't I get a break? Do I have to be a doctor everywhere and at anytime? I am not here to be a doctor. Can't you see I am in pain too?

Buddy tells me to be kind.

I turn to the priest and answer, "Sure. I'd be happy to see your sister."

Beverly's smile increases.

I find a pharmacy and struggle to get the medication I feel she needs. The names of the drugs are different than in the States, and the product information is in French, which I don't speak, write, or read. I pray and finally find the drug.

I give it to her, and she feels better.

The priest blesses me and says, "I'll conduct a special service at the end of our pilgrimage in Paris. Please attend."

"Of course, Father. I will. Thank you."

I don't call him Father Roy. I have tried once. It's painful.

My father's name was Roy.

We arrive in Lourdes, late in the night, tired. I have had enough of the rosary for the day. We eat and go to bed. I have just fallen asleep when there is a loud knock on our hotel room door. "Yes," I call from behind our door.

"Are you Doctor Roberts?" The inquirer has a deep voice.

"Yes."

"I need to see you. My wife is very ill." The voice is louder.

I open the door.

"I'm sorry to bother you. But I heard there was a doctor in your group. We're staying at a nearby hotel. My wife is really ill. I beg of you. Please help us."

My legs are weaker from the long day.

"Of course I will. Please give me a minute."

I close the door and get dressed.

"Jay, I'm so sorry. Do you want me to come?"

"No, Beverly. Please stay. I'll be fine."

"God bless you, Jay."

"Thanks."

Their hotel is farther than I expected.

"Can I help you?" asks the man when I stumble.

"Yes. That would be nice."

"I can't thank you enough. I'm so worried about my wife."

"It's okay. But are we almost there?"

"Yes, it's right here."

I examine his wife and know she needs Zithromax for bronchitis. We find a pharmacy, but it is closed. We go to a local police station, where an officer calls the pharmacist and the store is opened for us. I struggle, again, to find the right medication. I pray and find it.

Her husband helps me back to my hotel.

I fall into bed and sleep.

"Come on, Jay. Let's get an early start. I hope Peachy is awake." Beverly's voice bubbles with excitement.

Morning seems to come early in France. I look out our hotel window. The simplicity of Fatima contrasts harshly to the hectic congested street below. Merchant vendors pour onto the sidewalks and peddle candles, religious statues, crosses of all sizes, and "holy water" in plastic containers in the shape of Our Lady of Lourdes, others with a stamp of her image.

"Are you sure we are in the right place? Is this really the famous Lourdes?" Sarcasm in my voice is as evident as the smirk on my face.

"Yes. Come on now. Let's get ready." Beverly's voice is angelic.

My cynicism about Lourdes is changed to curiosity as we near the legendary healing baths and I see crutches, canes, walkers, braces, and wheelchairs discarded by a stream. My heart pounds.

Could this be the place for me?

Does healing really occur here?

Lourdes is a small village at the foot of the Pyrenees Mountains, famous for the apparitions of the Virgin Mary in 1858 to a fourteen-year-old girl, Bernadette Soubirous. The Grotto of Massabielle is the holiest site at Lourdes, the grotto where Mary appeared to Bernadette and the source of the shrine's healing waters. The bubbling waters of the miraculous fountain can be seen under a glass cover. Nine water taps dispense spring water for people to drink. The Order of Malta Knight clergy and volunteers transport afflicted travelers, known as *malades*, in wheeled carts each morning to the *Domaine* area, which covers several square miles and surrounds the grotto for Mass and activities. Each year about 350,000 pilgrims seek spiritual healing and miraculous cures for intractable ailments at the baths.

We stand amongst hundreds of pilgrims and dozens of malades and drink the spring water. The hum and muffled chants of prayer from the swarm of pilgrims soften the haste of vendors and pilgrims to collect the water.

"Jay, it's time to go to the baths." Beverly gently taps my shoulder.

"Sure. Let's go." I smile and look up at birds that dart about, reminding me of the playful Maya birds in the Philippines. "Yeah. I need to go to the baths."

I see the sick lady from last night. She limps toward the baths.

Hundreds of men of all ages, most with heads bowed, pray in a multitude of languages as they sit outside on long, wooden benches. As one man rises and is directed into the indoor bath area, a hundred buttocks scoot down the bench. I am in awe of the languages of prayer and do not mind my two-hour wait. But I feel a little overdressed in my short-sleeved, black silk shirt, khaki cotton pants, brown, slip-on, Top-Sider shoes, and thin, black silk jacket.

The sounds of prayers continue as I enter the bath area. The massive, dimmed room hums as men bathe. Partition walls provide partial privacy for the row of bath chambers, and small, off-white marble benches, aged but clean, offer a place to lay your clothes or to rest.

"Sir, what language do you wish spoken for your prayers?" a gentleman asks with a peaceful smile aglow.

"English please," I murmur, sounding like a question more than an answer.

I remove all of my clothes and stand in front of my private marble tub.

Two men stand around me, bow their heads, and pray in unison. Two other male attendants also pray and assist me into the cool water. They are middle-aged, wearing short-sleeved, white polo shirts, white shorts, and are barefoot. Their gentle, caring eyes look into mine with their heads now bowed in prayer.

I do not feel naked.

I am asked to pray and kiss a statue of Our Lady of Lourdes. The stone statue is eight to ten inches high. She wears a white veil and robe with a long blue sash tied around her waist. A rosary hangs from the right forearm and yellow roses are on the end of her robe just above her bare feet.

I comply.

After a full immersion, I stand up exhilarated. My attendants continue their chants and help me out of the water.

While I dress, I realize I am dry. I have just stepped out of the bath and used no towel. But I am dry. I can't explain the lack of wetness. It is contrary to the laws of nature. But never mind.

The men continue to pray.

An elderly fragile man enters. He grimaces as he attempts to stand straighter. His eyes are wide. He seems to shiver. The hum inside the room becomes louder. An increase in echoed prayers off the walls has magnified the droning sound.

Lord, give him peace.

I leave in prayer.

Later that evening, we stand amongst a thousand fellow pilgrims with lighted candles in a procession to honor Our Lady of Lourdes. The chaotic street scene of the morning has faded, snuffed out by the thousand lights of faith. Spontaneous songs and praises to God and Our Lady of Lourdes fill the air. The lights flicker in tempo.

A few hours later, the candles extinguish in succession, the music concludes, and the pilgrims seek shelter.

I do not want the evening to end.

"Jay, Jay," says Beverly, attempting to get my attention.

"Yeah, I know. Time to go."

Tonight, time seems to stand still.

Tomorrow, we have to catch a train to Paris.

The trajectory of the bullet train lands us in Paris at night. The countryside scenery has been blurred by the speed of the express transport.

We are tired; we eat then go to bed. I feel I have just fallen asleep when Beverly calls me. "Jay, come on. We're going to be late. Let's get Peachy."

It is early morning, Beverly's favorite time. She cherishes daybreak, her devoted time to read the Bible.

"Okay, Beverly."

I finish my coffee, my essential requirement in the morning. I do not want to go to church. But I do not want to disappoint Beverly.

Peachy is late as usual.

I smile as I remember Peachy's arrival at the JFK airport in New York. It was the start of our pilgrimage. We were about to board, still no Peachy in sight. A horn blared. A man shouted, "Out of the way, behind you."

There she was, Peachy, poised on a "people mover." Her silk scarf trailed behind her neck, her right hand grasped a purse the size of carry-on luggage. She was smiling.

"I'm here, don't worry!"

Her left hand waved, the right hand still locked on the purse. Her smile was frozen.

"Yes, the queen has arrived," I said with a grin.

"Please tell me all those suitcases are not full of shoes, or I'll start calling you Imelda Marcos," joked Beverly as she pointed to Peachy's luggage. She gave her a big hug and kiss on both cheeks.

"No, only half of them." Peachy laughed.

The memory of Peachy's grand entrance at the airport is cut when there is a knock on our hotel room door. She is at the door and finally ready to go to the church.

"Did you bring extra shoes?" I ask Peachy as we leave the hotel.

"What do you mean?" Peachy asks confused.

Beverly looks confused.

"Never mind. Bad joke."

It is a short walk to the church, the Chapel of Our Lady of Miraculous Medal. It is packed with locals and visitors. To our surprise, there are three seats available in the right front pew next to the center aisle. We would have preferred to be in the back, but I do not want to stand for a lengthy Mass. Father Roy has planned for us to have Mass at this church. He is to be the celebrant and to conduct the special service. Special Masses occur frequently in this church.

The Chapel of Our Lady of the Miraculous Medal is revered by Catholics as the site of three apparitions of the Virgin Mary in 1830 by Sister Catherine, a young novice of the Daughters of Charity. The Miraculous Medal, also known as the Medal of the Immaculate Conception, is a medal created by Sister Catherine and believed to bring special graces through the intercession of Mary if worn with faith and devotion at the hour of death. The medal is not a charm and should not be construed as being either "magical" or superstitious but should serve as a constant physical reminder of devotion.

In February 1832 a deadly cholera epidemic claimed the lives of more than 20,000 Parisians. The sisters of the Daughters of Charity distributed the first copies of the medal, and cures and protections were soon reported. When Sister Catherine's body was exhumed in 1933, it was found miraculously preserved. Pope Pius XII named her a saint on July 27, 1947.

The chapel was enlarged after the apparitions, to accommodate all those who wished to pray at the altar where the Virgin Mary promises prayers would be answered.

We sit on worn, rigid, brown wooden pews and see the incorrupt body of St. Catherine on display in a glass case on the right side of the altar. She is dressed in a black habit and lies on her back. A long black rosary is wrapped around her hands and draped on her left side. The large crucifix, at the end of the rosary, is below her knee.

The walls of the chapel are decorated with mosaics and murals. The majestic marble altar is embellished with golden sculptures and encrusted with medallions containing relics. A white marble statue of Mary stands over the altar. She is crowned with twelve stars and rays of grace lead from her outstretched palms to the white marble floor.

The altar of the apparitions is on the right side of the altar, next to St. Catherine. It is made of marble and decorated with precious stones. It was the main altar from 1815 to 1856. It was at this altar that our Blessed Virgin told Catherine, "Come to the foot of the altar. It is there that graces will be showered on all those who ask with confidence and fervor."

The mass is long but nice. Father Roy shares that as a small boy, his disfigured hand was healed by the water at Lourdes. Just before the dismissal prayer, an announcement is given that a special service is to be conducted.

Our row goes first. I reluctantly stand and move to the front of the altar as instructed. We line up in the same order as we sat in the pew. I am at the center of the altar, Beverly to my right, then Peachy.

We are told to bow our heads, close our eyes, and pray. I hear a commotion to my left but keep my eyes closed until I feel a presence. Father Roy stands in front of me. His healed right hand reaches to my forehead.

A warm bolt shoots through my body.

I fall backward. I do not try to stop my fall.

I am at peace.

"Jay, can you get up?" Beverly asks while she cries and kneels next to me.

I am on my back. The cool, ancient, tiled floor does not feel hard. I am not hurt but cannot move.

"Jay, Jay. Are you okay?" Beverly sobs.

A river of tears flow from my eyes.

The priest kneels down, lays his hand on my chest, and prays.

More tears flow. My arms and legs begin to move.

I arise, crying uncontrollably.

"Jay, are you hurt? You fell hard," Beverly says while holding onto me.

"No. I'm not hurt. I just need to sit down. Please help me out of here."

We sit outside on a stone wall under a shade tree facing the entrance of the church. People smile and nod at me as they leave the special service.

"If I knew that was the special healing service, I would have left the church immediately. I have never believed in that stuff," I say to Beverly and Peachy.

"Jay, I felt like falling too. But I kept praying not to fall. I wanted to be able to help you. I did not know it was a healing service." Beverly squeezes my hand.

"I didn't want to fall either. I left my purse in the pew and was too mindful of my money to let it happen. I'm ashamed to be so materialistic. God forgive me," Peachy says as she wipes tears from her cheek.

"I wish you'd both fallen. It's incredible, overwhelming, and peaceful. Next time, Beverly, don't worry about me, and Peachy, leave your purse in the hotel."

I am in no hurry to leave. We sit there for an hour until darkness falls. Crickets chirp and birds scurry for shelter in the tree above us. We are at peace amidst a sanctuary.

"Buddy, I feel his spirit."

"I know."

"Do you think he will heal me?'

"Be patient. Have faith."

"I will."

34

PALM SPRINGS, CALIFORNIA

2000

"Beverly, thank you for taking me to Europe, but we should have just stayed home and saved our money."

"No, Jay. I am glad we went." Beverly sits down beside me on our bed. Her head down, her hand rubbing my shoulder.

I wince and close my eyes.

I cannot understand. I felt his spirit in Fatima, Lourdes, and Paris; but I am still sick. He does not answer my prayers.

I recall our day trip to the Carmelite convent of St. Teresa in Coimbra, Portugal, with Father Roy and the other pilgrims. It was forty miles north of our hotel in Fatima. Sister Lucia of Fatima lives a cloistered life in the convent but receives requests for prayers. She is one of three children who claim to have witnessed a series of apparitions of the Virgin Mary in Fatima in 1917. It is believed that she reads and prays for every plea. Our written petitions were given to Sister Lucia. I begged to be restored to health.

"He's not a loving God. Or I'm not worthy of his help. I'm not worthy of any help." My voice is cold, and my eyes remain shut.

"Don't say that. You're worth the world to me. I would do anything for you."

"Then leave me alone." My words are intended to rip through her like a knife.

"I love you."

"Leave me alone. Please," I add with a sneer.

She kisses my forehead. I grimace and unlock my eyes.

She leaves but keeps the door open. I am about to yell at her to close the damn door. Buddy stops me.

I am mad at Beverly, God, and myself.

I am not working, but we are okay financially, at least for now. I could have given the money we used for the trip to a charity. It would have been put to good use.

It was a waste on me.

I should have spared my sons. I see the sadness in their eyes as they talk to me and embrace me. They try to act strong, but I can feel their pain. I have set them up for disappointment. I have caused them to hurt.

I bleed inside.

"Your boys love you," says Buddy.

"But they hurt." My voice trembles.

I close my eyes and cry inside with Buddy.

❧

I finish my fatherly advice tapes for my sons. I try to make the tapes positive and light despite my decay. I admire the stack of tapes and grin. I feel I've cheated God out of his timing for my silence.

I recline in my bed with my back supported by large pillows and stare out the windows at the backyard. The sky is bright blue, a light wind stirs the palm trees, and the laughter of my sons in the pool echoes off the surface of the water.

I do not smile. I remain wounded. I feel like garbage that needs to be disposed of soon before it stinks more.

The sun shines but my light dims.

"God, why do you not want me? Am I not good enough?" I shout.

I always wanted to say these words to my father. I couldn't to him but can to God.

I gasp for air between my cries. "God, I don't really hate you. Please, don't hate me."

I exhale in pain, as if all my air is released. I have no more fight in me.

I sleep.

At dusk, I awake. My body stings as if a thousand bees have pierced my skin. I pray the Lord's Prayer and stumble on "… as we forgive those who trespass against us."

I begin to feel a stir inside of me.

The Miracle Prayer of Father Rookey is heavy on my heart. I have not memorized the prayer but remember some of the words:

> Lord Jesus, I am sorry for my sins.
> Please forgive me.
> I forgive others.
> I invite you into my life.
> Heal me.
> I love you, Jesus.
> Mary, mother of God, intercede for me.
> Amen.

I add, "Thy will be done."

My hurt bursts with those words.

I close my eyes. My mind spins and thoughts flow as if in a swift current.

It has always been hard for me to pray "thy will be done" and really mean it. I would have to give myself completely to God, to surrender to him, and lose control over my life. It would be easier to pray for God's will to be done if I believed he was a loving God and wants good things. It would be harder if he were a punishing God and wanted bad things.

"God's will be done" is more than just words or language. It is a way of life. I must walk in his spirit. Be a light shining for God.

It is a scary thought to surrender control. I would have to submit to another father, him. I would have to let go of my defenses, the protective wall around me. I would be vulnerable. I would show fear. My wounds would be exposed.

My mind stops its spin.

I pray "thy will be done" and mean every word.

My heart quiets. My mind rests.

I sleep.

Later that night, I awake. Beverly is asleep next to me.

A sheer, white robe floats across our bedroom and hovers at the foot of our bed. I can see through the garment the sitting area of the room with the sofas and fireplace. The robe flows over me.

I feel a chill.

I do not shiver.

I smell sweetness in the air, like the sampaguita flower in the Philippines.

The sampaguita (Arabian jasmine) is the national flower of the Philippines. Its white, star-shaped flower opens at nights, produces a unique sweet scent, and symbolizes for the Filipinos purity, simplicity, humility, and strength.

Surrounded by the scent of the flower, I am at peace.

I feel light, as if I could float away,

I feel his presence.

I pray with Buddy, "Now I lay me down to sleep, I pray the Lord my soul to keep."

We sing, "Jesus loves me this I know, for the Bible tells me so."

The white robe floats through our closed bedroom door.

I close my eyes and continue to pray. *Oh God, please forgive me of all my sins. I do not understand, but I believe. Your will be done.*

I dream of happy times of running and jumping as a child on the beach in the Philippines.

I awake late in the morning. Beverly is not beside me in bed.

The room smells sweet.

She must have used a lot of perfume this morning.

I yawn, a deep yawn, like a bear out of hibernation. A tingle flashes through my body. I feel energized, like a recharged battery, and smile.

I stand and stretch. I shake my head in disbelief. My legs are strong. I raise my arms over my head and scream in delight.

"Oh my God, Beverly! Come here, Beverly!" I shriek.

"What? What's the matter?" Beverly shouts from the hallway.

"Look. Oh my God. Look," I yell as she enters the room.

I move my arms and legs powerfully. I begin to jog in place.

Her eyes widen and her mouth opens. "My God, Jay. Look at you. Thank you, Jesus," she cries and raises her hands above her head.

I run to her and we embrace.

Her legs buckle. Mine remain sturdy. We sit on the bed wrapped in each other's arms.

"What's wrong?" screams Ryan as he and Derek run into our bedroom.

"Dad! Mom! Are you okay?" cries out Derek.

Beverly and I stand.

"Look at your father," exclaims Beverly.

"Yeah, look at me," I bellow and jump up and down.

"Oh my God," Derek cries.

"Dad!" Ryan shouts.

I squeeze my sons with force as we embrace and cry. Beverly joins our hug and sobs. Praises to God pour out of our mouths as we all thank Jesus.

Later that day, I walk around the backyard and recline on a lounging chair. The sky is baby blue with few clouds. A thin patch of cloud glides overhead like a white flowing robe. It hovers over me for several minutes then flutters away like a stream of waving white handkerchiefs.

I know at that moment that I have to move on and let go of my anger.

"God loves me," I tell Buddy.

"I know he does. And you love him," he answers.
"I don't need to play with you right now," I whisper.
I smile and go back to our bedroom and gather the tapes.
"You can destroy those," Buddy speaks softly.
"I know. I will."

35

PALM SPRINGS, CALIFORNIA

2000

I am afraid to restart my practice.

What if I don't have the stamina to do the long hours? What if I get weak again? What if my patients don't come back?

I must have asked Beverly these kinds of questions a hundred times. She is patient with me. At the perfect time, she reminds me that I am *parang pinoy* (like a Filipino). There is a saying, "The Filipino is pliant as a bamboo." The Filipino character is felt to be similar to the bamboo because it has flexibility, endurance, and harmony with nature. It bends with the wind but can survive a storm.

I reestablish my private practice and hang my picture with pride. It feels right. The best way to show God's love is to flourish in life. He calls us to live. I want to bloom everyday.

My practice flourishes.

A new patient, Arnold Weinberg, enters my office and life.

Arnold is a handsome man in his seventies, with distinguished gray hair, strong bone structure, compassionate eyes and smile, and a firm handshake. He is kind, wise, strong, and gentle. He has a kind heart.

Arnold can also give a stern look and a sharp reproach if he feels you need or deserve it.

"Jay, what do you mean you're not doing epidural (spinal) injections? Do you know how much money you're throwing away? Besides, your patients would rather you to do their injections," he says as we eat lunch. We have a standing appointment for lunch every Thursday.

"You're right," I answer.

"Are you going to do them?"

"I'll think about it."

"What are you saying? Don't be a putz." His voice is very loud. Customers in the restaurant look at us. My face reddens.

"Well, at least you did not say a schmuck," I whisper.

"Then don't be one."

My head bows.

I am silent as I speak to Buddy.

"Buddy, keep me strong."

"Arnold cares for you like a father. You can trust him. He is a good man," Buddy whispers.

"Jay. Are you alright?" Arnold taps my hand.

"Yes."

"Jay, you know I cherish our time together. I'm proud of you. I want the best for you and your family. I love you." His voice softens.

"I know. Me too."

My eyes fill.

"Remember to do good in business and love your family," Arnold adds as he places his napkin on the table.

We leave. I feel like a son walking out with my father. It feels good.

Arnold speaks from experience. He is successful in business, and he loves his family.

I take care of his pain problems. He helps heal my wounds.

We have many wonderful lunches and talks. Until one day, the phone rings.

"Jay. Arnold has passed," cries Carol, his wife.

"I'll be right there."

Arnold had been sick for a while, but the call shocks me. My heart feels wounded.

Carol meets me at the front door. Her eyes are red, cheeks wet with tears. She shakes.

Carol is a feisty short lady. She can attack like a pit bull and be sweet as a Shih Tzu.

I ask and am permitted to go to Arnold in their bedroom. I pray for him: "God, our Father, you brought us into life and by your command we return to dust. May Arnold rejoice in your kingdom. May we be together again in one family forever. Amen."

Carol and I cry.

His memorial service is held in their home with family, friends, and a rabbi. I am asked to speak. I tell Buddy to keep me strong, clear my throat, and share the thoughts in my heart about Arnold, a good, honest, and humble man; a man who loved life and his family; who showed me kindness and love, at times with brutal frankness as a loving father would to a son; a man who is now at peace and free of pain.

I miss Arnold, especially on Thursdays.

In my private office, where I follow my own rules, not a board of physicians, I begin to pray with patients who want prayer. I do not force my faith on any patient. But I am not reluctant to acknowledge Christ.

"Dr. Roberts, I was deceptive to your receptionist," explains a patient who I have treated for neck pain. "I really don't have any more pain, but I told her I did to get this appointment. I'm really here for you to pray for me. But please charge Medicare for this visit."

"I'll be happy to pray. But I can't charge Medicare. There is no billable code for prayer. Glorious will be the day that there is a code," I say and I smile as I hold out my hands. There are no visible wounds.

We hold hands.

I pray, "Heavenly Father, you heal the brokenhearted and bind up their wounds. Help me to be your servant. Bless this patient. Take away her pain, her suffering and wounds. I pray this in your most precious name. Amen."

I now believe when compassion and caring are present, the power of healing is formed. There is already an increasing demand to integrate western and alternative medical treatment. But I believe we should integrate God's healing, to evoke his power for the care of our patients.

❧

Through my medical research, I become aware of photomedicine and the Thor laser system.

Photomedicine is the application of red and near-infrared light over injuries or lesions to improve wound/soft tissue healing and give relief for both acute and chronic pain. The treatment is non-invasive and harmless. It provides reduction in pain, inflammation, and edema; and it decreases healing time. My due diligence on laser equipment shows me that not all lasers are alike. The best in my opinion is the Thor laser system.

I go to London, meet, and am trained by the founder and leading physician of Thor laser, James and Karen Carroll. I am impressed by their knowledge of photomedicine and their patients' responses to the treatments.

Healing through laser therapy is approved by the FDA. I purchase a Thor laser system and help write protocols for physicians using the equipment in the United States. Most patients experience pain relief and improved healing time, all without side effects. My results parallel the findings in Asia and Europe.

In my opinion, laser therapy is a vital part of the future of medical care.

My patients are delighted that I am back practicing. I inform several of them of my diagnosis and my healing. They tell their families and friends about me, who then tell their friends. Patients in wheelchairs, severely disabled by CIDP and ALS (amyotrophic lateral sclerosis or Lou Gehrig's Disease) start to arrive at my office for a cure. They are desperate and come to me "as their last hope." I tell them prayer helped me and that I am not the answer, but God is. I pray with some, but some refuse. I am drained after each consultation.

Some patients ask me, "Why do you think you were so special to be chosen by God to be healed?" I tell them that I never thought I was special, and I don't know why I got the disease or why he healed me. But that I am thankful to be healed and know I have to practice again.

I stop telling what my illness was. I no longer have to know why I got sick or why God healed me. I am just thankful and believe in him.

❧

I have strength in my arms and legs. But I feel emptiness inside of me. I pray to God for guidance, for the answer to my burning desire to do something more for him.

My family shows me unwavering, unconditional love.

I become closer with my sister, Dona. She is a strong Christian and leader at her church. We weren't always fond of each other. I close my eyes and remember.

"Hi, Dona," I shout as I approach her. She stands next to her locker at school with a few of her girlfriends. Dona has perfect brown hair, a feat resulting from hours of preparation in early mornings, and a little pug nose. She is cute, but I don't tell her.

It is my first day at high school. Dona is a sophomore.

"Hi, Dona," I repeat and smile.

No response.

"Hey, Dona. Is he your brother?" giggles one of her friends.

My sister shrugs her shoulder and states, "Never mind. Let's get out of here."

She walks away. Her friends trail behind. Dona turns after a few steps and looks back at me. I see sadness in her eyes. I want to die. For three years, she's never talked to me at school.

Dona asks for forgiveness thirty-two years later when I get sick. She says she is so sorry and ashamed of herself. We hug and cry. I tell her I forgave her years ago. Then I reveal to her that I got revenge during those three years we were in high school together.

Popular guys, mainly jocks, would come up to me and ask if Dona had a date for that weekend. I guess macho guys are afraid of rejection.

If I didn't like them, especially if I had heard them boast about their girl conquests in the gym locker room, I would say yes even if she didn't.

My sister sat home on many weekends wondering why no one asked her out.

I smiled many times. Buddy told me I was wrong. I told him I knew it was bad, but I did it anyway.

❧

I continue to feel a need to do more, but I don't know what. I begin to pray several times a day, often short prayers like "Thank you for this day, Jesus. Guide me to do your work. Thy will be done."

John Cook, a patient, friend, and lawyer for the City of Indian Wells, California, enters my office. "Dr. Roberts, it's so good to see you again. I'm glad you're better," he says smiling.

"Me too." And then, surprising myself, I add, "But I feel emptiness inside of me like a hole in my heart. I have a burning desire to do something, to fill the hole, but I do not know what." I shake my head and place my right hand over my heart.

"Prison ministry. Join me in Kairos Prison Ministry," John states. His hands raise upwards, his eyes widen.

I feel a warm sensation flow throughout my body.

"Yes, that's it, I will!" I shout without concern over whether or not my patients in the waiting area or examination rooms can hear. "But what is Kairos Prison Ministry?" I ask with sudden bewilderment.

John laughs and shakes his head. "Let's get together soon, and I'll tell you all about it. But I really need help with my pain right now."

"Of course, but I must do the ministry. When can we get together?"

"Tomorrow."

"Great. Okay, now let me focus on you."

Later that night, I remember my prior wish for the prisoners to have my disease.

36

BLYTHE, CALIFORNIA

2000

I have to do the prison ministry.

I have never wanted to go to prison. I feel, like a lot of people, that prisoners deserve what they get and need to suffer. I meant it when I prayed to God to give my fatal illness to prisoners.

Now, I'm going to prison.

Kairos Prison Ministry is an ecumenical ministry to adults in medium and maximum-security prisons. The mission is to bring Christ's love and forgiveness to incarcerated individuals, their families, and those who work with them and to assist the incarcerated in the transition to becoming productive citizens. Kairos is a Greek word meaning God's special time.

I first attend a two-day Kairos qualifying/introductory weekend training program at the Methodist Church of Palm Springs. That is where I first meet Ed Carpenter.

Ed is a large man, a former longshoreman, a kind and spiritual man. He had a hard life before walking with Christ. He now is full of his spirit and feels a calling for prison ministry. Gwen, Ed's wife and angel, supports him and keeps him in line like Beverly does me. We four become dear friends. The Carpenters have been sent to us by God.

"Jay, I don't think I can do this ministry," Ed confides in me during a break on the first day of training.

"Why?" I ask, surprised.

"There is too much hugging. I'm not into hugging a man," he whispers.

"Well, I might not be able to do this ministry either," I admit.

"What? Why?"

"I overheard two of the men saying that we can only have one piece of lunchmeat in our sandwich and no lettuce, to get used to prison food. I like to eat," I whisper.

"I like to eat too," Ed chuckles.

"Ed, promise me that you won't quit if I don't."

"Okay. And you promise not to quit if I don't."

We shake. Ed leads us into a prayer for guidance and strength.

The program focuses on the basics of the ministry that would be presented in the prison. We learn the motto of Kairos: "Listen, Listen, Love, Love."

We eat little and sleep on the floor in the church's hall.

There are short talks and times for prayer to foster a team for Christ, one with the spirit of servanthood and humility. We are encouraged to recognize our limitations and acknowledge that with God's help, we can make a difference.

We become vulnerable as we pray and share together and find that we all have broken hearts, wounds that need healing. We need to let God enter our hearts and heal our wounds.

We are reminded of "I was in prison and you visited me" (Matt 25:36, NLT) and about how "Jesus washes his disciples' feet" in John 13:1-17.

We wash each other's feet.

I feel his presence as I am on my knees and wash the feet of a Kairos brother.

The prison rules are stressed. Some of the guidelines include:

a. No blue pants or blue shirts (prisoners wear blue).

b. No forest green pants or forest green shirts (guards wear forest green).

c. No tank tops or T-shirts (prisoners wear T-shirts).

d. All shirts with collars and no sayings or logos printed on them.

e. Do not take money, pocketknives, paging devices, beepers, car alarm activators, cellular phones, drugs, guns, expensive jewelry or watches, mints, medicine, or food, including gum and candy, into the institution.

f. Do not take any messages out of the prison. It may be a coded escape message.

g. Appreciate officers and other staff members' responsibilities.

Ed and I keep our promise. We both stay.

A few weeks later, an eight-week-team formation program is held to mold the team into a community recognizable as the body of Christ. It is highly structured, with a defined agenda for each Saturday meeting. The spiritual themes of the meetings include servanthood, vulnerability, the nature of God's love, the nature of our sinful love, humility, gratitude, compassion, and affirmation. There is time for praying, talking, listening, singing, eating, laughing, and crying.

We come to understand and know God as love and deepen this experience of God as a loving parent through our personal journey with Christ during those weeks of being molded into Christ's body.

It is the work of the Holy Spirit.

We must give unconditional agape love. Most of the inmates have had few, if any, visitors for years. We must introduce them to the powerful love of Christ.

After the Kairos Boot Camp, we are prepared to go to the prison for a four-day program. I will enter, along with twenty-two "outside" Kairos brothers, on Thursday morning and be "paroled" on Sunday night. Our volunteer team comes from a variety of social, economic, educational, and denominational backgrounds. Our religious experiences are varied. We learn to love when it hurts to love as well as when it is easy. We learn to love God with all our hearts and our neighbors as ourselves.

Ironwood State Prison is a medium-security, level-III facility in the desert, about thirty minutes away from the city of Blythe, California.

The first time I enter the security cage and the gates slam behind me, I feel trapped and pray that the gates will reopen. The gates do open but not behind me. They open in front of me and lead me deeper into the prison. After two more gates, I stand in an exercise yard of the prison.

There are five cement "houses" that face the brown, sandy, barren yard. Each cell has a small vertical window, a sliver of view to the outside. The facility has a designated capacity of 2,200 prisoners but has a total institution population of 3,945 (179%).

Inmates, segregated by race in their claimed area of the yard, stop to watch "the fresh meat" parade down the yellow-striped walkway and into a room that serves as the chapel. Officers with batons and pepper spray are on the yard; and those with rifles in the tower stand guard.

I carry an "alarm button." If I am in danger, I am supposed to press the alarm, and the "goon squad" will descend within two to three minutes. It is not that comforting to me since I think a lot of damage could be done in two to three minutes. After all, I have seen *The Shawshank Redemption*.

The prisoners are skeptical of us at first. They enter the program with hardened eyes, stiff backs, and gang postures. We are taught not to touch the inmates on the first day but to wait for them to extend their hand to us. Some of the inmates, most of whom are of color, have never allowed a white man to touch them before. They soon realize we do not want anything from them, a new concept for inmates.

There is a selection process, approved by the local chaplain and the warden, for the inmates to sign up for the program. The "bad" prisoners are sought, especially the leaders of the gangs.

Most of the prisoners do sign up out of boredom. It is a break in their daily routine for years. They hear there will be better food and good coffee.

Some come as a means to see and speak to their fellow gang members whose cells are in different houses. The yard has been in lockdown for eighteen months.

A few come to learn more about Christ but do not admit it at first. They do not want to show any sign of weakness or vulnerability.

We don't care for their earthly reasons. We know the Holy Spirit will work on them. We are here to witness God's work on them and on us.

One of the new prisoners I am assigned for the weekend is Asian. I try to talk to him the first day, but he remains mute, sitting in a defiant gang posture. After several attempts to find out where he was from, he leans into me, stares with cold dagger eyes, and says, "The Philippines, and so what!"

Without hesitation, I talk to him in Tagalog. His eyes widen. There is a hint of a smile on his hardened face. The stabs from his eyes blunt. I learn he is from the same province that I grew up in as a child. We talk loudly for thirty minutes.

"How many inmates are here today that can speak Tagalog?" I ask.

"I'm the only one. There are others in their cells, but I'm the only one here." He smiles and then asks, "How many of you outside guys can speak Tagalog?"

"I'm the only one. It's amazing that we are paired for today," I reply with a smile.

I want to pat his shoulder but do not. I wait for his hand to be offered.

"No. It's not amazing. It's God's doing," he announces with authority.

"You're right. You're absolutely right." My face reddens.

I am baffled. I am supposed to be introducing him to Christ, but he is reminding me of God's every presence and power.

God is great.

I am about to speak when he unfolds his arms and offers his hand. I extend my hand to give a firm shake. He is in control of the brief grasp, followed by his gang hand greeting that ends when his hand strikes his chest.

I just watch and smile.

We continue to chat nonstop.

We talk of childhood, about the beach where we both learned to swim, the food we miss, the coconut trees we climbed, the carabaos we rode, the bolos we swung, and the slingshots we made.

We do not talk of family.

We do not talk of why he is in prison.

He does ask me if I would pray for him.

I answer, "*Oh ho*" (yes with respect).

He responds, "Salamat po."

While we speak Tagalog, several of my outside brothers and inmates turn, stare, and shake their heads. Some smile. Some gaze upwards with raised hands.

Ed Carpenter beams at me and whispers, "Jay, I didn't know you have the gift of tongues."

"Ed, I'm not speaking in tongues. I'm speaking Tagalog."

"Well, the Holy Spirit is with you. I saw how that inmate opened up to you." Ed smiles and taps me on the back. His strong hand, from his longshoreman days, feels more like a slap.

A guard enters our room and orders all of us to the prison cafeteria for dinner. All the inmates line up and are patted down by several guards on the yard's walkway. We march in single file, take the thick plastic tray with food poured into the portioned areas that spill over to the adjacent spaces, and sit in order at round metal tables and stools that are bolted to the floor. Guards on the floor and in an inside tower with rifles survey for any untoward activity.

I thought the food would be bad. But I never expected the smell, a ripe odor, a mixture of food and body scent. We have three minutes to eat. I look at the tray, shake my head, and pray. The prisoners at my table tell me it is the prison variety of beef stroganoff. I hated beef stroganoff since I was in high school, and my sister cooked it weekly for months and months for a boyfriend that was to become her husband. Since she cooked it, we had to eat it.

My first meal in prison and it has to be beef stroganoff, cold stroganoff at that. I try not to show disrespect to the inmates who are devouring their portions. We are not allowed to share food. I wish I had my dog, Prince, who saved me at home when I was made by my parents to sit at the table, alone, until I cleaned my plate of stroganoff. I do the old routine of pushing my food around to make it look like I am eating something. I know the inmates are on to me.

I take a bite.

I cannot swallow it.

"Don't spit it out. Swallow it," Buddy encourages.

I swallow and gag.

The command to stand at the end of the three minutes is an appreciated order. I am the first at our table to stand, glad to surrender the tray and account for my spoon.

The Filipino inmate asks me if I liked the food.

I smile.

He laughs.

"Nothing like our adobo and pancit," he proclaims and rubs his stomach.

My stomach rumbles.

He continues to rub until he is lined up with the other prisoners outside of the cafeteria to be re-searched by the guards.

After the inmates return to their cells, we leave for a nearby church. I am pleased to see the prison gates open. I am displeased at our sleeping arrangements, sleeping bags on the floor. I admit I am more of a Four-Seasons-Hotel guy with one-thousand-thread-count sheets. But the worst is the noise, men snoring and farting. I have a sudden respect for their wives and hope that I never subjected Beverly to those sounds.

The worst offender is David Stewart, who sounds like four freight trains combined on one track. At one in the morning, I plead with him to leave the room. His cousin, Mike Lawliss, agrees. David complies and sleeps the rest of the night in his pickup truck.

After a meager breakfast, David forgives me for the "push to the curb." He understands. "I have been pushed out of rooms before," he says and gives me a hug.

Later that morning, I inform our weekend leader that I will be sleeping in a nearby motel. I promise to remain each night at the church until the conclusion of the evening prayer and return early each morning before prayer service. I assure him I will not miss any activities.

"No. Everyone sleeps at the church. It is for bonding and fellowshipping," the leader adamantly declares.

"I do not fellowship or bond with any man while I sleep." My voice raises a bit.

"It is against the rules," adds the leader.

"Then I'm sorry, but I'm breaking that rule."

And with that, I become the first "sleeping rebel" of our Kairos group.

Later that night, as I check into the motel, Ed Carpenter enters the lobby with a smile. "I'm with you, buddy. I need to get some sleep. I need my own room, my own bed. I guess we're the bad boys." Ed laughs.

"Yeah, I guess so. Sleep well. See you tomorrow morning."

It is a Motel 6 that feels like a Four Seasons compared to the room at the church.

My body thanks me the moment I sink onto the bed. My mind rests without the noises from men. My stomach thanks me when Ed and I eat breakfast at a nearby Denny's before we go back to the church in time for morning prayers.

Years later, all the Kairos brothers will sleep at a motel.

The next morning, as I enter the exercise yard, a group of Asians approach me. They do not cross the double yellow lines, the out-of-bounds markings. A guard in the tower, rifle poised, is my backup security.

They are Filipinos and speak to me in Tagalog. They have multiple life sentences. They shout, "*Mabuhay po!*" They bless me with long life and give it with highest respect.

"*Mabuhay din ho.*" I bless them with long life with respect.

They smile, chuckle, and walk away.

I wonder if wishing long life to an inmate with a life sentence without the possibility of parole is a blessing or an insult. I pray that I did not disrespect them. Showing respect and revealing no fear or vulnerability are crucial and fundamental to survival in prison.

I also wonder how they knew I could speak Tagalog. I have never met them before, and I have only been in prison for one day.

I am amazed at the incredible communication in prison. When the Filipino inmate that I met the day before entered his house and cell, he somehow communicated that the tall white man from the outside can speak Tagalog. And the message went from house to house after lights out without telephone, computer, or mail. There is a definite way to pass information in prison. I do not know how. But I am new to prison and have not earned the right to know such information. Not yet.

I learn another lesson later that day. Prisoners are observant. They notice everything, little or big. I guess it is part of their survival package.

"Jay, I've noticed you have not peed all day. Are you afraid to go to the bathroom?" asks an inmate, a member of the crime gang known as the Bloods.

"Absolutely not. In fact, I was just about to go," I reply and avoid looking into his eyes.

"Well, if you are concerned, I can go with you."

"No. That's okay. I don't need any help. But thanks anyway."

I get out of my chair and head to the bathroom before he can offer me help again. I do not want to disrespect him. But there is no way I want his help to pee.

The truth is, I have been holding my urine for hours. I saw the bathroom earlier and do not look forward to the experience. The front of the bathroom is one big window for guards, and everybody, to see everything. There are no partition walls, no doors, and no toilet paper. Just toilets stuck out of the floor.

I pee faster than I have ever before. In that situation, you forget about any advice on how many times you should shake it! My instrument goes back inside my pants in record speed. Several inmates smile at me. I never ask why. I prefer to think it is for acknowledging my rite of passage or for knowing how long I waited by the volume of flow.

Then another lesson. No soap and no paper towels. I find out that the inmates bring their own sheet of paper with them. But there is no mention of soap. A flash of all the handshakes I have done for two days nauseates me.

We have been told not to bring in any supplies.

I express my "medical" concern for cleanliness to the leader of our group. Toilet paper and soap are then supplied upon request to the outside team members. But we are given only a few sheets of paper at a time, and the supply runs out before the end of the day.

"Buddy. I've accepted the rationing of food. But I draw the line with toilet paper. It's like camping. You do your business quickly. But there are no trees, bushes, or leaves."

"Behave. You'll be fine."

Later, a key is given to a senior member of our outside team that opens the officers' bathroom down the hallway. The outside team is allowed to use this room.

Ah, paradise found!

I walk back to the chapel. My back is stiff; my steps, strong and sturdy. "Everything okay?" the Blood asks.

A fellow gang member smiles.

"Yep. Just fine." I smile and stare into his eyes. My gaze aborted with visions of my father's eyes in his.

"Is everything fine?" he asks again.

"Yes. Thanks. Now where were we? Let's get back to our discussion." I want the focus off of me. And I do not want to show any fear.

I can hear my father's command.

Be strong.

The Blood brother leans toward me and says, "Be strong, you'll be fine in here. I've got your back."

I almost fall out of my chair. Those are my father's words coming out of a black inmate's mouth, minus having my back. I fight to keep my mouth closed and my feet planted. I'm sure glad I already peed. I might have lost it then.

Much later, I'm told that the Blood brother is a shot caller.

A shot caller is the boss, the leader of the pack, who makes decisions for the gang. It is the highest position in the pecking order.

I bond with the Blood brother. He's a tall, muscular, ebony-skinned, hardened man who rarely smiles. His eyes can pierce through you.

We talk and pray one-on-one together as part of the program and learn that we have something in common, abusive fathers, and learned to keep secrets, to hide wounds. He was violated as a child by an uncle, the brother of his father.

He has never told anyone of his abuse before. It would have made him weak and vulnerable to his gang. He could be taken out, because of the "shame," and overthrown as the shot caller.

I am shocked that he told me. I know it has to be the Holy Spirit working through me. I seem to say the right words at the right time. And I know when to say nothing, just listen.

He had thought his heart was dead and that no one loved him, including God. When I told him God loved him as much as he loves my sons, he felt his heart anew. He looked into my eyes and knew I spoke the truth.

He offered his hand, and we prayed. He tried to wipe his tears, but I held his hands. He cried and bowed his head. We sat in silence for several minutes.

His hands grip mine with controlled strength. He looks up, stares back into my wet eyes and gives a little smile, increases his grip strength with a few shakes, and releases my hands. He takes in a deep breath. His eyes glance around the chapel room to see if anyone has been watching.

No one has.

He turns back to me. A huge smile exposes his perfect set of white teeth. We stand and leave the room for a break. He whispers a thank you as we step into the yard.

I answer in a low voice, "You're welcome."

I stand outside the door.

He walks to the black area of the yard. His gang members welcome him with their sign. He talks with exaggerated hand gestures; his fingers, fixed in a posture duplicated by other gang members.

He is in his environment, his home for the past fifteen years. He is strong and in control. He is a different person on the yard than I witnessed inside the room. But he has the same heart. And that heart has just felt unconditional agape love, God's love.

I pray for guidance to help my Blood brother, Chris.

As I pray, I remember I have not always helped my blood brother, Robbie. He was my father's favorite.

I was beaten and told to be like him. I resented him and even tormented him.

❧

Robbie is afraid of the dark. He is in first grade. I am in fifth. At night, I turn the bedroom light off and close the door. He screams and remains frozen, immobile in terror.

I am beaten and go play with Buddy.

❧

The image of my father's eyes in Chris's eyes haunts me that night in the motel room as I sleep.

❧

The bright reflection of light from the butcher knife shines across my father's face. He does not move. The stench of beer heightens as air is forced out between his puffed out lips during each exhalation. He will not stir for hours. I have time. My grip on the knife is firm, insured by a two-hand hold. I try. I try again. The knife remains at my eye level. I try again and again to stab his eyes. The knife will not move. He is right. I am weak. I am weak.

❧

I awake soaked in sweat, my hands clutched in fists. It is two in the morning. I watch the hours pass on the clock, relieved at the first sign of daybreak. A strange feeling comes over me. I feel safer in prison.

The first time I walk the exercise yard, I'm surprised to see outdoor showers.

"Hey, you guys don't have it so bad in here," I joke to some inmates who walk with me.

It's not advisable to walk the yard alone. Your back needs protection. Inmates walk in packs of not more than six. If more than six inmates are spotted together on the yard, untoward activity is suspected by the guards. Gunfire could be used to disperse the crowd.

We are taught that during a riot, we are not to "fall" as the prisoners are ordered. The inmates learn to dive off any paved surface and preferably land on sand. They could be down for hours and easily be burnt by hot pavement in the desert, especially during summer months. We are told to remain standing and slowly walk backward to the nearest wall. Our backs should be at least six inches from the concrete wall to avoid being hit by ricocheting bullets. If we fall down by mistake, we are to stay down. Any movement detected by the guards in the tower will be shot at.

"Jay, those showers are only used after a disturbance on the yard when we're pepper sprayed. They are not for showering at will," an inmate says and shakes his head.

"Okay. Okay. I am learning." I try to offset my ignorance of prison life.

We enter one of the inmates' cells under strict supervision by guards. I can stretch my arms across the width of the cell and touch both walls. There are metal bunk beds, a small metal table bolted to the floor, a tiny metal sink, and a metal toilet without lid next to the metal door with bars. The design allows for complete view of the cell by the guards. A string crosses the space from which laundry is hung. A small television perched on a shelf blares and flickers. There is no refrigerator. No visible cooking device, although later I learn there are improvised hot plates. The inmates are very creative. All types of devices are made, some for good use, some not. It is a cage, a cell, not a home.

A bad odor permeates the cell. Then a toilet flushes in the next cell.

"Jay, it's not that bad. We do our best. We survive." The inmate and his "cellie" fist pump.

"I can see that you do make do with what you have." I do not know what else to say.

They are like caged animals as they take a few steps from one end of their cell to the other. I do not want to tell them that their cell is horrible. They are in their early twenties and "LWOPs" (life without parole). This is their home for life.

But the inmates read my thoughts.

The horror is in my eyes.

They try to reassure me, to comfort me. They're fine in their cells.

They do not know that part of my devastated look is guilt for having wanted them to suffer even more with my disease.

I am ashamed of myself.

I remember, "Judge not, that you be not judged. For with what judgment you judge, you will be judged; and with the measure you use, it will be measured back to you" (Matthew 7:1-2, NKJV.)

I ask Buddy, "Who am I to judge them, to want my illness to be added to their punishment?"

"You're a good person. You were angry at the time. They will understand. Ask for forgiveness," he encourages with a whisper.

"Are you kidding? They'll hate me. I am here to show them God's love. And now, you want me to let them know how much I hated them."

"Yes. Tell them. Ask them. They will understand."

"Or take me out in a second."

"No. You made a mistake. They will forgive."

A tap on my shoulder sets my friend deeper inside of me.

"Jay. Are you okay?" asks one of the inmates.

"Yes. I'm fine. Just thinking." I smile.

"Don't look so doomed. We're fine."

"I know you are. My mind was on something else for a moment."

"Anything that we can help you with?" asks the other inmate.

"Maybe. But we have to get back to the chapel. Thanks for showing me your home." I smile as well as I can.

"Officer, we're ready to leave," I announce.

As we walk back to the chapel, Buddy keeps at me. "Just tell them."

"Okay already. I will."

Later in the day in the chapel, I have a heavy heart. I know I have to ask for forgiveness.

Our chapel room is about twenty by eighteen feet. It has concrete walls with smudged white paint, secured overhead fluorescent lights, and a concrete floor. No windows. A paper cross is taped on the front wall. The central air-conditioner fails to keep the room cool.

There are thirty-six prisoners and eighteen outside men in the room.

Six inmates in prison blue and three outside brothers sit on plastic chairs around a circular table. Paper and a small, dull pencil are supplied to take notes. My "table family" has prisoners from the Crips, Bloods, Asian, Hispanic, and White gangs. There are five other table families in the room, with more African Americans than Hispanics, Whites, Orientals and Asians, and Native Americans. The tables are known as "families" of Mark, James, John, Luke, Matthew, and Peter.

It is a tight squeeze.

We pray for God's guidance.

Our assigned discussion at that time is forgiveness of others.

There is dead silence at our table.

I swallow and speak.

"I have to ask forgiveness of others." My voice is low.

They lean toward the center of the table.

"I have to ask forgiveness from all of you." My voice becomes hoarse.

Their eyes shift. Their bodies remain still.

"I had a fatal illness. I prayed to God to give my illness to prisoners, to you, a plea to God out of ignorance and despair." My throat dries.

They remain motionless.

"I was so wrong. I now understand that God loves you as much as he loves my sons." My eyes water, and my stomach feels like a horse kicked it.

Their eyes drill into mine.

"I am sorry. I ask for your forgiveness."

I bow my head.

"Buddy, help me. I don't want to cry."

"It's okay to cry," he gently whispers.

I weep inside. I close my eyes. One by one, they all say, "I forgive you."

Then Chris prays, "God, protect Jay. He's a good man. He's in pain. Please help him."

I hear others add, "Amen."

"Jay, please stand," Chris requests as he places his hand on my shoulder.

I stand and receive hugs from Bloods, Crips, Asian, and White gang members, my family brothers.

My heart feels warm.

A wound has healed.

God is present.

When I arrive back home from the four-day prison program, I stand in front of the refrigerator, open the door, and stare inside. It reminds me of my sons when they come home to visit from college. They stare into the refrigerator. When I ask what they are looking for, the answer is always, "Nothing, just looking."

Beverly sees me at the refrigerator. "Honey, what are you looking for?"

"Nothing, just looking." I smile.

She gives me a kiss.

The next few days, I continue to think of the brothers I met in prison when I open the refrigerator, enjoy the privacy of a bathroom, use a fork and knife to eat, place a napkin on my lap, eat tasty and identifiable warm food, and walk anywhere I want and whenever I want beyond the defined steps in a cell.

I have also come to realize that we all have made good and bad choices, some worse than others. I wonder if my choices would have led me to prison if I had lived in the hood, did not know who my father was, was sold for sex for my mother's drug habit, had all my relatives in prisons, and the only family I knew was my gang.

❧

I return to prison monthly for a one-day reunion and prayer-and-share time and twice a year for the Thursday-to-Sunday week-end program.

I do not judge the prisoners. They have been tried and sentenced. I do not discuss their conviction or possible innocence. I do not want to hear a confession to a crime that could land me in court to testify against the prisoner. I am there to visit and show Christ's love for it states in Matthew 25:36 (NLT), "I was in prison and you visited me."

I begin to receive letters from the inmates by means of a secured P.O. box. The prisoners are not allowed to know my home address. The letters are written on all types of paper, any paper the prisoner could obtain. Some use pens, others pencils. Some with tear stains, others with food stains. All are heartfelt and appreciated.

The letters speak of gratitude for visiting them. Some are explicit in enlightening me to the significance of our time together, which transferred them from being suspicious with a gang attitude and posture the first day to holding hands and praying with a white man the next day. They inform me I am the first man who ever really listened to them and did not want anything from them. They have never shown weakness or vulnerability to anyone in prison before, but they have cried, hugged, and laughed with me.

One letter stands out in my mind. An eighteen-year-old prisoner, recently incarcerated with a life sentence, asked me to continue to pray for him. I had prayed with him during my last prison visit. He is young and handsome. The night he wrote his letter to me, he slept with his clothes and shoes on. The word is out that he would be "punked." At the end of the letter, he praised God and stated that it was already morning and nothing happened to him but to please continue to pray for him. Tears smudge his writing.

When I next visit him in prison, he has black eyes and bruises.

He asks for continued prayers.

I pray with misty eyes.

He never writes again.

37

CALIPATRIA, CALIFORNIA

2004

I am transferred to Calipatria State Prison, along with Ed Carpenter and several of my other Kairos brothers. Calipatria State Prison stands in the desert three miles from Calipatria, California. It is a maximum-security, level IV facility designed for a capacity of 2, 208 people but with a population of 4,271 (193%). Two inmates in bunk beds share a cell designed for one. The facility resembles Ironwood State Prison but with more barbwire fences and wall perimeters, more electronic security, and more staff and armed officers. A $1.5 million electrified fence, which could cause instantaneous death for escapees, was installed in November 1993. The fence was redesigned after a number of birds died by electrocution. I guess the free-flying birds were valued more than the escaping birds.

Ed and I have vowed to stick together. We have had each other's back like "cellies" since our boot camp, strengthened in prison at Ironwood.

I learned that *we* are the church. No matter what building or parcel of land, including in prison, *we* are the church. Worship is our spirit connecting with God's spirit. I have lacked affirmation, which is critical for my spiritual growth. My Kairos brothers, especially Ed, affirm me. I feel God's spirit within me.

I have seen and now believe that love is the expression of God within us. We are each filled with the spirit of God equally. "There is one body and one Spirit..., one God and Father of all, who is above all, and through all, and in you all." (Ephesians 4:4 and 6, NLT).

I feel blessed. I have a loving family, wonderful friends, and a great practice. I am free and can open a refrigerator.

I am committed to the ministry.

I never thought I would be a farmer planting seeds or a fisherman casting out nets in prison for Christ.

"Here I am, Lord. I come to do your will."

I have witnessed God's work.

In three days, I watch rival gang members talk and pray together, see peace on the faces of hardened prisoners, hear cries to Jesus for help from the inmates, witness forgiveness after years of hatred, sing and dance the Hokey Pokey with maximum-security prisoners, and observe an outside group of men from diverse backgrounds united in Christ learn when to listen and when to speak the right word at the right time.

At the end of each day, we form a large circle and hold hands. Whites, Bloods, Crips, Mexicans, and Asians interlock hands in peace and sing *Surely the Presence of the Lord.*

> *Surely the presence of the Lord is in this place. I can feel God's mighty power and His grace. I can hear the brush of angels' wings. I see glory on each face. Surely the presence of the Lord is in the place.*
>
> —Wolfe, Lanny, "*Surely the Presence of the Lord,*"
> Lanny Wolfe Music, 1977

We sing it twice; on the second time, all of the interlocked hands are raised above our heads and smiles cross many of the inmates' faces.

The Spirit of God is upon us.

He surely is in our place!

Prison has changed me. My family, friends, and patients comment that I seem more at peace and have become a better listener.

During one of my prison visits, a guard almost assaults me. I have to use the bathroom. I run down a hallway, slide around a corner, and encounter a guard positioned to strike my head with his baton. He had heard the rapid footsteps from a presumed inmate and was prepared to protect himself. His eyes widen. He evokes the name of Jesus in a non-pious shout, lowers his stick, then shouts, "You're not in Disneyland. Do not run, especially toward an officer."

My throat tightens. My tongue is parched. My response, "Yes, sir!"

I still have to pee.

On another prison visit, I become aware of the vastness of skills locked up in the cells. I walk with some inmates around the exercise yard during a break from our prayer-and-share meeting. I overhear two of the inmates talking about safes.

"I can't open a safe in my office. I have not used the safe for years and forgot the combination. I think there's money inside, but I do not know how much," I confess.

"I sure wish you could bring it in here. I could open it in no time," boasts an inmate.

"Yeah. My fingers itch. I could open it in seconds. I used to—"

I halt the other inmate's declaration. I don't want to hear a confessed crime.

"Well, it sure would be great to use your expertise. But I don't think I can get that safe past the guards." I point to the tower.

"Yeah, but it sure would be fun." The inmate kicks some sand but not enough for the guard to spot.

As we continue our slow walk, I notice all the inmates have the same swagger, regardless of race. But they hang with their race for survival.

Later that day, in the safety of the chapel room, I mimic the prison swag, much to the amazement and delight of the inmates.

Months and years pass and we remain committed to the Kairos Ministry. Exhaustion and outside-life pressures tempt each of us, at times, to quit, but the strength of our group of Christian men from different churches and backgrounds, with our prayers and encouragement, keeps most of us strong. Our group, diverse in flesh, is united in spirit.

The friendship among Ed Carpenter, his wife Gwen, Beverly, and myself blossomed like a prize-winning rose and strengthened my spiritual walk. One night, Beverly and I were getting ready to go out for dinner with the Carpenters. I was selecting a tie when I saw Tatay's tie hanging in the back of the tie racks. I had kept the tie for years but never wore it. I removed the tie, and held it to my heart. I knew Buddy was right. Nanay did love me. I forgave her, but it took another year before I gave the tie away.

I am often asked, "Why do you do prison ministry? Can't you do something safer?"

I answer, "I don't *want* to do it. I *have* to do it."

And it brought me Ed and Gwen Carpenter.

✤

During the next four-day program, I give the forgiveness-series talk to the prisoners. The room looks like the chapel at Ironwood State Prison except for an elevated portion at the front of the room where the crucifix is taped on the wall and the wooden podium stands. It also has six tables and chairs for the thirty-six prisoners and eighteen outside men to sit around as table families named after the same apostles. It is a tight squeeze with a similar air-conditioner that struggles to keep the room cool. The race mixture of the inmates is still more African Americans than Hispanics, Whites, Orientals and Asians, and Native Americans.

I stand in front of the inmates and outside brothers, behind a wooden podium.

A brief prayer, a deep breath, and Buddy commanding me to be strong combine to help my mouth open.

"Hi. I am Jay Roberts, a layperson, and a sinner. Forgiveness includes acceptance of self. I thought I was a good Christian, but I was wrong. I was suddenly hit with a fatal neurological disease. I could not believe the doctor's diagnosis. You see, I'm a physician, and I could not possibly have that fatal disease. I had done nothing wrong. I was a good guy. I may have sinned before but not major sins. Well, the diagnosis was correct, and within one and a half years, I became progressively paralyzed, not being able to use my arms or legs. I was near death. I was very mad, very mad at God. I did not want to die." My voice cracks.

"I wanted to live and be with my wife and two sons. I thought I was strong in faith, but I was not. I was so angry and didn't believe I deserved this fate. I swore at God and told him that those bad prisoners deserve my disease, not me. I said, 'Give my disease to those prisoners who are more of a sinner than me.'"

My knees buckle a bit.

"At the weakest point of my condition, I prayed to God for forgiveness. I no longer felt that I was less of a sinner than anyone else, even you inmates. I submitted myself to the saving grace of Jesus Christ. I fell asleep praying. I awoke the next morning able to move my arms and legs. I thanked God for my healing. I felt sick and ashamed of wanting my disease to be given to you."

My eyes fill.

"When invited to be a part of Kairos Ministry, I felt a bolt of warmth go through me. I knew that God wanted me to be in this ministry. I was able at my first weekend in prison at Ironwood State Prison in Blythe to ask for forgiveness from the inmates in the room. I was forgiven and felt God's love."

My tears swell.

After a few blinks of my eyes, I proceed.

"I am still a sinner, one who continues to fall. I still feel guilty for my sins. I do not want to sin. I know now that Jesus Christ died for my sins and for all of our sins. Acceptance of myself and receiving the healing power of Jesus Christ has helped me in my life, a life that now includes being a part of Kairos. Forgiveness of yourself will also be powerful and healing."

I take a deep breath and continue.

"Forgiveness also includes acceptance of God's forgiveness. The Bible is filled with statements assuring us that God forgives us of anything we might have done if we are willing to ask for that forgiveness and accept it. Some of us have decided it would be hard for God to forgive us. This is not the case. We must remember that love and forgiveness are God's nature. Not to forgive is what would be hard, so hard that God was unable to hold back his forgiveness even when it cost him his son. It is probably our enormous pride that keeps us from accepting forgiveness. In our self-centeredness, we see our evil, our sinful acts, as being so exceptional, so great, that what God did for us is not enough to wipe away such sin. We are, in fact, saying, 'Jesus, you haven't done enough for me yet. Dying on that cross was not enough to answer for what I have done.'" My lower lip trembles.

I bow my head. After a short pause, I stand straighter.

"And forgiveness includes forgiveness of others. I have told you I received forgiveness from prisoners in Ironwood. But I have needed to forgive someone in my family, my father."

I take a deeper breath, lock my knees, and stiffen my back.

"He beat me with various forms of objects, including wire clothes hangers, belt buckles, and even a whip. He beat me with emotional whippings as well. I never felt a soft touch from him or ever heard him say that he loved me. I hated my father. But now, I want to forgive him."

My knees start to flex. My fingers burrow into the side of the wooden podium.

"All of us have prayed the Lord's Prayer many times. Let me ask a question. How would we stand if God answered that prayer with a 'yes!'? Think about it. We pray, 'forgive us our trespasses as we forgive those who trespass against us.' Jesus goes on to emphasize this point by saying, 'If you forgive others the wrongs they have done to you, God will also forgive you. But if you do not forgive others, then God will not forgive the wrongs that you have.'"

My eyes cloud.

"To forgive those who have hurt us and to ask forgiveness from those who we have hurt can be risky. It requires becoming vulnerable to the other person. And when we become vulnerable, we sometimes get hurt. I understand the risk is greater in prison. Your key to survival is to show no vulnerability. To do so could be fatal."

I pause.

Some of the prisoners gaze downwards. Others stare straight ahead.

"God loves the person I hate with the same love he has for me. I can't love the person I hate with my own resources, but when I forgive that person and pray good for him or her and ask God to fill me with divine love and compassion for that person, Jesus can and does make it possible for me to love."

More heads bow.

"I told you I want to forgive my father. But I waited too long to tell him. He died before he could hear my words of forgiveness. I now wish I had told him. I hope you will not wait to forgive."

More inmates gaze downwards.

I think they have also been told as a child, "Be strong. Men do not cry."

After my talk, I instruct the prisoners to bow their heads and contemplate for a few minutes on what my talk meant to them.

I have never talked about forgiveness of my father before.

When I was assigned the topic of forgiveness, I did not want to do it.

I sit in a corner with my head bowed and hands folded and pray for God to continue to guide me and to help me speak the right words to the prisoners now that they know of my wounds. My heart warms and I feel a hole is closing.

After the long silence, all heads rise, most eyes wet. Break time is announced. Coffee and cold, flat cinnamon rolls are served. The prisoners are delighted. I cannot eat or drink. My stomach is in knots.

I follow a Blood, Anthony, into the exercise yard. He is tall and strong and has a polished, shaved head, dark chocolate tattooed skin, and fierce eyes. We have just prayed together in the chapel. As we held hands in prayer, he told me a white guy could never have touched him on the outside. He whispered to me that he could relate to my story. He also has a mean father. He hates his father too. His eyes seemed to water as he spoke. His grip tightened.

Outside in the yard, I touch his shoulder. I had wanted to tell him I would pray for him and ask for him to pray for me. My touch freezes him and my voice. I had forgotten we were no longer in the private chapel room.

He is a leader in his gang. A white man cannot touch him. If a white man does touch him, he would have to "deal with it." Or else, his gang would deal with it and take the offender and him out.

He orders, "Jay, just step away. Get away from me."

I look around and see several black inmates glare at us with anger.

"I'm so sorry. Will you be alright?" I ask as I recoil my hand.

"Yes. But walk away now," he barks and he walks into the black area of the yard.

He is not harmed after some fast talking and chest pounding.

After returning to the sanctuary of our chapel, Anthony shakes my hand and reminds me of the danger of touching him in the yard. I had broken a serious prison rule. It could have cost him his life.

Giving the forgiveness talk was a difficult challenge, but it was rewarding. I had to become vulnerable, something I was taught not to do. Many prisoners identified with my struggle. They were surprised to be able to relate to me, a white man from a "privileged home."

"Jay, thank you for sharing. I want to shake your hand. I have never touched a white man before or allowed one to touch me. On the outside, I was your worst enemy. You do not want to know what I did," voices a tall, strong, fierce-looking Crips brother.

"You're welcome. And you're right. I don't want to know what you did."

"Jay, I want to thank you too," adds a rugged Bloods brother.

"Sure. I also don't want to know what you would have done to me on the outside."

"You're right." The Bloods brother smiles.

It is God working through me. Two members of rival black gangs in the same prison, who tried to harm each other for years, now talk to each other and touch me. The next day, we all hold hands and pray in a circle. I witness God's work that day.

I am his servant.

Later that afternoon, I am informed by gang leaders, inmates that heard my forgiveness talk, that I can safely go anywhere in the exercise yard. No one would harm me.

"Go ahead. Walk anywhere and you'll see," boosts a Crip.

"Yeah. No one will dare touch you. The word is out that you're protected," adds a Blood.

"That's right," chimes a Mexican gang member.

"Yep. Even in our area," proclaims a white skinhead with a swastika tattoo on his forehead.

"That sounds great, but I'm comfortable right here." I clear my throat.

"You're not afraid, are you?" asks the Blood.

"No. I'll walk around later," I respond, trying not to have a crack in my voice or allow my knees to buckle.

A few hours later, I do venture out. I feel confident as I walk into the black-only area of the exercise yard. Black prisoners perform chin-ups. Their ripped abdomens shine.

Everyone stops.

The guards in the towers are on alert.

I walk over to a chin-up bar. I unloosen my shirt, jump up, and grab hold of the bar.

Oh God, what am I doing?

"Buddy," I call for help.

"Be strong. I am here," he whispers.

I have not done a chin-up since high school. I try to pull myself up. No success. I try again. No luck. All of a sudden, I feel pressure on both sides of my ribcage.

Oh, that doesn't hurt so bad.

I expected stabbings by shanks to be more painful.

I glance at my sides as I maintain a firm grip on the bar. I am going up and down as if performing multiple chin-ups. The hands of two black prisoners compress my chest. Long fingers dig into my ribs as they lift me up and down on the bar.

Cheers ring out from the yard.

It isn't until later, with my shirt tucked back in as I walk away from the black area, when my legs feel weak, not my arms. I know that I am a white man who entered the black exercise area and touched their bar. And I came out alive. I do feel protected.

God is with me.

❧

Despite giving the forgiveness talk and witnessing God's work, I struggle in my spiritual walk, and resist forgiveness of others. Through Kairos Prison Ministry and with my Christian brothers' prayers, I am able to tear down my wall. As I remove stones from my wall—stones of fear, envy, mistrust, self-pity, stubbornness, and pride—I feel light in my heart. The temptation to rebuild is strong, especially when vulnerable or hurt. But the last stone of my wall, hatred, is the hardest to remove. It is large and heavy and keeps my father out and Buddy safe.

I know I must remove the stone.

I know for God to forgive, I must forgive. "For if you forgive men their trespasses, your heavenly Father will also forgive you. But if you do not forgive men their trespasses, neither will your Father forgive your trespasses" (Matthew 6:14-15, NLT). "And whenever you stand praying, if you have anything against anyone, forgive him, that your Father in heaven may also forgive you your trespasses" (Mark 11:25, NKJV).

My failure to forgive and my continued hatred of my father distresses me more than I initially realized. I lose weight. I feel suffocated even outdoors in fresh air, sense gloom inside, and have an ominous heaviness on my heart, like the weight of a tombstone.

I have pleaded for the prisoners to forgive, but I have not. I cannot look into the inmates' eyes. I still want to hate my father.

I stop going to the prison for a few years but stay connected to the prison ministry. I attend the weekly prayer-and-share meetings with my outside Kairos brothers, and the monthly Kairos board meetings.

I go to weekly Mass and serve as Lecture and Eucharistic Minister. I read the Bible more and attend a Bible class with Beverly and the Carpenters.

I find that the evidence of God's love for me has been all around all along. Only I could not see it. I could not find Jesus. I discover, at those times when I see only one set of footprints in the sand, it is God who carries me. He never leaves me. He is always there. I do not find Jesus. He is not lost or hidden. He awaits an invitation to enter my life.

My Kairos brothers, inside and out, pray that I will return to prison. I often think of the inmates. I feel I have abandoned them. My heart is heavy.

I pray for strength to return to prison. I feel the same warmth in me as when I first heard of prison ministry. I know he wants me to return.

I obey.

The inmates greet me with respect on my return. Some shake hands, some fist pump, some give hugs. They are all there, at least all that I remembered. Most are "lifers without" and will be there for years and years.

It doesn't take long for the inmates to pick up right where we left off years ago, with forgiveness. It has to be forgiveness. It couldn't have been servanthood, vulnerability, or any other number of topics. No, it has to be forgiveness.

God does work in mysterious ways. I guess he knows what I need. I guess he knows I am ready.

A large, dark chocolate Muslim prisoner looks deep into my eyes. He has his strong hands on my shoulders. He had heard my forgiveness talk a few years ago and related to it. He senses my continued difficulty with forgiveness of my father. He says, "Jay, just do it. Forgive your dad." He shakes my shoulders gently and repeats his plea, "Just forgive him." His eyes cry for submission.

It is at that moment I know that I can forgive my father. It takes a Muslim prisoner in a level-IV maximum-security prison to shake me at the right moment and say the right words to release me from my own imprisonment. He has given me my key to release me from my prison.

We walk outside into the exercise yard, packed with prisoners. I look up. Small black birds, like the ones on the island, fly overhead.

I feel free. I am in prison but feel I can soar.

Then alarms blast.

Prisoners drop.

Guards scramble.

A "disturbance" has occurred on the yard. I remain standing and inch back toward the concrete wall. I stop about six inches from the wall and look up at the guard tower.

Rifles are poised for fire.

I am free but definitely not in Disneyland. I stand like a statue and pray.

Lord, help us, guide us, and protect us.

A blaze of brightness shines through my heart. Alarms stop, prisoners rise. We return to the chapel.

Our program for the day ends, and I watch the inmates stroll back to their cells. Prince, the Muslim prisoner, turns and nods at me. His eyes stare into mine as if looking into my soul and seeing my secrets, my deepest wounds.

I pray to God for strength. I know that he has watched me build my wall and that only through his grace can my final stone be removed. I ask him in to remove the stone and mend my wounded heart.

His hand comes upon me and the stone of hatred is blasted. A blaze of brightness shines through my heart.

The stone is gone.

Later, I put part of the stone back, out of fear, triggered by a nose, a vision of my father's nose.

It takes years for me to throw it back down.

It takes a visit to a cemetery.

EPILOGUE

ONALASKA, WASHINGTON

2010

Bright orange and red leaves of medium-size maple trees sway below the taller, dark green forest trees that line I-5 North Freeway and Washington State Route 508. I landed earlier in Portland, Oregon, and am en route to Onalaska, Washington.

"Buddy, I can't do this. I'm going to tell the driver to turn around."

"Jay, be strong. You can do it. You need to do it," he says.

As I approach Shoestring Cemetery, I sit taller in the backseat and look out the Town Car window. A flock of birds fly overhead in a V formation. The sky is dark. A mist blankets the countryside. Rain is in the forecast. I feel calm despite the impending storm outside.

The driver opens my door and I step out. I feel a chill and zip my jacket up. I am alone. No one else walks the sacred grounds.

I search over tombstones and wonder if there are good and bad memories buried in each grave.

Happy memories of my past several years rush through my head.

Ryan graduated from USC and Hastings Law School in San Francisco. He has a successful law firm in South Lake, Texas, near Dallas. He is married to our dear Emily. They have two children, my pride and joy, Maxwell Jay and Kate Belle. I am the first Grandpa Roberts to see the birth of a grandson. They are expecting a second son.

Derek graduated from USC, where he also played basketball. Then he played professional basketball and modeled in the Philippines for two years. He subsequently returned to the States, graduated from SMU's MBA program in Dallas, Texas, and is a senior management consultant for telecommunications in San Francisco, California. He is engaged to the love of his life, Anna. They are to be married soon.

Beverly, my angel, advisor, and protector, has stayed at my side. She obtained a MFCC degree at Loma Linda University in Riverside, California, and has been providing psychotherapy for troubled and abused children for several years. She heals their wounds. I adore her. I feel I do not deserve her but am thankful God knows I do.

Sad memories come into my mind, including the passing of my father-in-law, mother-in-law, Rody, and Nanay.

I have a good relationship with my sister Dona and an okay relationship with my mother. I am still resentful that my mother taught me love hurts and that my dad beat me because he loved me.

My brother Rob resembles my father in looks and temperament. I avoid him.

I continue my search. I have found the tombstones of my grandmother, great-grandmother, aunts, and uncles but not the one I seek.

And there it is. I have found it.

Thirty-two years have passed since my father's funeral, and this is the first time I have returned to his burial place.

The clouds darken, the sky roars, and rain sprays the land. My hair and clothes are wet. My mouth is dry.

The spray stops, but it is gloomy outside and inside of me.

The air is frigid. My stare is cold.

Suddenly, a small light shines on my father's grave. I turn and look upwards. A sliver of sunlight shines through a small break in the black clouds.

As I refocus on the grave, the spot of light widens.

"Why couldn't you have told me just once that you loved me? Why didn't you hold my hand and take me for a walk in a park, or show me how to swing a baseball bat, or throw a ball, or dribble a ball? Or why not just a simple gentle touch? Do you know that just one sign of love from you, I would have gladly taken more beatings."

I turn my back on him and scream and scream.

Moans, guttural noises, and wounded-animal-like sounds pour out of me.

Birds nearby take flight.

My legs weaken as I look again at the gravesite.

"I do not hate you anymore. I do not love you, but I do not hate you."

God, give me strength.

My legs and back stiffen.

"I forgive you, Dad."

My head bows.

Tears flow.

As I walk back toward the Town Car, I feel free like the birds that soar overhead.

My stone of unforgiveness, which kept me captive all these years, has fallen and has been buried with my father.

More tears flow.

I am strong.

I did not quit.

Men can cry.

A smile consumes my face.

A rustle of grass behind me halts my walk and erases my smile. I glance back and see a hand on top of the grave. The hand with its thick, stubby digits and brownish-yellow hair scratches and crawls across the grave toward me. There are no windows to slam and latch to protect me.

My eyes widen as the hand jumps.

My eyes refocus. A wild rabbit, with its dirty brown-and-yellow paws, hops further along the gravesite and into the adjacent meadow.

My smile returns.

My walk resumes with a wider stride as I look to my next mission for today. I must talk to Robbie and explain about the walls that surrounded me and kept him out and ask him to forgive me.

The sky darkens. Thunder snaps and sounds like the crack of a bullwhip.

I jump into the Town Car for protection.

"Let's go." My voice strains.

Another thunderous crack of a whip lashes. I flinch.

"I said let's go. Please!"

The driver nods, and we leave Shoestring Cemetery. I flinch at the sound of another thunderous crack, but I never look back. *Some wounds are not easily sutured, some impossible. I forgave but cannot forget.*

As I ride to meet my brother, I look out the car window. The sky darkens but my mind clears.

I close my eyes.

The deep rumble of the thunder vibrates in my ears like the bass and soulful voices of the prisoners as they sing. Some of the words resonate loud and tremble.

> Break the chains…deep within me
> Lord…set me free
> Heal the pain…deep within me
> Lord…set me free
> Make a change…deep within me
> Lord…set me free
> Let love reign…deep within me
> Lord…set me free
> Break the chains…deep within me
> Lord…set me free

My chains are broken, and I am set free.

I am happy and at peace but fear Buddy, my protective angel and friend, will go away. A price for my freedom.

He says he will never leave me. We are one.

He has never grown. He is still a child.

We don't play anymore. But we still talk.

I am afraid people will think I am crazy if I tell them about Buddy.

He says they will understand. I am not so sure.

I need to talk to him some more.

Tomorrow.